DESIGN CAPITAL

The Hidden Value of Design in Infrastructure

Sherry McKay has a PhD in architectural history from the University of British Columbia and is Professor Emerita in the School of Architecture and Landscape at the University of British Columbia and the inaugural Chair of the architecture program in SALA (2006–09). She served as book review editor for Building Research & Information, UK and co-editor of the West Coast Modern House Series. Recently published is "West Coast Land Claims," a chapter in *Canadian Modern Architecture, 1967 to the Present.*

AnnaLisa Meyboom is an Associate Professor at the University of British Columbia in the School of Architecture and Landscape Architecture (SALA). Her research interrogates future applications of technology in the design of our built environment. She holds a degree in engineering from University of Waterloo and a Masters of Architecture from the University of British Columbia. She designs and writes about future infrastructures and the use of advanced digital tools in the design and fabrication of architectural form.

Routledge
Taylor & Francis Group
NEW YORK AND LONDON

Cover Image: Robert Maillart, Salginatobel Bridge, Schiers Switzerland, 1929-30. Photo: Rama, Rama, CC BY-SA 2.0 FR, via Wikimedia Commons.

First published 2023
by Routledge
605 Third Avenue, New York, NY 10158

and by Routledge
4 Park Square, Milton Park, Abingdon, Oxon, OX14 4RN

Routledge is an imprint of the Taylor & Francis Group, an informa business

Library of Congress Cataloging-in-Publication Data
Names: McKay, Sherry, author. | Meyboom, AnnaLisa, author.
Title: Design capital: the hidden value of design in infrastructure /
Sherry McKay, AnnaLisa Meyboom.
Description: New York, NY: Routledge, 2022. | Includes bibliographical
references. |
Identifiers: LCCN 2021062124 (print) | LCCN 2021062125 (ebook) | ISBN
9780367565466 (hardback) | ISBN 9780367565435 (paperback) | ISBN
9781003098287 (ebook)
Subjects: LCSH: Public works--Design and construction. | Engineering
design--Economic aspects. | Infrastructure (Economics)--Social aspects.
Classification: LCC HD3850 .M35 2022 (print) | LCC HD3850 (ebook) | DDC
624--dc23/eng/20220111
LC record available at https://lccn.loc.gov/2021062124
LC ebook record available at https://lccn.loc.gov/2021062125

ISBN: 9780367565466 (hbk)
ISBN: 9780367565435 (pbk)
ISBN: 9781003098287 (ebk)

DOI: 10.4324/9781003098287

Typeset in Franklin Gothic ATF
By American Type Founders Collection

Publisher's Note
This book has been prepared from camera-ready copy provided by the authors.

ACKNOWLEDGEMENTS

We would like to acknowledge the valuable contributions from those who have worked on both the content and form of *Design Capital*. We are especially appreciative of our editor Vikki Killington's thoughtful and careful editing of the text, Colette Parras' creative and superb graphic design and Jana Tyner's undeterrable sourcing of images and publication permissions. We are grateful to Sara Stevens for her contribution to the initial discussions of the concepts and avenues of investigation pursued in the book and Michael Goldberg for his helpful comments on an early version of Chapter 5 and the discussion of extrinsic value. We are also appreciative of the support of our editor at Routledge, Katheryn Schell, and her understanding throughout the long covid-19 year of the book's final production. Finally we would like to acknowledge the financial support of UBC from their UBC Scholarly Publication Fund.

CONTENTS

1

INTRODUCTION

Currently, designers are unable to make a case for excellence in design of public infrastructure. They have neither the tools nor a strategy to demonstrate the value of design in the face of public criticism of any perceived spending on that which might be considered unnecessary. Competition for scarce government funds and a general public perception of infrastructure as mere efficiency, as well as wariness of wasteful use of tax revenues, has often left design ill-considered. Nevertheless, beautifully designed infrastructure brings value that far exceeds its initial construction expenditure. Can one put a value on the design of the Pooley or the Pont Neuf bridges? What if the historic fountains of Italy had been built as merely functional and economically sensible? What would society have lost? We are depriving future generations of the social and cultural value of design when designing our public infrastructures to be only functional in the economic sense.

Designers need the ability to argue for the value of the contributions that they bring to a project: 'design capital', as we are terming it. This book aims to define design capital in this context of infrastructure in the public realm and, in naming it, give it power. By naming and defining it, our intention is that design capital will become part of the discussion and realization of every infrastructure project. In addition to defining the concept of design capital, this book studies the process, mechanisms and strategies involved in realizing design capital; it presents both historic and current examples of design approaches that have imbued infrastructure, both large and small, with a predisposition to accrue such capital. We further argue that if public infrastructure is to accrue significant design capital, then it must be conceived with design in mind from the outset. It is our hope that through this discussion of both concept and precedents, designers and decision makers can articulate a stronger case for the value of design in public infrastructure.

THE PROPOSITION

This book looks at the intersection of infrastructure and design, and supplies the context within which we identify and understand the role of design in infrastructure as being both urgent and significant. It also establishes the economic advantages of design in the material manifestations of infrastructure.

New forms of infrastructure provision and regulation have arisen which have redefined infrastructure's function as a public good: it is now recognized by design theorists and practitioners that infrastructure has social and behavioural consequences and supports new cultural formations. This is what makes design, which considers such factors, so critically needed. Infrastructure spaces, such as those associated with transportation networks, are a shared, common realm.[1] But, at the same time, there is huge pressure on governments to spend public money prudently; as a result, many governments are reluctant to invest in design, because of the concern that it could be perceived as wasting the taxpayer's money. It is for this reason that the discussion of design capital is both timely and germane. Private corporations and entities will spend money on branding and design because they operate in a business environment and thus recognize the value to their organizations, but government agencies have rarely understood the value of design; even those that have seen the importance of design often lack the tools to convince the public of its value. Infrastructure is related to modes of production and influences social behaviour. It is conceived of as a public good: it is available without subtraction[2] to many without added cost, and it is non-excludable, meaning once it is built no one should be excluded from its service. Therefore, in looking at issues of equity in society, infrastructure and its design is of vital importance to ensure that all service users are able to benefit from the advantages it provides. Typically, its cost is borne and extent determined by various arrangements between the state and private interests.

During the 1800s, infrastructure was focused on transportation, communication (telegraph, telephone) and energy. It was constructed to facilitate industrialization and involved various forms of public/state ownership or controlling order to provide standardized services in fulfillment of "universal obligations."[3] In the 19th century, infrastructure produced a certain pattern of urban form: regularized, rationalized, functionally zoned, and integrated from core to suburban periphery and beyond.

In contrast, the 21st century has been described as the disintegration of the 19th century integrated city ideal in a 'splintering' of previously integrated public systems and monopolies into more private sector involvement to better serve the post-industrial economy.[4] Over the last thirty years, infrastructure provision has changed in form and governance.[5] It is in this new, post-industrial context that this book examines the relationship of design and infrastructure. The term 'post-industrial' became prominent in the 1970s to identify major social, economic and political changes experienced by cities, regions and nations. It refers to the reconfiguration of production from the manufacture of goods to service provision and the corresponding increase in professional and technical occupations.[6] Other descriptors have also been used for the post-industrial shift, including post-Fordist, knowledge economy, experience economy, network society, information society and consumption society.[7] Each of these terms has had significant consequences for thinking about infrastructure and design.

These large economic shifts are evidenced in the urban regeneration policies and programes introduced in the European Union and elsewhere in the developed world that sought to encourage an 'urban renaissance' in the interests of sustainability and global competitiveness, as well as neighbourhood renewal to improve the physical, environmental, social and economic conditions in residential areas.[8]

There are two key points in this seismic shift in the economy from a design perspective. The first is that, "[i]nfrastructures are inevitably imbued with biased struggles for social, economic, ecological and political power."[9] The second is that, with this shift, there has been a recognition of knowledge as a valued form of (human) capital, one which adds to material capital[10]; design is one of the creative industries and a form of knowledge. Infrastructure is what enables society and its production regimes, be they service, tourism, entertainment or financial industries.

THE ARGUMENT

Currently, infrastructure is being reassessed as a design issue, an object requiring the attention of architects, landscape architects and urban designers.[11] There are several factors encouraging this interest, among them the sense that the design professions have been marginalized by the engineering protocols that prevail in city building, the awareness of new opportunities arising from the urban regeneration policies and projects introduced by governments across the developing world and the ascendency of public-private partnerships.[12] There is growing competition among both public entities and private developers to attract investment in a globally competitive field and new demands created by the scale of the required response to ecological/environmental disasters. The reassessment of infrastructure is also influenced by the belief that cultural and social considerations in city-building are crucial in shaping the experience and economic feasibility of amenity and service provision. The present economy and government policy constitute new forms of project sites that are large in scale and complex in execution: as exemplified in brownfield sites needing remediation and regeneration propositions involving multiple stakeholders. Remediation and multiple stakeholders call for the involvement of environmental and social considerations respectively. These multi-faceted projects usually involve various levels of government and complex public-private financing and regulation arrangements. They also call for multidisciplinary, synchronized collaboration among the design and other professions.

WHY DESIGN + INFRASTRUCTURE

There are precedents for the current interest in infrastructure as a topic of contemporary design discourse—interest occurred in modern architectural theory in the late 1950s and 1960s. Practicing on the cusp of postmodernism, English architects Peter and Alison Smithson extolled the beauty of large-scale infrastructure like the freeway systems in Tokyo in their Team Ten Primer (1968),[13] pointing out infrastructure's role in city-building and place-making. Although this fascination with infrastructure was pervasive through the 1950s and '60s, it was largely focused on megastructures, and hence visualized in discrete architectural forms.

However, the attention to infrastructural systems and the value that design can bring to these assemblages of infrastructure and more conventional architectural programes is prescient.

After a hiatus, consideration of infrastructure within the design disciplines returned in the late 1990s and proliferated in the first decades of the 21st century, as evidenced in an increasing number of conferences, books and articles dedicated to the subject of infrastructure.[14] Notable among them are the Landscape Urbanism Conference (1997),[15] "Infrastructural Urbanism" (1999),[16] The Landscape Urbanism Reader (2006),[17] Ecological Urbanism (2010),[18] Fast Forward Urbanism (2010),[19] Extrastatecraft: The Power of Infrastructure Space (2014),[20] Next Generation Infrastructure (2014),[21] Infrastructural Monument,[22]Landscape as Infrastructure (2017),[23] Infrastructure Space (2018),[24] and Driverless Urban Futures (2019).[25] While the focus varies among these cross-disciplinary works, they all propose a collaborative, design-led approach to infrastructure in the urban restructuring caused by de-industrialization, urbanization, and the growth of environmental, ecological and sustainability agendas. As landscape architect Charles Waldheim, among others, has convincingly argued infrastructure is now deemed the basis for urban order with economic, political and social consequences.[26] Design expertise is posited as necessary. The design disciplines have the ability to craft the specifics of place within the dispersive impulse of global networks.

By the 1990s, practitioners had begun to formulate their experience with projects of increasing size, multiple funding partnerships among private and public entities, and the growing complexity of programe adjacencies and demands. This is evidenced in the work of Stan Allen; in 1997, Allen published "Infrastructural Urbanism," which outlined how design expertise could be inserted into urban infrastructure through defined interventions that would affect the life of the city.[27] The resultant megastructures were intended to perform as icons, real estate enhancers and local development 'triggers.'[28] The architect's specific expertise would give "an immediate identity to the site" via the "ability to fix form and structure with high levels of precision."[29] In Allen's view, as much as "infrastructural urbanism" was a technical proposal, it was also "an aesthetic proposition."[30] Architecture and landscape architects, Allen argues, have expertise in infrastructure design, not only historically, but also currently in their ability to integrate technical objects produced by the instrumentality of engineering "into a meaningful cultural and aesthetic framework," to work with territorial organization and functionality, and to provide imaginative responses to the infrastructure crisis of the 21st century.[31] These claims are supported by both philosophical concepts and built projects.

Similarly, architect and urban designer Roger Sherman argues that architects must reassert their role in shaping urban experience and embrace infrastructure as something beyond an "optimized singular function."[32] Sherman also, in noting the rise of public-private partnerships, claims an economic advantage in the inclusion of the architect in infrastructure provision:

> Freeing Infrastructure to assume a more leveraged approach to providing public amenities absent the fixed-sum metrics of efficiency and optimization, privatization signals a shift from its limited role of service providing to a more entrepreneurial one of destination making. [...] this new privatized model is directed toward supplying and evoking desire for what is not there (yet). It looks for opportunities, hidden in plain sight, for disruptive innovation. From new forms of (public) parking and recreation to mobility centers, it explores modes and mixes of access and excess, opening private property to (qualified) public use while building in excess capacity for wider community participation/enjoyment.[33]

In the introduction to the book Infrastructural Monument, published by MIT Center for Advanced Urbanism in 2016, Alexander D'Hooghe, professor of architectural urbanism at the center, makes a strong case for the involvement of the design disciplines in infrastructure. He identifies two major problems in contemporary infrastructure projects: firstly, the dangers of taking a purely mono-functional approach, which prioritizes technical over cultural needs and is hierarchical in process; secondly, assigning design a token, after-the-fact role. D'Hooghe argues that, in America, the concern about infrastructure is not only functional, but also cultural since infrastructure creates spaces intended to be used in common by many (a new form of the medieval English commons).[34] This failure to see the cultural as well as functional aspects of infrastructure is attributed to the restricted disciplinary knowledge brought to infrastructure:

> Engineers and planners designed these with a single use in mind that did not include an awareness of their roles as the sole remaining "commons" of society. While designed to connect, much transportation infrastructure, for example, engenders a sense of discontinuity from the surrounding world.[35]

This mono-functional approach also sees design as an appliqué, an afterthought. As D'Hooghe beautifully explains:

> [D]esign cannot introduce this cultural dimension if it is only conceived as a form of decoration–adding a few big screens, brighter material or ornament, something done after the transportation engineers and planners have done their homework and established routes, mostly on narrow cost and functionality considerations, mixed with the mitigation of stakeholder indignation. A transportation infrastructure as a cultural commons must be wired for a diversity of users (commoners) not only to enable their access but in fact attract them.[36]

This rethinking of infrastructure is marked by a number of propositions regarding the contribution design might make to the urban realm. It could, for example, enhance mobility with social life and differentiated places within the flow of movement.[37] A mono-functional form prioritizing "efficient mobility of goods or labour" could be recast by a series of talented designers into "a realm of culture, public space and landscape form."[38]

In Landscape as Infrastructure (2017), Pierre Bélanger proposes considering infrastructure as both human and natural material, arguing for "infrastructural ecologies [...] a synthetic landscape of living, biophysical systems that operate as urban infrastructure to shape and direct the future of urban economies of culture into the 21st century."[39] He points out the urgency of "rebalancing an over reliance on technology and technological systems" with a consideration of ecological, cultural and economic factors. Bélanger is one of many who point to the need to consider the seemingly intangible aspects of infrastructure, its ability to foster sociability or provide new spatial experiences, for example.

The essays in Infrastructure Space (2018) elaborate on many of the same arguments concerning the role of the design disciplines in infrastructure construction; generally, they plot "plausible common ground between architecture and infrastructure."[40] Infrastructure is described as a complex process that "entangles engineering, architecture and social, technical, economic and political issues into an amalgamated hyper-structure of material matters that concern us all."[41] And while it requires "the problem solving of engineers," infrastructure is something that also benefits from "the architect's skill of questioning given problems and in so doing craft innovative research methodologies."[42] Because infrastructure is recognized as involving social conditions, politics, ecology and a host of cultural considerations which are deemed outside the professional expertise of civil engineering, it requires not only technical skills but also design expertise.[43] It is argued that infrastructure has the ability to influence and instil habits and behaviour[44] and that the professions of architecture, landscape architecture and urban design are equipped, via their educational routes and experience, to work collaboratively to respond to social and cultural needs.[45] As Henrik Ovink declares, "Design is key for showing clearly and comprehensively the added value of investments across sectors and scale and over a period of time. [...] Design in that sense is both the 'cultural' process as well as the economic outcome."[46]

WHAT WE ADD TO THE ARGUMENT

In contemporary design theory, designers argue that infrastructure should be coupled with not only the means of production and distribution but also recreation and ecology at territorial scales. They contend that it can be endowed with the potential for more than one function and for future, possibly opportunistic, programming. This is exemplified by the Viaduc des Arts in Paris (Figure 1:1 and 1:2), where in the 20th century social and economic value was perceived in a disused, 19th century railway viaduct in central Paris and repurposed into a series of artist studios and boutiques, while a parkway replaced the elevated railway track as part of an extensive promenade plantée.[47] The Tabiat Bridge in Tehran (Figure 1:3) reimagined a simple pedestrian bridge, commissioned to connect two urban parks bifurcated by a major expressway, as an extension of parkland, thus converting a technical object of passage into a public space and social amenity.[48]

Many of the claims that have been made about the positive contribution that the design professions make to infrastructure are supported by

1:1 Patrick Berger. Viaduc des Arts (1988-96), Paris, France.

1:2 Patrick Berger. Viaduc des Arts (1988-96), Paris, France.

1:3 Diba Tensile Architecture.
Tabiat Pedestrian Bridge (2014), Tehran, Iran.

both philosophical concepts and built projects. Likewise, many authors have highlighted the crucial role of designers due to their knowledge of social and cultural factors and the consequential added value they contribute by applying that knowledge to infrastructure. However, to date there has been no clear outline of how that knowledge is acquired. And, although the economic advantages of design are mentioned, they are not underpinned by methods of economic assessment. This book aims to fill these knowledge gaps; in addition to naming, identifying and defining design capital, it also elucidates how to create it and, finally, how to value it economically.

But first, the potential to accrue design capital begins with a notion of what good design is.

BUT WHAT IS GOOD DESIGN?

In speaking of design, it becomes necessary to broach the subject of "what is good design?" Design should not be confused with stylistic attributes or subjective expression, it involves objective aspects or impartial considerations. This is, of course, an expansive topic which is given more extensive discussion in Chapters 6 and 7, but several characteristics of good design can be clearly identified. The first and easiest to identify is appropriate durability. Attention to longevity significantly affects detailing and material choice. It makes sense for any significant, publicly-funded infrastructure to be built with materials that are fit for purpose and will have an appropriate longevity determined by environmental and sustainability considerations.

The second factor in good design is its contribution to the environment, whether it be a complex urban environment such as Blackfriars Station—the new rail and pedestrian crossing of the Thames in London—or a more pastoral site like the Millau Viaduct in France. Blackfriars Station accommodates multiple modes of public transit in a high-volume interchange that offers views to the river and little upheaval in the existing urban fabric. In the case of the Millau Viaduct, the bridge creates a carefully considered event in a rural scene: an event of sufficient aesthetic consideration to become an attraction in itself. The specific contribution to the environment is, in all cases, context dependent.

The third factor in good design is its cultural and social response and expression. This factor is more complex than the others, but the most important in resolving the social and cultural relevance of infrastructure. A skilful designer is one who can translate culture into built form while at the same time maintaining all the technical and functional requirements of the brief. This interpretation is a process of design and the design outcome reflects this process. There is no 'neutral' form: anything that is built makes a statement about who we are as a society and what we value. Infrastructure tends to persist for future generations to judge. When something is poorly built due to prioritizing fiscal considerations, it conveys society's lack of concern for future generations in the interest of minimizing costs, a myopic and uncivil attitude. When budget is the sole or dominant determinant of design, and cheapness its only aspiration, design is diminished in its ability to participate in other social and cultural uses. Finance becomes the singular basis of evaluating infrastructure and so endangers durability and longevity. Building infrastructure according to bare economic criteria leaves a barren legacy for future generations.

The complex determinants of good design are demonstrated in the Erasmus Bridge, where many of the concerns defining the production of contemporary infrastructure are successfully responded to / resolved.

EXAMPLE: THE ERASMUS BRIDGE

Completed in 1996, the Erasmus Bridge (Figure 1:4) provides us with a substantive example of infrastructure with significant design capital whose value to the public has been assessed post-construction via a research project.[49] The methodology used for this is elaborated on below and is explained further in Chapter 5 ,"The Economics of Design Capital". TU Delft used the Contingent Valuation Method to estimate the willingness to pay (WTP) of the population of the Netherlands for this piece of infrastructure. The study found that the public's willingness to pay for the increased costs of the enhanced design over the most economic bridge to be significantly more than the cost of the bridge by a factor of four to five.[50] The additional cost of the increased design quality, as compared to the base cost of the most economic bridge design, was 18 million euros; however, the public was willing to pay between 69.7 million and 95.7 million euros above the base price of the bridge. Such studies begin to reveal the 'design capital',

1:4 UNStudio. Erasmus Bridge (1990-96), Rotterdam, The Netherlands.
Photo: Ronald Tileman.

as we term it, of a piece of infrastructure. While this study does not factor in any increase in business activity or in land values (and therefore taxes), the public's perception of a monetary value for design is demonstrated. The bridge has clearly accrued design capital, as evidenced on the one hand by the public's willingness to pay and on the other by aspects of social importance related by the media and the local society's reference to the structure. It is not considered simply a transportation link but has taken on social significance to the people of the Netherlands—not only locally in Rotterdam but also across the country. It is worth understanding a bit more about this bridge and how it came to accrue this significant design capital.

To explain the bridge and its context, the bridge spans the two banks of the Meuse River to unite North and South Rotterdam, accommodating and coordinating several modes of mobility: pedestrian, cycle, automobile, and tram, while its southern, bascule bridge section allows river passage for over-height ships. Its engineering feats have garnered praise: the 800-metre bridge deck was the longest suspension bridge in the world in 1996, and was the tallest in the Netherlands; the bascule bridge was purportedly the largest and heaviest in Western Europe and the largest panel construction of its type in the world.[51] It was touted as a "record-breaking bridge" and its asymmetrical pylon and cable system, 32 cables on the long side and 8 on the shorter, celebrated.[52] Beneath its deck, the bridge was augmented with a shop, restaurant, and parking. The architect, Ben van Berkel, had the credentials and cultural capital of his profession and experience; he had worked in the office of the highly celebrated bridge designer, Santiago Calatrava, and had designed at least two bridges independently prior to the Erasmus Bridge project.

Van Berkel's expertise was highlighted in Architect Magazine, which noted that the Erasmus Bridge was a "comprehensive structure" with several demands (construction, urbanism, infrastructure, and public functions), successfully achieved via integrative design (five concrete pylons of different shapes, railings, landings, details of fixtures and joints and maintenance).[53] The visual function of the bridge's design was noted—the play of light across the cables, the sweep of concrete stairs meeting the curve of the pedestrian-level landing, the dematerialization of the structure by the night-time illumination design and the resulting virtual interior space. All of these factors "contribut[ed] to the bridge as a "square in the city."[54]

As the name given to the bridge signals, it was intended to serve as more than a simple segment in a transportation system. It was given a distinctive form, the canted pylon and cables inviting metaphoric references to a swan and harp respectively which contributed to its functioning as landmark and icon. However, Erasmus Bridge was bestowed with cultural significance not only in name, but also in its deployment as a brand for Rotterdam and site for major cultural events. It was opened by Queen Beatrix of the Netherlands, and is now part of the city logo, featured on souvenirs and commercials. The bridge is used as a significant backdrop for activities such as city-wide marathons and other sporting events and has created a place of engagement within the city. It is not only a landmark to look at (or from) nor is it just a destination and conveyance: the Erasmus Bridge has become the locus for a site of urban development.

The imageability of the Erasmus Bridge was recognized by all levels of government (municipal, regional, national) as one of several incentives and strategies for the urban regeneration of South Rotterdam. The federal government understood the potential of the bridge to act as an incentive for private investment in the area; the bridge formed part of a strategy for not only the regeneration of South Rotterdam but also the redefinition of the city as a whole. On a national scale, this private investment and development was instrumental in securing the global competitiveness of the Netherlands. To this end, the public sector assumed responsibility for public spaces and infrastructure, and provided the bulk of funding for the Erasmus Bridge. Politicians were persuaded to support the most expensive of three bridge options by the argument that the regeneration in South Rotterdam was good for Holland as a whole.[55] It was one among several tactics adopted to ensure the success of the whole initiative.

By 2015, South Rotterdam development had attracted around the bridge a number of new buildings by well-known architects: Renzo Piano, KPN Tower (2000); Mecanoo, Montevideo Tower (2005); Alvar Size, New Orleans (2010); OMA, De Rotterdam (2013). The professional design credentials and brand power of these star architects are clearly emphasized in the literature that addresses the success of the redevelopment of the area generally.[56] Consequently, the cost of the bridge was therefore evaluated alongside the larger social, economic and physical context of its site. The national government was willing to fund the Erasmus Bridge because it contributed in terms of both function and imageability to a high-quality public realm and as a consequence would garner specific investment opportunities and contribute to the economic success of Rotterdam.

Various studies of the urban regeneration of South Rotterdam, of which the Erasmus Bridge was a significant part, refer to the importance of high-quality buildings, public realm and living conditions, cultural and spatial components, infrastructure, and the role these have had in improving economic investment and the social status of the area.[57] These comprehensive commentaries on the success of South Rotterdam, and the fact that "[t]he Erasmus Bridge became a symbol of Rotterdam Renaissance as a whole,"[58] highlight the large physical, economic and political context in which this single piece of infrastructure was conceived and evaluated. In this case, the issue of gentrification (further discussed in Chapter 3, "Infrastructure in Context: Globalization and Gentrification") was addressed from the outset. Clearly stated goals, well-conceived strategies and tactics, and coordinated government initiatives (including local input and effective implementation policies) all contributed to the positive evaluation of the Erasmus Bridge.

The Erasmus Bridge discussion introduces salient issues raised by the intersection of infrastructure and design that are developed in subsequent chapters. The celebration of the bridge within the design community, but also more widely across political agencies, business sectors and the public at large, speaks to the value and benefits that design possesses. The ability of design capital to operate as a form of currency across different types of value is explored in Chapter 2, "Design and Other Forms of Capital". As part of a larger strategy for economic growth, urban re-tooling and global investment, the Erasmus Bridge has also raised concerns about the possible repercussions of rising property values, and the dislocation of local populations by more wealthy ones. How infrastructure contributes—or not—to this is the topic of Chapter 3, "Infrastructure in Context: Globalization and Gentrification". As monument and icon, but also as support for public spaces, the bridge points to the ability of infrastructure to create place, and not just systems of efficient mobility, as we examine in Chapter 4, "Infrastructure in Context: Placemaking." The post-construction evaluation of infrastructure regarding a "willingness to pay" by Delft University research raises questions about public funding assumptions and regimes. We have identified that what is needed now is a means of assessing the value of design pre-construction, and this is the subject of Chapter 5, "The Economics of Design Capital." The credentials of the designer of the Erasmus Bridge, his education, experience, and critical success among the design disciplines, all contribute to the bridge's cultural and social success. It also suggests that it is pertinent to understand how the skills required to create design capital via infrastructure are acquired. How this disciplinary expertise is accomplished is presented in Chapters 6 and Chapter 7, "Creating Design Capital." Chapters 8, 9 and 10 discuss case studies of small- medium- and large-scale infrastructure and examine their potential to accrue design capital.

CONCLUSION

The argument presented in this book is premised on the fact that designers, such as architects and landscape architects, are trained to bring social and cultural considerations to bear on any given project—as such, they are predisposing the built form to accumulate design capital. This integration of social and cultural values with practical consideration is what contributes additional non-economic value to the infrastructure. This value, however, cannot be presumed as inherent to any infrastructure; it is conferred by a society that recognizes in it some cultural or social desirability. Bridges are perhaps an easy way to make this point: while some bridges will become socially significant structures, immediately resonant with place and meaning, not all will; so too will be the case with most infrastructure. What creates a socially significant structure depends on a variety of factors such as purpose, location, its relationship to landscape, and its design. This book looks at how to create this relationship between infrastructure and social significance.

We believe that making the value of design explicit and defined will contribute to an increase in the quality of our environment. If designers can make this argument and demonstrate the increasing and multifaceted value of infrastructure over time, then policy makers will be provided with sound arguments for investing in it and good design is more likely to be facilitated. Clearly, in the competition between cities to attract talent as well as durable prosperity, it is beneficial to be able to design a built environment that is predisposed to contributing to design capital. The question, then, is how can we think and talk about the work of infrastructure designers in terms that make design's immense value apparent to the decision makers and the public at large?

This book examines design capital as it pertains to infrastructure and situates it within the current context of financial austerity, short-term prioritizing, and mono-functional focus. We study design capital through the lens of case studies of varying scales and historical time periods. It is hoped that once the argument is made and understood for these studies that it can be extended to other infrastructural investments and eventually buildings. We believe that this argument holds for all aspects of the built environment but have chosen specific examples at different scales to make our case. Historic examples give a demonstration of the continuing value of an initial investment in design and provide a valuable demonstration of the long-term potential of this approach. Our premise is that by articulating what gives infrastructure design capital, and by providing historic and current examples of design approaches that have imbued infrastructure with a predisposition to accrue such capital, infrastructure more broadly can be similarly evaluated. It is hoped that through this discussion, designers can make a stronger case for the value of design in public infrastructure.

NOTES

1. Stan Allen, Meredith Baber, and MIT Center for Advanced Urbanism, eds., Infrastructural Monument, First edition (New York: Princeton Architectural Press, 2016).
2. 'Without subtraction' means that it is not diminished by another person's use which is an important concept with regard to a public good.
3. Robert Millward, "European governments and the infrastructure industries, c.1840-1914," European Review of Economic History 8, no. 1 (April 2004): 3-28. https://www.jstor.org/stable/41377947. Industrialization in the 19th century saw the massive expansion of railway track, telegraph and then telephone lines, electric stations, gas and water works—all but water being new services based on technological innovations.
4. See, S. Graham and S. Marvin, Splintering Urbanism: Networked Infrastructures, Technological Mobilities and the Urban Condition (New York: Routledge, 2001).
5. Chris Couch, Olivier Sykes, Wolfgang Börstinghaus, "Thirty years of urban regeneration in Britain, Germany and France: the importance of context and path dependency," *Progress in Planning 75* (January 2011). https://doi.org/10.1016/j.progress.2010.12.001
6. Daniel Bell, *The Coming of Post-Industrial Society: A Venture in Social Forecasting* (New York, Basic Books, 1976); H.V. Savitch, *Post Industrial Cities: Politics and Planning in New York, London and Paris* (Princeton NJ: Princeton University Press, 2014); Douglas V. Shaw, "Chapter 18: The Post-Industrial City," in *Handbook of Urban Studies,* ed. Ronan Paddison (Thousand Oaks: Sage Books, 2000).
7. David Harvey, *The Limits to Capital* (Oxford: Blackwell, 1982); David Harvey, *The Condition of Post Modernity* (Oxford: Blackwell, 1989); W. F. Lever "Chapter 17: The Post-Fordist city," in *Handbook of Urban Studies,* ed. Ronan Paddison (Thousand Oaks:Sage Books, 2000).
8. Couch, Sykes and Börstinghans, "Urban Regeneration," 19.
9. Panos Constantinides, "Introduction: Historical Review of Infrastructure Development," in *Perspectives and Implications for the Development and Information Infrastructures* (Hershey, PA: IGI Global, 2012) 1-18. See, Graham and Marcin , *Splintering Urbanism*, 11.
10. Dirk Czarnitzki, Bronwyn Hall, Raffaele Oriani,"The Market Evaluation of Knowledge Assets in US and European Firms," 2006. https://eml.berkeley.edu//~bhhall/papers/CHO05_mktval.pdf
11. This can be evidenced by publications such as: *ExtraStatecraft,* 2014; *Infrastructural Monument,* 2016 and *Infrastructure Space,* 2019. It is also seen in conferences: Center for Architectural Urbanism, MIT Infrastructural Monument Conference, 2013; Lafarge-Holcim Conference 2016.
12. Stan Allen, "Infrastructural Urbanism," in *Points and Lines: diagrams and projects for the city,* ed. Stan Allen (New York: Princeton Architectural Press, 1999). Roger Sherman, "Battery Power: Recharging Architecture's Causes and Effects," in *Infrastructural Monument* (New York: Princeton Architectural Press, 2016).
13. Alison Smithson, ed., *Team Ten Primer* (Cambridge, MA: The MIT Press, 1968). This publication is a collection of essays and discussions by Team Ten members between approximately 1953-63. Membership in Team Ten varied over the years and was a loose grouping of individuals who shared a direction of thought rather than a single ideology. Members initially included: Georges Candilis, Aldo van Eyck, Gian Carlo de Carlo, Peter and Alison Smithson, Shadrach Woods, Ralph Erskine. Peter and Alison Smithson first published an essay "Team Ten Primer" in *Architectural Design* in December 1962, which highlighted the role of infrastructure in design thinking and of design in an approach to infrastructure, although they emphasize comprehensibility via design.

14. A similar hiatus is also noted in the use of the term more generally. See H. William Batt, "Infrastructure: Etymology and Import," *Journal of Professional Issues in Engineering* 110 no. 1 (January 1984) https://doi.org/10.1061/(ASCE)1052-3928(1984)110:1(1)
15. "Landscape Urbanism" Conference at the Graham Foundation, Chicago, 1997.
16. Stan Allen, "Infrastructural Urbanism," *Points and Lines: diagrams and projects for the city*, ed. Stan Allen (New York: Princeton Architectural Press, 1999).
17. Charles Waldheim, *The Landscape Urbanism Reader* (New York: Princeton Architectural Press, 2006).
18. Mohsen Mostafavi and Gareth Doherty, *Ecological Urbanism* (Baden: Lars Müller Publishers,2010).
19. Dana Cuff and Roger Sherman, *Fast-Forward Urbanism: Rethinking Architecture's Engagement with the City* (New York: Princeton Architectural Press, 2011).
20. Keller *Easterling, Extrastatecraft: The Power of Infrastructure Space* (London and New York: Verso Books, 2014).
21. Hillary Brown, *Next Generation Infrastructure* (Washington, DC: Island Press, 2014).
22. Stan Allen, Meredith Baber, and MIT Center for Advanced Urbanism, eds., *Infrastructural Monument,* First edition (New York: Princeton Architectural Press, 2016).
23. Pierre Bélanger, *Landscape as Infrastructure* (London and New York: Routledge, 2017).
24. Ilka Ruby and Andreas Ruby, eds., *Infrastructure Space* (Berlin: Ruby Press, 2017).
25. AnnaLisa Meyboom, *Driverless Urban Futures: A Speculative Atlas for Autonomous Vehicles* (London and New York: Routledge, 2019).
26. Charles Waldheim, *The Landscape Urbanism Reader* (New York: Princeton Architectural Press, 2006), 39.The publication had been preceded by the "Landscape Urbanism " Conference, held at the Graham Foundation in Chicago in 1997. See also Charles Waldheim, "Landscape Urbanism: A Genealogy," *Praxis: Journal of Writing + Building" No. 4 Landscapes (2002):* 10-17, https://www.jstor.org/stable/24328948.pdf
27. Stan Allen, "Infrastructural Urbanism," in *Infrastructural Monument* (New York: Princeton Architectural Press, 2016) 55.
28. Allen, "Infrastructural Urbanism" in *Infrastructural Monument*, 56, 57. He mentions the projects Gwangquo Pier Lakeside Park and Taichung Park Suwan South Korea
29. Allen "Infrastructural Urbanism," in *Infrastructural Monument,* 58.
30. Allen, "Infrastructural Urbanism," in *Infrastructural Monument,* 56.
31. Allen, "Infrastructural Urbanism," in *Infrastructural Monument,* 48-51.
32. Roger Sherman, "Battery Power: Recharging Architecture's Causes and Effects," in *Infrastructural Monument* (New York: Princeton Architectural Press, 2016), 85.
33. Sherman, "Battery Power: Recharging Architecture's Causes and Effects," 87.
34. Alexander D'Hooghe, "Transportation Infrastructure as Our Commons," in *Infrastructural Monument,* eds. Stan Allen, Meredith Bader and MIT Center for Advanced Urbanim (New York: Princeton Architectural Press, 2016) 15.
35. D'Hooghe, "Transportation Infrastructure," in *Infrastructural Monument,* 16
36. D'Hooghe, "Transportation Infrastructure," in *Infrastructural Monument,* 16.
37. D'Hooghe, "Transportation Infrastructure," in *Infrastructural Monument*, 18.
38. Allen, Bader, and MIT Center for Advanced Urbanism, "Preface," *Infrastructural Monument*); D'Hooghe, "Transportation Infrastructure," in *Infrastructural Monument,* 19, 16.
39. Pierre Bélanger, *Landscape as Infrastructure: A Base Primer* (Abingdon, Oxford and New York: Routledge, 2017).
40. The book originated in the Lafarge-Holcim-Lafarge 5th International Forum (Detroit) in 2016.
41. Francois Charbonnet and Cary Siress, "Shades of Gray and a Green Thumb with Out-of-the-Blue Couplings," in *Infrastructure Space,* iii.
42. Chabonnet and Siress, "Shades of Gray," in *Infrastructural Space,* viii.
43. Chabonnet and Siress, "Shades of Gray," viii; Milica Topolovic, "Land as Project: On Territorial Construction," in *Infrastructure Space,* 158.
44. Ricky Burdett, "Infrastructures of Equality Versus Inequality," in *Infrastructure Space,* 306-313.

45. Henrik Ovink "Transformative Capacity of Resilience: Learning from Rebuild by Design," in *Infrastructure Space,* 342.
46. Ovink, "Transformative Capacity of Resilience," in *Infrastructure Space,* 342.
47. The Viaduc des Arts was commissioned by the City as part of a larger redevelopment of the disused railway infrastructure in eastern Paris initiated in 1979, which by 1983 included the Promenade Plantée—a 4.2 km planted walk way on former rail lines between Bastille and Vincennes. The Viaduc des Arts, which formed the eastern section of this promenade, was initiated in 1988, its elevated park opened in 1989. The 67 renovated vaults beneath, designed by Patrick Berger, between 1994 and 1997.
48. The Tabiat Bridge, was the result of a competition held by the city of Tehran in 2009 and won by Leila Araghian and her studio. Diba Tensile. It was completed in 2014
49. Roy Heijnsdijk, "The Iconic Value of Infrastructure Projects: A Case Study to the Iconic Value of the Erasmus Bridge" (Delft, Netherlands, Technical University of Delft, 2015).
50. Heijnsdijk, "Iconic Value," 17.
51. City Guide Rotterdam, "Erasmus Bridge Rotterdam," https://www.cityguiderotterdam.com/things-to-do/sights/ersamus-bridge, access March 30, 2021.
52. City Guide Rotterdam, "Erasmus Bridge."
53. "Erasmus Bridge, UN Studio," *Architect Magazine,* posted December 20, 2013. https://architectmagazine.com/project-gallery/erasmus-bridge
54. "Erasmus Bridge, UN Studio," *Architect Magazine.*
55. Urban and Economic Development (URBED) and Marco van Hoek, "Regeneration in European Cities: Making Connections. Case Study of Kop van Zuid, Rotterdam (The Netherlands)," (April 2007, updated March 2008), 23.
56. URBED and van Hoek, "Regeneration in European Cities," 2, 23.
57. URBED and van Hoek, "Regeneration in European Cities," 2, 3.
58. URBED and van Hoek, "Regeneration in European Cities," 32.

2

DESIGN AND OTHER FORMS OF CAPITAL

WHAT WE MEAN BY DESIGN CAPITAL

The term 'design capital' serves to reposition the seemingly mute asset of design as an expressible value. It aims to demonstrate that design itself can be shown to have a value as powerful as any short-term consideration such as time efficiency or maximizing immediately apparent financial profit.[1] Design capital is a way of capturing the various assets of design and the manner in which they can operate within a system of exchange usually restricted to economic capital.[2] Design, as an aesthetic practice, is generally understood to be outside any economic evaluation because aesthetics is considered a disinterested pursuit (that which is uninterested in economic gain) that responds to a set of value judgements. These value judgements arise not from necessity or monetary gain, but from a moral or ethical basis. Aesthetics is, therefore, believed to escape the logic of economic interest. However, this is arguably a function of how we, as a society, have thought of design.[3]

Some insight into how design considerations might function economically is suggested by the work of sociologist Pierre Bourdieu. In his 'theory of practice,'[4] Bourdieu "suggested that all actions, even those understood as disinterested or of no purpose, were to be conceived economically as actions aimed at the maximisation of material or symbolic gain."[5] Our term, design capital, can be discussed and interpreted in the context of Bourdieu's formulation of types of capital.[6] While it stands as a concept without this discussion, it gains specificity and clarity of meaning when positioned relative to the other intangible but nevertheless potent 'capitals.'

Bourdieu is helpful for our exploration of the value of design in infrastructure in three ways. Firstly, he posits that there are different forms of capital that appear to be uneconomic by social agreement but do, in fact, contribute to economic capital and have an economic logic. Secondly, he argues that these different forms of capital circulate within different social groups, or fields, and function to ensure social cohesion and a hierarchy between differentiated social groups, which is set by dominant social groups. Thirdly, while different forms of capital work with economic capital within different social groups, these different social groups may come to value the same object, but according to different codes of evaluation. There are, for example, different aesthetic codes determining symbolic and social value and these differences are embedded within social class hierarchies. Ultimately, the symbolic and other values produced by design are part of an economic logic.

Bourdieu's concepts of social and cultural capital were developed to explain how certain social practices produce and maintain systems of status and power and distinctions between social classes, and ultimately have an economic logic, or profitability.[7] Social capital refers to the actual and potential resources connected to an individual's networks of both institutional relationships and acquaintances: who you know, and the networks within which you are able to operate. Cultural capital refers to objects and styles of expression or performance, the ways of doing something. Of the various forms of cultural capital—embodied, objectified and institutionalized—we are especially interested in its objectified and institutionalized forms.[8] According to Bourdieu, the cultural capital embodied in an individual or group, acquired via education for example, is legitimated and bestowed by institutions (for example, academies or licensing boards) and objectified through art and other products. Cultural capital comprises the social assets of a person (education, style, etc.) which promote their social status within a defined group.

Cultural capital operates within a system of exchange, where cultural knowledge confers status and power, and its objectified forms entail material and symbolic goods that society (or a social group within society) considers desirable. Design capital resides in the recognition of the cultural or symbolic significance of its objectified form, rather than necessarily in its use or need. This recognition of a value, which is deemed disinterested (that is, not concerned with monetary gain) is, we argue, of significant value.

One of the functions of cultural capital is to confer status and power by inhabiting the form of both material and symbolic goods that are deemed 'worth seeking by society.' One of the functions of cultural and social forms of capital is the appearance of disinterest; this obfuscates the advantages each bestows and the systemic inequalities each serves to ensure.[9,10]

Bourdieu argues that all types of capital, in fact, contribute ultimately to economic capital. Different forms of capital have different forms of risk: cultural capital is more uncertain than economic capital because it must rely on social capital for recognition and legitimacy; economic capital is risky because its value will fluctuate in the long term. Design capital, like cultural capital, has the potential to ensure long-term value. We find these theoretical concepts useful in articulating the mechanism by which infrastructure accrues social and cultural significance through its design aspects. We have used the term 'design capital' to refer to this socially and culturally conferred value.

However, the defining and use of the phrase 'design value' in reference to Bourdieu does raise a problem. While Bourdieu concludes that social and cultural forms of capital are agents of economic development, he insists that within the societal framework that he discusses, cultural production of any form—art or literature, for example—must appear to eschew economic capital. He argues this subterfuge is necessary because it allows the unequal access to economic capital to appear natural and it maintains power over scarce resources among an elite. Here, we are attempting to define design capital as a means of giving heretofore unacknowledged, culturally valued aspects of built form an economic value so that it can be considered in decision making. This departs from conventional notions of (elite) cultural production being disinterested or unmotivated by economic gain, an idea which was formulated in aesthetic theory and then academies in the 16th century and which persists today.[11] While this unspoken rule is clear in the fine arts and literature, it is also found in architecture. Le Corbusier, for example, always spoke of architecture as disinterested and as possessing a quality of the indefinable. Whereas most culturally valued architecture (as practised in the world today) must deal with economic considerations as a primary concern, the academy and award systems almost completely eschew such discussions, often seeing them as an impediment to design creativity and assessment, and to the true practice of architecture as cultural production. This approach is in keeping with other fields of cultural production. There are, however, challenges to the elitist aspects of the academy and established professional award systems, as evidenced by public outcry about significant cost overruns in major public projects and attention given to projects solving budget limitations via design in professional publications and awards. These challenges suggest, as Bourdieu observed, that "the characteristic aura of traditional cultural elites is being demystified."[12]

The language of Bourdieu's sociological analysis has been taken up by urban theorists, historians and others to parse the full economic advantages won by intangible considerations, such as social benefit and cultural prestige accruing from design attuned to what Bourdieu has termed "habitus": the everyday life patterns associated with, and encouraged by, the built environment amongst other influences. Similarly, in this book, it is through this idea of design capital that we will analyze how infrastructure might function in the current economy (post-industrial, tourist-seeking, amenity- and entertainment-promising) and how economic value in relation to social good might be assessed for infrastructure.

Writing in 1995, Sharon Zukin asserts: "Cultural capital [is] as "real" as investment capital in its effects on society."[13] Her book, The Culture of Cities, explores how cities used culture as an economic base in the post-industrial economy of the 1970s and 80s. She explains the "symbolic economy" of this era as "[t]he growth of cultural consumption (of art, food, music, tourism) and the industries that cater to it fuels the city's symbolic economy, its visible ability to produce both symbols and space."[14] She notes that "the symbolic economy features two parallel production systems that are crucial to a city's material life: the production of space, with its synergy of capital investment and cultural meanings, and the production of symbols, which constructs both a currency of commercial exchange and a language of social identity."[15] Zukin is contextualizing the discussion of urban design and city building within the post-modern period.

The question of what constitutes the value of design has also arisen more recently in the literature on 'the experience economy.' This literature points to an answer to the question, why would one pay more for something than what is warranted by bare necessity? In Brandscapes: Architecture in the Experience Economy (2007), Anna Klingmann discusses 'added value,' which she defines as that which distinguishes architecture from mere building: design aspects which extend beyond mere functionality and utility. Design value includes "the multiple meaning structures ranging from symbolic and experiential significance, aesthetic appeal, as well as the elevation of social prestige and institutional status."[16] For example, the added value of architecture "enhances status and cultural recognition, institutional status and social prestige of their owners" while providing "aesthetically pleasing experiences to visitors," and has the "ability to change the social, political, cultural, and economic status of its beneficiary."[17]

However, Zukin observes that, "we shouldn't jump to the conclusion that the producers of symbols (artists, architects, designers) have much power. As in any other market economy, clients wield more power than producers. Those who deal out the symbols—the Disney Company, BIDs [Business Investment Developments], museums—are in control."[18] As such, for the topic of design capital, who (whether individual, corporation, or public sector/local government) determines the purpose / intent of a commission is critical. While designers of infrastructure have the ability to implement this intent, ideally their intent is gathered from reading the social desires of those for whom they are designing. Accordingly, this book is addressed to all involved in making decisions in infrastructure design and especially the clients—the governments and funders. Infrastructure, as an agent in spatial production, is conventionally thought of in terms of its instrumental value, and rarely is consideration given to the full social and cultural values it might assume.[19] Our interest, however, is not with the ephemeral aspects of added value as "advertisements and destinations."[20] Added value can offer a sense of social belonging and cultural identity.[21] We prefer the term, design capital, to highlight the complex social and economic relationships and spheres in which this value of design is recognized and produced. Design capital seeks, ideally, to create a sense of belonging for multiple social groups and cultural identities.

HOW DESIGN CAPITAL WORKS

The need and impetus for the concept of design capital is evident in contemporary discourse on infrastructure. Most of the essays in Infrastructure as Architecture (2010), for example, identify the need for an updated (post-industrial, ecologically sound, expanded) conception of infrastructure and postulate an equally recalibrated design as the means of meeting those needs. The needs referred to include environmental health, social well-being, and cultural aspirations; multi-functionality and site specificity;[22] a "working with nature and natural processes, improving social contexts, and serving local constituents;" the creation of contemporary publics;[23] consideration of social impacts as integral to the effectiveness of design;[24] the inclusion of cultural activities and processes and "extra-functional amenity spaces;" and "to consider infrastructure as cultural production."[25]

Design is the means of satisfying those complex, multiple functions. Many of the authors in Infrastructure as Architecture speak to this. Dana Cuff argues that infrastructure must be accepted into "the design fold;"[26] Katrina Stoll and Scott Lloyd contend that design ensures "appropriate intervention" and the failure of existing infrastructure is a design issue;[27] Alexander d'Hooghe, claims that infrastructure is an "artifact" with cultural references and not, as many believe, a system of engineering and transportation planning.[28] Additionally, in Next Generation Infrastructure: Principles for Post-Industrial Public Works (2014), Hillary Brown identifies the need to "rethink the way architects design," and to "question current design assumptions."[29] She also recognizes the need to convince planners, financiers and public officials to fund this more comprehensive criteria for infrastructure design/construction. The recognition of design capital assists in bridging the gap between those new design conceptions and their implementation.

INFRASTRUCTURE PARTICIPATION IN OTHER SOCIETAL ECONOMIC MODELS

It is commonplace for costs (construction and associated considerations) to be prioritized when planning new infrastructure, with the result that efficiency and minimizing material use in structural determination are privileged. But, as infrastructure in general is increasingly a participant in new economic models, other factors apart from initial costs should be considered. The necessity of this is evidenced by the growing outcry of neighbourhoods regarding planned local infrastructure projects, which are increasingly likely to be built in denser urban areas. This forces infrastructure to engage with a broader social discussion, but currently the typical delivery mechanisms and infrastructure design approaches have no way of engaging in this conversation. The less tangible forms of value-creation have been identified as essential to urban development. Recent studies, which have identified "brandscapes," "consumption society" and "tourist enclaves" as current models of economic generation, have also developed new tools to identify and affirm the formerly neglected, intangible aspects of economic and social regeneration.[30] While these types of approaches are not what we are proposing, we can still learn from the precedents that they discuss, as they show that there are methods for acknowledging economic value in design quality. These methods can assist in identifying not only what tourists, consumers and business interests want, but also the wishes of local inhabitants. This follows the lead of other disciplines, such as sociology, which have developed analytical concepts that provide a language for naming and discussing the intangible values attributed by society and its institutions to design capital.

CONCLUSION

Currently, demand for an enhanced consideration of infrastructure is growing. There are assertions of the public and community nature of the work, the advantages of multi-functional projects, the inclusion of environmental and sustainability assessments, and the consideration of local concerns. But none of these perspectives, although perceptive and prescient, have convinced many policy makers, government officials, taxpayers or infrastructure's neighbours of the role of design in realizing an infrastructure of mutual benefit. This is where our concept of design capital is so critical: by allowing us to evaluate the long-term advantages of design in the construction of infrastructure. It seeks both to offer and justify an alternative to the engineering, zoning and conventional framing of infrastructure and also to vindicate budgets that incorporate these seemingly intangible, 'difficult-to-assign-dollar-values-to' advantages of infrastructure construction.

Design capital invites us to consider the economy of infrastructure in a broader interpretation than merely fiscal, one which allows us to include design as an asset or value that ultimately contributes to economic capital. We conceive design capital as a means of empowering those wishing to make the argument for good design to overcome the reliance on traditional conventions of persuasion (such as economy, functionality and pragmatism) by allowing the estimation of infrastructure values to include a broader range of benefits. These benefits, often considered intangible, include environmental, cultural and social gains. Defining a term—'naming' the value so to speak—gives the whole community a specific, tangible asset to refer to in making the argument for design. It is a powerful tool that has, until now, been lacking. While engaging in this discussion runs the risk of 'devaluing' design in the sense that it has been assigned a monetary value, it is a risk worth taking in the pursuit of a well-designed and equitable environment.

NOTES

1. Pierre Bourdieu, "The Forms of Capital," in *Handbook of Theory and Research for the Sociology of Education,* ed. J. Richard (Westport, CT: Greenwood, 1986), 241-58. Bourdieu claims that symbolic and social capital contribute to economic gain eventually. Symbolic, social and cultural forms of capital are intended to appear disinterested but are in fact masquerades for the accumulation of economic capital via regulations embedded within social relations which they also seek to maintain.
2. Economic capital refers to the command of economic resources: money, assets, labour and property.
3. The word "disinterested" often arises in this context. In aesthetic theory, that of Emile Kant for example, disinterested refers to a contemplative attitude rather than a pecuniary concern. Bourdieu questions this disinterest in economic considerations.
4. Pierre Bourdieu, *Outline of a Theory of Practice*, trans. Richard Nice (Cambridge UK: Cambridge University Press, 1977).
5. Bourdieu, "The Forms of Capital." The key texts are: Pierre Bourdieu and Jean-Claude Passeron, *Reproduction in Education, Society and Culture*, trans. Richard Nice (London: Sage, 1977); Pierre Bourdieu and Loic Waquant *Invitations to Reflexive Sociology* (Chicago: University of Chicago Press, 1992).
6. Pierre Bourdieu, "The forms of capital," *Cultural theory: An anthology*, eds., Imre Szeman and Timothy Kaposy (Chichester: Wiley-Blackwell, 2011), 81-93.
7. Social and cultural capital are related to but different from economic capital in that the latter refers to the command of resources (money, assets, property.)
8. For an elaboration on these terms, see: Pierre Bourdieu, "Forms of Capital," in *Handbook of Theory and Research for the Sociology of Education*, ed. J. Richardson (New York: Greenwood, 1986), 241-258. Briefly, embodied refers to cultural capital in "the form of long-lasting disposition of the mind and body"; objectified refers to cultural capital in "the form of cultural goods" (e.g. books, machines, etc.) and institutional cultural capital a special kind of objectification that "confers entirely original properties on the cultural capital it is presumed to guarantee."
9. The role of cultural capital is to reproduce the social structure and the advantage of specific social groups. Hence cultural capital has an economic value but also produces social hierarchies and social relations.
10. Randal Johnson, ed. "editor's introduction" in Pierre Bourdieu, *The Field of Cultural Production* (New York: Columbia University Press, 1993), 7. The editor is referring to Pierre Bourdieu, *In Other Words: Essays Towards a Reflexive Society*, trans. Matthew Adamson (Cambridge and Stanford: Polity Press and Stanford University Press, 1990), 22.
11. Bourdieu is especially critical of Immanuel Kant's aesthetic theory in this regard.
12. Bourdieu, referenced in Anna Klingmann, *Brandscapes: Architecture in the Experience Economy* (Cambridge MA: The MIT Press, 2007), 44. Klingmann is interested in individual practices of consumption as challenges to established elite culture rather than the practices of public institutions here.
13. Sharon Zukin, *The Cultures of Cities* (Oxford: Blackwell, 1995), ix.
14. Zukin, *Culture of Cities*, 2.
15. Zukin, *Culture of Cities*, 23-24.
16. Klingmann, *Brandscapes*, 66.
17. Klingmann *Brandscapes*, 66.
18. Zukin, *Culture of Cities*, 292.
19. Knowledge of the social and cultural ramifications of design is often missing in the education and methodologies of major players in the defining of the form and presence of infrastructure, such as engineering disciplines.
20. Klingmann, *Brandscapes*, endcover.
21. Klingmann, *Brandscapes*, 67.
22. Katrina Stoll and Scott Lloyd, eds., *Infrastructure as architecture: designing composite networks* (Berlin: Jovis, 2010), 5.

23. Dana Cuff, "Architecture as Public Work," in *Infrastructure as architecture*, eds., Stoll and Lloyd, 11-12, 21.
24. Urban Think Tank, Alfredo Brillembourg and Hubert Klumpner, "Slum Lifting: AN Informal Toolbox For Architecture as Infrastructure," *Infrastructure as architecture, eds.*, Stoll and Lloyd, 27.
25. Bureau E.A.S.T., "Cultured Infrastructures," in *Infrastructure as architecture,* eds., Stoll and Lloyd, 89, 94.
26. Dana Cuff, "Architecture as Public Work," in *Infrastructure as architecture*, eds., Stoll and Lloyd, 18, 21.
27. Katrina Stoll and Scott Lloyd, "Performance as Form," in *Infrastructure as architecture,* eds., Stoll and Lloyd, 52.
28. Alexander d'Hooghe, "The Objectification of Infrastructure: The Cultural Project of Suburban Infrastructure Design," in *Infrastructure as architecture,* eds., Stoll and Lloyd, 78.
29. Hilary Brown, *Next Generation Infrastructure: Principles for Post-Industrial Public Works,* forward David Orr, (Washington, D.C.: Island Press, 2014), xi-xii.
30. Klingmann, *Brandscapes*; Mark Jayne, *Cities and Consumption* (New York and London: Routledge, 2006).

3

INFRASTRUCTURE IN CONTEXT: GLOBALIZATION AND GENTRIFICATION

The creation of design capital in infrastructure inevitably brings with it the issue of gentrification. If design quality is successfully added to a place, it will make that place more desirable and the area may gentrify. The important question to address then is whether or not it is possible to consider infrastructure and its accruing of design capital without creating gentrification and all its associated negative attributes?

WHY LOOK AT GENTRIFICATION, GLOBALIZATION AND ICONICITY?

Infrastructure invariably plays a significant role in highly publicized, largely urban, redevelopments. These projects often prove divisive; their supporters cast them positively as renovation, regeneration, revitalization or renaissance projects; by contrast, their detractors see them as a retaking of the place by the wealthy or as misplaced government investment.[1] Be it Gehry's museum infrastructure, the Bilbao Guggenheim (Figure 3:1), Ben van Berkel's transit infrastructure for Rotterdam South and the Erasmus Bridge (Figure 1:4), or the variously-authored leisure infrastructure for Oslo's Fjord City, all have involved the redevelopment of brownfield sites with unprecedented investment, which is often global and invariably involves multiple levels of government. These infrastructure projects also frequently involve the branding and marketing of iconic structures, and the associated forces of gentrification and globalization. Indeed, many authors understand iconic buildings as a genre of architecture specifically linked to globalization.[2] The profit and tax-generation ambitions of such iconic projects also often rely on gentrification; this funding and gentrification dynamic could easily similarly apply to iconic infrastructure.[3] All of the projects cited above also participated in the design-led urban regeneration agenda that had become prominent by the late 1990s.[4] While the literature on both globalization and gentrification is enormous, and that on iconicity more specialized but no less polarized, it is necessary to broach these issues in assessing the attribution of design capital to infrastructure and our claims that it is a significant contributor to the public good.[5] Since iconicity may also play a role in infrastructure design it is important to examine its function in the assessment of good design. In this way, a broad discussion of the benefits and detriments of investing in good design, undertaken for the public good, can be understood.[6]

GENTRIFICATION

Investments in infrastructure are often considered to be for the public good; gentrification, by contrast, is often associated with negative social outcomes for the original inhabitants of the communities which experience its impact. As infrastructure and gentrification are often linked, it is pertinent to discuss this linkage and whether it is possible to invest in infrastructure while mitigating the negative aspects of gentrification.

Generally, the current understanding of gentrification has evolved from a rather ad-hoc strategy of working-class neighbourhood incursion and resident displacement in the late 1950s and 60s as a result of the movement of middle-class individuals in search of housing opportunities to the large-scale, multi-function urban redevelopment and population dislocation as public policy by the late 1980s.[7] In referencing the gentry in its initial coining (by Ruth Glass in 1964), gentrification has ever since implied class struggle as part of its definition.[8] By the 2000s, gentrification was recognized as having nuanced formations according to strategies involving the economic, cultural and social capital of its protagonists.[9] In addition, gentrification has come to be understood as not only affecting housing but also its supporting network of commercial, transport and leisure sectors. While the literature is united in its identification of gentrification as an outcome and aspiration for most, if not all, of the celebrated regeneration projects of the late 20th and early 21st century—in which infrastructure is often a salient component—it is divided in its assessment of it.[10] Some argue, like the public-policy makers from across the political spectrum that promote it, that gentrification is a positive process of urban improvement.

Others, like community activists, neighbourhood groups, social scientists and 'leftist' cultural geographers, argue that gentrification can lead to "exclusionary landscapes reinforced with middle-class sensibility."[11]

Negative assessments of gentrification are tied to the complex role played by the expansion of international financial investment in urban redevelopment and the attendant social inequality and economic disparity that often results. Gentrification[12] and globalization (of residents, tourist-supporting infrastructure, and design practice) are both processes and results. In such regeneration developments, the often-promised social mix does not appear to materialize, or at least not effectively; any proposed community creation is instead, it is argued, replaced by accumulation opportunism, and with it a loss of "place."[13] This is especially true when neighbourhoods are redesigned so that public space is co-opted for the needs of consumers and place-marketing is pitched to a global, not local, audience. In these instances, local populations are displaced (with the demolition of both their housing and social networks) and housing prices inflate.

By contrast, positive features of successful investment in development and planned (or consequential) gentrification are usually identified with increased tax revenues from the purchase of locally provided goods and services. There are also incentives for lower-income households to stay owing to neighbourhood improvements, and increased employment for lower-income groups, often as a result of the increase in municipal services. These factors all contribute to creating economically diverse neighbourhoods of mixed-income groups.[14] Positive assessments, though, often come with caveats. Many of these beneficial outcomes depend on safeguards such as rent control, a cap on annual increases in real property taxes and addressing the issue of affordable housing for the poor to prevent existing population dislocation.[15] These caveats were noted back in 2005 by Atkinson and Bridge, who observed that "[g]entrification as a process of investment and movement by the wealthy may have modified or positive effects in cities characterized by strong welfare regimes, enhanced property rights and mediation, and low competition for housing resources."[16]

In contemporary urban regeneration projects, gentrification has been adopted as a public policy tool which both justifies market forces and public-private enterprises; ideally, it should also direct market processes toward benign outcomes.[17] Property tax uplift, it is argued, is necessary to improve the services available to all residents, increased public services and, theoretically, social capital transference. Such positive outcomes are associated with the 'liveable city' rhetoric of bids by municipal governments aiming to compete globally.[18]

While Glass identified gentrification in 1964 as more isolated, small-scale incidents of middle-class individuals moving into working-class neighbourhoods, "by the 1990s gentrification had evolved into a crucial urban strategy for city governments in consort with private capital in cities around the world."[19] It subsidized private market transformation of the urban built environment.[20] Neil Smith highlights the qualities of contemporary urban redevelopment that distinguish it in its evolution from the neighbourhood transformations by individuals in the 1960s to the comprehensive restructuring of enormous swaths of the urban fabric by municipal or national governments in the last 30 years. Smith argues that gentrification has become "a way of transforming whole areas into new kinds of landscapes that initiate a comprehensive class-infected urban remake."[21] This transformation is implemented by global networks of finance, real estate and property developers, and their local counterparts, business interests and municipal or national governments. In aiming to attract tourists, investors and affluent consumers within competing urban economies, the new kinds of landscapes depend in large part on gentrification. Therefore, they must appeal to the symbolic codes and spatial amenities that this intended social group expects. Infrastructure is a key element of not only the material landscape of gentrification but also its symbolic forms. Regeneration is not only an investment of economic capital: it is an investment of symbolic capital. Because of its public role, infrastructure has the opportunity to be more inclusive in its programming of space and cultural referencing. Just as design can be used to create exclusionary infrastructure, such as benches that deter unintended use, it can also be used to encourage more inclusive infrastructure.[22]

GLOBALIZATION

Globalization is an integral part of the gentrification associated with large-scale urban regeneration efforts. Smith, for example, identifies gentrification as "a sector of productive capital investment" in new metropolitan-scale urbanism and hence a particular instance of "the globalization of production."[23] Globalization has also coincided with the international practice of architectural firms, the worldwide influence of post-Bretton Woods institutions such as the International Monetary Fund and the World Bank, and technological developments in mass media. There is a common belief that globalization is a process that leads to homogenized cities and places wherever it operates.[24] But what exactly is meant by globalization?

Contemporary international or global institutions tailor their definitions of globalization to their specific realms of operation. The United Nations Committee for Development Policy offers a specifically economic (and neo-liberal) formulation:

> Globalization is] the increasing interdependence of world economies as a result of the growing scale of cross-border trade of commodities and services, the flow of international capital and the wide and rapid spread of technologies. It reflects the continuing expansion and mutual integration of market frontiers [...] and the rapid growing significance of information in all types of productive activities and marketization are the two major driving forces for economic globalization."[25]

The World Health Organization examines globalization in terms of its interests in health:

> [T]he increased interconnectedness and interdependence of peoples and countries, is generally understood to include two inter-related elements: the opening of international borders to increasingly fast flows of goods, services, finance, people and ideas; and the changes in institutions and policies at national and international levels that facilitate or promote such flows. Globalization has the potential for both positive and negative effects on development and health."[26]

Globalization was introduced into academic discourse in the late 1950s and early 1960s; the word "global" was popularized in the 1970s and in common use by the 1990s.[27] When Saskia Sassen published *The Global City* in 1991, she commented that she had adopted the word "global" rather than "world" to distinguish this new type of city from the previous cross-border economic processes of earlier empires or inter-state trade. In contrast to these prior examples, Sassen argues that the new, global city is to be understood as "a result of privatization, deregulation, digitalization, the opening up of national economies to foreign firms, and the growing participation of national economic actors in global markets."[28] Contemporary urban regeneration projects are an example of the globalization she identifies. She also notes that globalization is mutable, its development alterable, and only accounts for part of what happens in cities.[29]

Anthony D. King, however, questions the extent to which the terms globalization and global (or homogenized) culture actually apply. He observes that what is considered "global" is "not applicable to everywhere, equally, with the same signification."[30] Instead, King and others posit the existence of a plurality of experiences, receptions and productions of 'global' cultures, with multiple responses to the processes of varied globalizations—economic, media, technological, and others. Indeed, by the start of the 21st century people were writing about the diversity rather than the homogenization of culture.[31]

German philosopher, sociologist and critical theorist, Jurgen Habermas, offers an expanded definition:

> By 'globalisation' is meant the cumulative processes of a world-wide expansion of trade and production, commodity and financial markets, fashions, the media and computer programs, news and communications networks, transportation systems and flows of migration, the risks engendered by large-scale technology, environmental damage and epidemics, as well as organised crime and terrorism.[32]

Alternatively, anthropologist Arjun Appadurai distinguishes different options:

> While global capital and the system of nation-states negotiate the terms of the emergent world order, a worldwide order of institutions has emerged that bears witness to what we may call

'grassroots globalization,' or 'globalization from below.' The most easily recognizable of these institutions are NGOs (nongovernmental organizations) concerned with mobilizing highly specific local, national, and regional groups on matters of equity, access, justice, and redistribution. These organizations have complex relations with the state, with the official public sphere, with international civil society initiatives and with local communities.[33]

Habermas' definition of globalization, which is generally the meaning associated with the word and the basis for its critique, clearly implies infrastructure—the bridges and airports, for example, that allow flows of commodities and people, the museums and banking structures that service tourism or attract finance. But infrastructure is also evident in Appadurai's "grassroots globalization," the local and informal service provision that is a positive contribution to a more equitable world. Saskin's "globalization of economic activity" and "the new type of organizational structure" that it entails also implicates infrastructure, in the forms of digital and optic networks and banking protocols.[34] King's questioning both of the terms "globalization" and "global", and in whose interests they are coined and used, cautions about generalization while positing alternative receptions of "global" products and their support infrastructure. This more nuanced understanding of globalization reveals that infrastructure has varied opportunities for supporting the public good: it, like the process of globalization, has the potential to make negative but also positive contributions to city and place making.

What is also relevant to the topic of infrastructure and its ability to accrue design capital is the relationship of these multiple processes of globalization to culture. King argues that there are "globally produced cultures and culturally produced views of globalization."[35] He also proposes that "the reception of global culture may be hybridized, indigenized or subjected to a process of translation."[36] All of which is to say that 'globalization' produces different cultural responses and different modes of reception and consumption—that is, meaning-making. These differences will be at play in the conveyance of value, design value and of the importance of design capital to infrastructure.

ICONIC STRUCTURES

Iconic structures are perhaps the most visible urban landmarks of the processes of urban regeneration and its forms of gentrification and globalization. Since the 1990s, iconic structures often purposefully represent global companies and depend on the financial flows of capital. They may perhaps become one of the most defining aspects of the postmodernist age.[37] These postmodern icons are diffuse in meaning and their veneration secular, no longer possessing the stable meaning and devotional veneration of past icons. Iconic structures, particularly (but not exclusively) buildings, have been identified in architectural discourse as powerful markers in landscapes and cityscapes, creating neighbourhood identities and providing global reference points. They function within the circuits of media-recognized 'starchitects,' tourism and financial capital, and they anchor city regeneration schemes. Iconic structures have been defended by architectural theorist and historian Charles Jencks as enigmatic signifiers, new kinds of monuments that have shed the impossible task of consecrating permanence and shared, often local, memories in an era sceptical of all overarching or unifying explanations (metanarratives); they and their architects, he proposes, seek global attention.[38]

Of the Bilbao Guggenheim, for example, Jencks notes that "developers and mayors could see the economic logic of the sculptural gesture, with its many enigmatic signifiers and the same method could be applied to any and every building." (Figure 3:1) This, he argues, raised a semantic problem—"how to invest the idea of decorum and appropriateness [when] an expressive museum could take the place of a cathedral or public building."[39] Bilbao Guggenheim was economically successful, costing £100 million to build but generating £400 million in its first two years. However, success was understood not only in terms of profitability, but also in the surrounding public and media sensation, its ability to attract tourists and to garner professional acclaim for its creative risk-taking. Jencks explains:

> Global society and its largest corporations, those commissioning these expensive landmark buildings, in turn force architecture to be mediated by the mass media—TV, Sunday supplements, airline magazines, international weeklies (Time). Partly global clients must

use the media to organize consent and raise a huge amount of risk capital, and the 'star architect' is essential in getting this attention.[40]

While there were fears that the local art community would suffer from public funds being directed from them to this single, international institution, this has not occurred and a more complex set of benefits to the arts community has in fact resulted.[41]

However, iconic buildings are often assigned banal functions. Context, site and the local economy are frequently disregarded and, as a consequence, iconic buildings do not perform as promised, either economically or socially. Sometimes these buildings fail to garner praise from the design profession or to attract media attention. The economic downturn in 2007-08 caused a reassessment of the iconic building and provoked a flurry of negative evaluations in the professional and academic press for their inappropriate functions, inflated budgets and cost overruns, gratuitous form, and poor design.[42] And there loomed over all the colossal failure of the Millennium Dome, which by 2006 had led many civic bodies to abandon, at least temporarily, the ambition of the iconic building with its high-risk and high-cost overruns.[43]

In his riposte to these criticisms, Jencks argues that the failure of some iconic buildings was due to inappropriate signification: what ensures their success, he argues, are enigmatic signifiers, a form that elicits multiple metaphors which resonate meaningfully with both local and global audiences. Jencks's reference to local and global audiences points to the tension that the enigmatic is intended to resolve. However, this tension is the product of more than the choice of signifier and a building's success is determined by more than design backed up by mass media attention. As demonstrated by the several failed iconic buildings highlighted in Miles Glendinning's *Architecture's Evil Empire? The Triumph and Tragedy of Global Modernism*, appropriate risk evaluation and a host of local, social and budgetary realities must also be considered.[44] For infrastructure to earn the accolades of being considered an iconic landmark and urban regeneration tool contributing to the greater good, it will need to consider all these design elements in order to acquire enduring value and to accrue design capital.

3:1 Bilbao, Spain with Frank Gehry's Bilbao Guggenheim in foreground.
Photo: Brianna Laugher.

3:2 Renzo Piano. The Shard (2012) London, UK.
Photo: Daniel Chapman.

WHERE DOES INFRASTRUCTURE FIT IN THIS DEBATE?

Infrastructure is a likely participant in globalization. It is highly visible in, and necessary to, urban regeneration projects where it often serves an iconic or landmark purpose. Its scale demands huge capital investment, often sourced internationally where it is seen as a reliable investment with good demand and a predictable revenue. Infrastructure, as part of a network, is able to serve not only the contemporary needs of global flows of people, capital and culture, but also the fabric of the historic city.[45] Infrastructure disperses and directs the flow of people and goods, provides amenities, and impacts physically and economically upon local neighbourhoods and distant networks. It can also be a significant landmark and urban feature and part of 'design-led' regeneration.[46] The Gateshead Millennium Bridge that crosses the Tyne to Newcastle is an example, as is the Shard in the Southwark borough of London, of the 'design led' renaissance.[47] (Figure 3: 2) Here, both bridge and building figure in assessments of regeneration schemes and their gentrification outcomes.[48]

The Gateshead Millennium Bridge was intended not only to connect Gateshead with Newcastle but also initiate the redevelopment of a disused industrial warehouse area into a cultural precinct. The bridge was financed by national and EU funding, with the latter specifically dedicated to infrastructure and service investment.[49] The cultural precinct in question was centered on two buildings, both the result of international design competitions managed by the Royal Institute for British Architects (RIBA), and both in part funded by National Lottery Grants. One building, the BALTIC Centre for Contemporary Art, was a retrofitted mid-century flour mill designed by Ellis Williams Architects and opened in 2002. The second, the Sage Gateshead Concert Hall by Foster + Partners (named after significant funding from the Sage Group), was opened in 2004. The BALTIC Centre, concert hall and bridge were all projects of a culture-led regeneration programme. The art centre and concert hall were also intended as anchor tenants to encourage private development between them. This culture and infrastructure-led urban regeneration is currently attracting investment interest and a developer-led project for an arena, hotel, and other leisure and entertainment venues on the site is currently under review. (See Chapter 8 for further discussion.)

The Shard, a 72-storey mixed-use 'iconic' building in Southwark, London, designed by Renzo Piano (2009-2012) is an example of global flows of capital and gentrification outcomes of urban regeneration. (Figure 3:2) The Shard replaced a 25-storey 1970s standard office complex. It accommodates 26 floors of high-quality office space, 18 floors of luxury hotel and 10 of luxury residential apartments, three restaurants and a viewing platform. Several players and initiates were involved in its creation. Its great height (and profitability) was a response to the UK government's announced encouragement of tall buildings at transportation hubs and to overturn opposition to the interest in 'exceptional design' in 1998. The planned significant reinvestment and refurbishment of transportation hubs in London would provide access for employees working in the building and encourage development around it. The London Bridge Station in Southwark was completely renovated between 2009 and 2017 and accommodated the Shard access in its redesign. The renovation was the result of the business acumen of the local developer owning the original 25-storey building and being able to fund the project with foreign investment due to the favourable view of London as an investment venue. Upon completion, the regenerated Southwark quarter was renamed the Shard Quarter and new luxury hotels and apartment buildings began to appear in its orbit. The Shard, with its investment (and subsequent 95% ownership) from Qatar, is clearly the result of globalizing capital. The Shard and London Bridge Station, with its quick access to Gatwick and Luton Airports as well as Crossrail, have been a catalyst for gentrification in the form of luxury hotels and apartment buildings.

Infrastructure in the context of regeneration and gentrification has also been discussed by Leary and McCarthy in *The Routledge Companion to Urban Regeneration*. In the introduction to "Part 3: public infrastructure and public spaces", McCarthy comments on "the importance of public infrastructure and public space in urban regeneration" and highlights "the interconnections between physical, social and economic aspects." He elaborates on the role of infrastructure and green space in placemaking, noting "their effectiveness as proxies for wider amenity and quality of life, since these often feature as elements of a set of measures intended as estimates of the 'desirability' of global cities as places to live and work."[50]

However, an iconic structure does not necessarily develop the culture of place that is sought out by global corporations, tourists and locals alike.

To nurture the culture of a place and represent it in new infrastructure involves an attitude toward design development which is different from that needed for producing generic or iconic buildings. The topic has been studied sufficiently in the design community to understand the pitfalls. We hope that governments promoting and guiding development will direct investment with an eye to social equality and cultural sensitivity, leading to better outcomes for all.

INFRASTRUCTURE REDEVELOPMENT: WHO BENEFITS?

In many of the redevelopment examples cited, global competitiveness is visible in design amplified in iconic structures. Bilbao's Guggenheim and London's Shard are just two examples; both are notable signifiers of, and market lures for, their redevelopment sites, with one a brownfield harbour and the other an "underutilized" city-centre borough. Both are the salient iconic features within comprehensive plans that involved different degrees of public/private cooperation and funding.[51] Both redevelopments, publicized as urban regeneration or renaissance, can be argued to include gentrification as an intentional urban strategy and to have a scale determined by global flows of capital.[52] Bilbao's revitalization was premised on "actively engaging in globalization strategies," using a "project-based approach" and featuring architects with name-recognition.[53] High-value structures, including iconic buildings with their attached architectural celebrity, were demanded by those involved in urban regeneration.[54] In Kyoto and Sydney, regeneration included "high quality railway design"; this has been identified as a contributor to the success of the schemes, a necessary complement to the correct assessment of real-estate market strengths.[55] In Manchester, it was found that infrastructure as part of brownfield redevelopment can assist in the restoration of the social fabric of the community. Successful regeneration schemes mean that areas previously deprived of infrastructure now acquire meaningful infrastructure, such as well-designed transit stations, and this confers symbolic capital on the area. Many urban design researchers have concluded that "having the necessary infrastructure in place is essential."[56]

3:3 Urban Think Tank (U-TT). Caracas Metrocable (2010).
Photo: Iwan Baan.

Infrastructure can play a galvanizing role in discussions on who should be the benefactors of urban redevelopments. In the late 1990s, Caracas proposed a highway that would connect the city centre to suburban enclaves. Projected on its most efficient course, the highway would have bisected a favela community, displacing the residents in its wake. In enhancing the convenient and rapid mobility of a prosperous middle class and the ensuing dislocation of the poorer favela residents, this proposal would have contributed to gentrification in the city. However, it was the catalyst for an alternative project that, because of its socially-aware design, was able to successfully redirect resources to a different infrastructure scheme serving a different constituency and arguably producing a more equitable public good.

Small-scale infrastructure can have a large impact on improving social equity. Urban-Think Tank's Caracas cable car system, comprising five station structures and associated cultural facilities and social amenities (2003-10), enhanced impoverished neighbourhoods of the city's San Agustin favela, giving residents access to jobs and services as well as public meeting places.[57] (Figure 3:3) While the project was local in its focus and instigation, it was nevertheless connected to global networks of funding, expertise and publicity in its execution. Funding was sourced from municipal programmes, international foundations (German Federal Cultural Foundation) and corporate players.[58] The founding members of Urban-Think Tank, architects Alfredo Brillembourg and Hubert Klumpner, were both educated in the US as well as Venezuela and Austria respectively; they maintain professional connections with American and European institutions, have won prestigious international awards, work as government advisors, and undertake multi-institutional research.[59] Many of the products used in the construction of the cable car infrastructure were developed in collaboration with European manufacturers.[60] Urban-Think Tank mobilized publicity via international symposia, exhibitions and publications to attract endorsement and support from those who might facilitate the project. The professional press, including web-based publications, drew a global audience. The design was not only functional but, by garnering attention in the professional design press and award system, added distinction (in both the traditional and Bourdieu's sense of the word) and value to the neighbourhood, both specifically and as an example of architectural intervention of global significance.[61] Global and professional recognition of the Caracas Metrocable are just two aspects of its design that contribute to its design capital. The architectural language devised for the cable car stations and associated structures refers to local practices in materials, assemblage and choreography across the neighbourhood. The structures were kept within the financial means of the community via an economy of means, reduced maintenance costs and sustainability strategies: dry or cistern-fed toilets, windcatchers, natural daylighting and LED night illumination.[62] The stations were also envisioned as landmarks, or beacons, within the favela. One in particular, built on the site of a former water tank, a barrio icon, references its form and iconic function.[63] So, while the cable car system has many of the characteristics of urban redevelopment, including global flows of capital and expertise, private/public joint venture funding, and even iconicity, it differs in its minimal negative imprint and dislocation of local populations, its disinterest in speculation and gentrification, and its resolutely local scale, architectural language and iconography. It resists gentrification by being responsive to "real public needs."[64]

Estudio Teddy Cruz + Fonna Forman's tactical design of housing and community infrastructure for the San Ysidro neighbourhood of San Diego is another example of development that responds inclusively to the needs of the local community. (Figure 3:4) "Living Rooms at the Border" (2001-18) serves the neighbourhood's needs for a range of services, including affordable housing and educational opportunities, while meeting the community outreach objectives of the University of California at San Diego (UCSD). Several levels of infrastructure were designed to embed housing within a network of social supports. An on-site church was repurposed as a theatre which supported not only a resident theatre troupe but also provided training in theatre arts; basic, linear open-air pavilions accommodated classrooms for UCSD internship programmes and a coffee kiosk providing barista training, while another linear structure offered office space for immigration services and two larger linear apartment buildings bracketed the site.[65] The site was also well served by the Blue Line of the San Diego Metropolitan Transit System, and so conveniently linked to UCSD as well as the city and its opportunities. The project was considered in its planning stages not only at the level of function and economy, but also design. The linear design of all the new structures allowed for permeation of the site by pedestrian alleys formed by their interstitial spaces; it also

3:4 Estudio Teddy Cruz + Fonna Forman. UCSD-Casa Community Station: Living Rooms at the Border (2020), San Ysidro, California, US.

afforded a unifying framework for an array of infill and stackable elements responsive to programmatic need. These strategies added design value to the spatial and flexible arrangement of services. While the project was of a neighbourhood scale and designed to resist gentrification, with funding primarily state-sourced and administered by a non-profit organization (Casa Familiar), it did nevertheless participate in globalization. Cruz and Forman's research is founded on an understanding of the global forces at work in the North-South divide and addressed pragmatically through his work on the Tijuana / San Diego border; their work has been exhibited internationally and they are involved with globally linked institutions like UCSD and Harvard. Casa Familiar is, however, positioned as a small-scale, small-economy, locally-determined alternative to the large-scale, globally financed and speculative developments characteristic of many renaissance or regeneration projects.

CONCLUSION

Gentrification is not a foregone conclusion when the public realm is redesigned well, but there is a significant association between the two. The most problematic feature of gentrification is displacement of the local population because they can no longer afford the increasing rents in the area. While this is to some extent dependent on economic forces, there are several important aspects that have to do with the design of the project. These aspects all, ultimately, address the question: who does this design benefit? The focus should be on the local community first—an imperative that investors and government sometimes lose sight of. To prevent this, the local community should have a voice in the creation of the project, rather than being simply asked for an opinion on the appearance of the development after it is designed. Secondly, the framework of the project should ensure the maintenance of housing and services for the local inhabitants and, ideally, offer a significant improvement in services. This must be carefully framed and contractually codified so that the intention is carried all the way through the project. This involves a commitment by all involved in the project and as such, it is not an easy fix. However, this offers a sustainable approach which will ultimately be of value to the city and its inhabitants.

NOTES

1. For an overview of the types of regeneration projects (for example, those led by or focussed on entrepreneur, housing, culture and leisure, or sustainability) see A. Tallon, *Urban Regeneration in the UK* (London: Routledge, 2010). Tallon also notes that the focus of regeneration projects has evolved over time, and with them would be the role of infrastructure. For negative assessments, see Miles Glendinning, *Architecture's Evil Empire? The Triumph and Tragedy of Global Modernism* (London: Reaktion Books, 2010) and Neil Smith, "New Globalism, New Urbanism: Gentrification as Global Urban Strategy," *Antipode*, 2002. Richard Rogers, for example, used the term, renaissance, in his 1998 White Paper "Toward an Urban Renaissance" and between 2001 and 2008 he served aschief advisor on architecture and urbanism to Mayor of London Ken Livingston.
2. See, Charles Jencks, "The iconic building is here to stay," *City* 10, no. 1 (April 2006).
3. See in Michael Leary and John McCarthy, eds., "Part 3: Public infrastructure and public space," in *The Routledge Companion to Urban Regeneration* (London and New York: Routledge, 2013), 209-302. Charles Jencks, "Toward an Iconography of the Present," *Log* (Fall 2004): 102-03.
4. Tallon, *Urban Regeneration*, 246.
5. By 2008 several anthologies had been written about gentrification including: Loretta Lees, Tom Slater, Elvin Wyly, *Gentrification* (New York and London: Routledge, 2008); Rowland Atkinson and Gary Bridge, eds., *Gentrification in a Global Context: The New Urban Colonialism* (New York and London: Routledge, 2005).
6. See, Tim Butler and Garry Robson, "Social Capital, Gentrification and Neighbourhood Change in London: A Comparison of Three South London Neighbourhoods," *Urban Studies* 38, no. 12 (2001): 2145-2161. For a good synoptic discussion of these positive and negative aspects of gentrification, see: Lees, Slater and Wyly, Chapter 6. "Gentrification: Positive or Negative?" in *Gentrification*, 196-238. Research is based on both empirical studies of specific neighborhoods and theoretical framings, primarily from the disciplines of sociology, geography and political science.
7. The term "gentrification" was coined to characterize the movement of middle-class individuals into working-class inner-city boroughs of London by Ruth Glass in 1964. By 1996, Neil Smith identified gentrification as a public policy tool and urban strategy of municipal and state governments. Ruth Glass, "Introduction: Aspects of change," in Centre for Urban Studies, ed., *London: Aspects of Change* (London: MacKibbon and Kee, 1964); Neil Smith, "New globalism, new urbanism: Gentrification as global urban strategy," *Antipode* 34, no. 3 (2002): 427-450;S.B. Laska and D. Spain, eds., *Back to the City: Issues in Neighbourhood Renovation,* (New York: Pergamon Press, 1980); J. Palen and B. London, eds., *Gentrification, Displacement and Neighbourhood Revitalization* (Albany: State University of New York, 1974); Neil Smith and Peter Williams, *Gentrification of the City* (Boston: Allen and Unwin 1986).
8. Lees, Slater and Wyly, *Gentrification*, 249-50.
9. See, Tim Butler and Garry Robson, "Social Capital, Gentrification and Neighbourhood Change in London: A Comparison of Three South London Neighbourhoods," *Urban Studies* 38, no. 12 (2001): 2145-2161.
10. For a good synoptic discussion of these positive and negative aspects of gentrification see: Lees, Slater and Wyly, Chapter 6. "Gentrification: Positive or Negative?" in *Gentrification*, 196-238. Research is based on both empirical studies of specific neighborhoods and theoretical framings, primarily from the disciplines of sociology, geography and political science.

11. Neil Smith, in Lees, Slater and Wyly, *Gentrification*, 195.
12. Gentrification is the mechanism or process by which dislocation of the poor results from the in-migration of wealthier groups, resulting in an increase in taxes, rents and property values. It is also associated with the transformation of the neighbourhood or area according to middle-class tastes, hence a reference to the gentry. The term entered contemporary theoretical discourse with the 1964 writing of Ruth Glass, a cultural geographer, who described the gentrification of Islington, an area in North London. While Glass described small-scale, ad hoc gentrification and private gentrifiers in her 1964 publication cited above, 30 years later gentrification is seen as a larger urban strategy used by city governments seeking global investment.
13. Janet Abu-Lughod, ed., *From Urban Village to East Village: The Battle for New York's Lower East Side* (Oxford: Blackwell, 1994).
14. J.P. Byrne, "Two Cheers for Gentrification," *Howard Law Journal* 46, no. 3 (2003): 405-432, quoted in Lees, Slater and Wyly, *Gentrification*, 195.
15. Lees, Salter and Wyly, *Gentrification*, 198.
16. Rowland Atkinson and Gary Bridge, eds. *Gentrification in a Global Context*: The New Urban Colonialism (London and New York: Routledge, 2005): 16-17, cited in Lees, Slater and Wyly, *Gentrification*, 234.
17. Stuart Cameron, "Gentrification, housing differentiation and urban regeneration: 'Going for Broke in Newcastle upon Tyne," *Urban Studies* 40:12 (2003): 2367-2382.
18. Liveable Rotterdam, see Justus Uitermark, Jan Willem Duyvendak, and Reinout Kleinhans, "Gentrification as a governmental strategy: Social control and social cohesion in Hoogvleit, Rotterdam," *Environment and Planning A:1* (2007): 125-141;129.
19. Infrastructure figures in the discourse of many academic and design professions, many of them identifying its detrimental consequences. Historically, those negative aspects include the furthering of imperial expansion and colonization where the latter often involves the settler society in a gentrification. Le Corbusier's plans for Algiers in the 1930s focused on immense infrastructural projects that included a viaduct/housing hybrid, continuous housing slabs and an iconic business tower, all scaled to the imperial rather than local investment capacity and fashioned for settler not indigenous occupation. Its huge bridging structure overstepped the indigenous old city, casting it in shadow and surrounding it with gentrification. It served the imperial project. Although World War II and Algerian Independence ensured that it was never built, it bears an uncanny resemblance to contemporary renovation schemes.
20. Neil Smith, "New Globalism, New Urbanism." Smith links gentrification with neoliberalism.
21. Smith, "New Globalism, New Urbanism," 443.
22. Mike Davis describes benches in Los Angeles, for example, that prevented the homeless from sleeping on them in The *City of Quartz: Excavating the Future of Los Angeles* (London: Verso, 1990).
23. Smith, "New Globalism, New Urbanism," 446.
24. For example see, Kenneth Frampton, "Towards a Critical Regionalism," in *The Anti-Aesthetic Essays on Postmodern Cultrure*, ed. Hal Foster, 1st ed. (Port Townsend, Wash: Bay Press, 1983).
25. Gao Shangquan, "Economic Globalization: Trends, Risks and Risk Prevention," United Nations CDP Background Paper NO.1 ST/ESA/2000/CPP/1, accessed June 15, 2020, https://www.un.org/en/development/desa/policy/cdp/cdp_background_papers/bp2000_1.pdf.
26. The World Health Organization, "Topics: Globalization," accessed June 1, 2020, https://www.who.int/topics/globalization/en.
27. Anthony D. King, *Spaces of Global Cultures: Architecture, Urbanism, Identity* (London and New York: Routledge, 2004), 24. Saskia Sassen's extensive bibliography to her 2001 *The Global City* cites 1 title with globalization before the first edition in 1991 and 18 before the second in 2001 and 20 titles with the word global before 1991 and 43 before 2001. See Saskia Sassen, *The Global City: New York, London, Tokyo, 2nd ed.* (Princeton and Oxford: Princeton University Press, 2001).

28. Sassen, *The Global City*, xviii.
29. Sassen, *The Global City*, xvii, xxii.
30. King, *Spaces of Global Cultures*, 30. King observes that market capitalism may disperse products and technologies widely but consumers may use them differently and hence consumer cultures are multiple. Likewise, he questions if mass events and mass culture are signs and sources of a global culture. See *King, Spaces of Global Cultures*, 26-57.
31. Diana Crane, Nobuko Kawashima and Ken'ichi Kawasaki, eds., *Global Culture: Media, Arts, Policy and Globalization* (London and New York, 2002), cited in King, *Spaces of Global Cultures*, 31.
32. Jurgen Habermas, *The Divided West* (Cambridge UK: Polity Press, 2006), 175, cited in Robert Adam, "Globalization and Architecture," *Architectural Review* 222, no.1332 (February 2008): 74, electronic version accessed April 29, 2020.
33. Arjun Appadurai, "Grassroots Globalization and the Research Imagination," *Globalization* (Durham and London: Duke University Press, 2001), 16-17.
34. Sassen, *The Global City*.
35. Anthony D. King, ed., *Culture, Globalization and the World-System: Contemporary Conditions for the Representation of Identity* (Minneapolis: University of Minnesota Press,1997), x.
36. King, Culture, *Globalization*, x.
37. Charles Jencks has written extensively on the iconic and symbolic aspect of architecture and postmodern architecture, in particular in *The Language of Post Modern Architecture* (New York: Rizzoli, 1977), *Towards a Symbolic Architecture* (New York: Rizzoli, 1985) and *The Iconic Building* (New York: Rizzoli, 2005). In part, Glendinning argues, these iconic buildings are the result of EU funding and Union-wide competitions for "City of Culture" which, like the Olympics or World Expos, seek to attract tourists and investment. Glendinning, *Architecture's Evil Empire*, 7-18.
38. Charles Jencks, "The iconic building is here to stay," *City* 10, no. 1 (April 2006): 4.
39. Jencks, "The iconic building," 4.
40. Charles Jencks, *The Iconic Building: The Power of Metaphor* (London: Rizzoli, 2005), 8-9. See also, Charles Jencks, "Towards an Iconography of the Present," *Log* (Fall 2004).
41. Biatriz Plaza, Manuel Tironi and Silka N Haarlch, "Bilbao's Art Scene and the 'Guggenheim effect' Revisited," *European Planning Studies* 17, no. 11 (2009), https://doi.org/10.10801096543210903208606.
42. Anon., "End of the Iconic Age," *Building Design* (July 23, 2004.); Silber "Architecture of the Absurd," *Architect's Journal* (November 19, 2009): 25; Marc Treib, *Architectural Research Quarterly* xi/ 2-4 (2007): 223-36; Charles Jencks, "The Truth about Icons," *The Architect's Journal* 9 (September 2004): 20-24; Kenneth Frampton, "The Work of Art in the Age of Commodification," *Commodification and Spectacle in Architecture. A Harvard Design Magazine Reader*,ed. William S. Saunders (2006), ix-xviii; Graham Morrison, "Look at Me!" *The Guardian* (12 July 2004).
43. There was a rash of articles in the professional, and occasionally the popular, press between 2004 and 2009. See footnote 42.
44. Glendinning, *Architecture's Evil Empire*.
45. Adam, "Globalization and Architecture."
46. Tallon, *Urban Regeneration*, 246.
47. Tallon, *Urban Regeneration*, 245.
48. Keller Easterling, *Extrastatecraft: The Power of Infrastructure Space* (London: Verso, 2016), 11.
49. National funding came from the Millennium Fund, a public body established to distribute National Lottery Funds. EU funding came from the European Regional Development Fund which had the purpose of transferring funds from richer regions to undeveloped ones.
50. McCarthy, Introduction to "Part 3: Public infrastructure and public space," in *The Routledge Companion to Regeneration*, 211-215.
51. Jorg Pliger, *Bilbao City Report*, CASE report 43 (2007). Accessed May 23, 2020, https://www.eprints.lse.uk/3624/Bilbao_city_report_(final). Up-market housing also accompanied these developments.
52. Neil Smith argues that "by the 1990s gentrification had evolved into a crucial urban strategy for city governments in consort with private capital in cities around the world. It subsidized private market transformation of the urban built environment." Smith, "New Globalism,

New Urbanism," 443. One of the few social programmes initiated by Bilbao Ria-2000, the non-profit publicly sponsored partnership that manages the large-scale regeneration of identified areas, involved the significant revitalization of the historic centre of Bilbao, Casa Viejo, which consequently gentrified. Jorg Pliger, *Bilbao City Report*,

53. Pilger, "Bilbao City Report," 17.
54. Adam, "Globalization and Architecture," 74-77; Will Hurst, Charles Gates and Damian Arnold, "End of the Iconic Age?" *Building Design* no. 1635 (July 23, 2004), accessed April 29, 2020.
55. Chris Hale, "Mass Transit is the Anchor: Transit-focussed urban regeneration across the Pacific Rim," in Leary and McCarthy eds., *Routledge Companion to Urban Regeneration,* 217-229, quote from 217.
56. Tim Dixon Noriko Utsuka and Hirokazu Abe, "Critical Success Factors in Urban Brownfield Regeneration: Bringing 'hardcore' sites in Manchester and Osaka back into use," in Leary and McCarthy eds., *Routledge Companion to Urban Regeneration*, 241-250, quote from 248.
57. Urban-Think Tank was founded in Caracas, in 1998 by Alfredo Brillembourg and Hubert Klumpner. It is a research collaborative. Brillembourg graduated from Columbia University with a BA in Architecture in 1984 and an MSC in Architectural Design in 1986. He also has a second design degree from the Central University of Venezuela, 1992. Klumpner also has a Columbia degree. https://u-tt.com/about/alfredobrillembourg and https://u-tt.com/about/hubertklumpner.
58. Suzanne Stephens, "Urban-Think Tank," Architectural Record (October 16, 2008), https://architecturalrecord.com/articles/6448-urban-think-tank.
59. Both were educated at Columbia Graduate School of Architecture, Planning and Preservation in the 1990s and Brillembourg has taught at Harvard GSD, and the Swiss Institute of Technology. See, Stephens, "Urban-Think Tank." By 2010 Brillembourg was Chair of Architecture and Urban Design at the Swiss Institute of Technology, Zurich. https://.architizer.com/blog/inspiration/stories/alfrdo-brillembourg-expanding-architecture. Note Alfredo Brillembourg and Hubert Klumpner, *Urban-Think Tank: Unsolicited Architecture* (Berlin and Stuttgart: Hatje Cantz, 2021).
60. Austrian ropeway manufacturers Dopplemayr and engineers Silman and Associates and Transolar were involved in the production of the cable car structure, engineering and solar panels. See, David Sokol, "Over Site: How Caracas's New Cable-Car System is Making the City's Favelas More Visible," *Architonic* (July 29, 2010), https://architeonic.com/en/story/david-sokol-over-site-how-caracas's-cable-car-system-ismaking-the-city-s-more-visible In addition the Paris-based graphic design firm, Integtral Ruedi Bauer et Associés, consulted for the vertical gym in the Baruda neighbourhood of the favela.
61. In 2008 the Caracas project appeared in the Spring/ Summer issue of *Harvard Design Magazine* devoted to "informal architecture." Awards for the project specifically and the informal settlement it elucidates include: the Venice Biennale of Architecture Golden Lion, 2012, the Holcim Gold Award for Latin America in 2011 and the Holcim Global Silver Award for Innovative contribution to ecological and social design practice in 2012. See the biographies at https://u-tt.com/about/alfredobrillembourg and https://u-tt.com/about/hubertklumptner.
62. See, Sokol, "Over Site."
63. The station at Hornos de Cal, which is a beacon and lookout, is a newly fashioned icon on the former water tower's site. See, https://archello.com/project/metro-cable.
64. See, Zukin and Hou, referenced in Leary and McCarthy eds, T*he Routledge Companion to Urban Regeneration*.
65. See, Ray Juard, accessed June 13, 2020, https://www.nbcsandiego.com/news/local/ed-salon-living-rooms-at-the-border-sanysidro (November 30, 2019); Inga Kiderra, accessed June 13,2020, https://www.ucsd.edu/feature/community-station-opens-at-us-mexico-border (February 17, 2020); casa familiar, accessed June 13, 2020, https://www.casafamiliar.org/livingattheborder.

4

INFRASTRUCTURE IN CONTEXT: PLACEMAKING

Much of the concern with gentrification from the 1970s to 2000s has centred upon its dislocation of existing residents as well as its homogenizing effect. While dislocation of residents has been discussed in the previous chapter, the loss of character and 'localness' is also a significant issue: gentrification often destroys the distinctive character of an area and replaces it with an alternative lacking reference to former local social groups or culture.

ASPECTS LEADING TO 'PLACELESSNESS'

When the term, gentrification, was conceptualized in 1964, it referred to the making of a different, more exclusive place for more expensive real estate.[1] As globalization developed, gentrification has led to an increasing homogenization of places due to a common set of economic factors, 'desirable' inhabitants and real estate practices. As global capital influences how cities are made, investment is more commonly manifest as financial returns and not a socially or culturally inclusive contribution. This, however, is not a given: strong planning policy can offset the most locally detrimental consequences.

While the homogenization of the built environment is often attributed to globalization, it was also a critique levelled at the modern movement of the early 20th century. However, there are differences. The Congresses of Modern Architecture (CIAM), sought consensus across its international members of best practices with respect to optimized, innovative construction technologies and the economies of mass production in the interest of improving working-class living conditions through mass housing and community buildings.[2] However, shared technologies and aesthetic ideologies contributed to a certain stylistic homogeneity across building types and even regional or national contexts. By the mid-20th century, the formal vocabulary of avant-garde modern architecture as represented by CIAM members was co-opted by corporations and governments in the interest of appearing innovative, efficient and current—that is, as a deliberately constructed image of their cultural and political modernity. The current globalization of capital, expanded reach of institutions, deregulation in banking and developments in real estate have both amplified and revamped the homogenized architectural outcome of the first six decades of 20th century modernism.

Currently, homogenization of the built environment arises from different pressures, policies and objectives. The built environment of today is more comprehensive, inclusive of a range of functions and much larger in scope. It now embraces not only residential areas but also contemporary leisure spaces and less tangible cultural regeneration. As Tallon notes:

> Increasingly globalization and diffusion of leisure and cultural regeneration strategies are encouraging the homogenization of culture in city spaces [... the] serial replication and homogenization of the urban landscape have been encouraged through the rolling out of similar types of leisure and cultural strategies, events and flagship buildings across cities.[3]

In addition, the large scale of current regeneration projects means that only certain firms with experience of development on this scale are competing for the projects; this means that only a handful of firms are producing major swathes of cities globally. The economic parameters of public funding, private financing and notions of profitable building types, ownership patterns and marketing oversight determines what gets built and for whom. While there are debates on the degree to which homogenization of space is global (see King above), the issues raised point to the need to discuss the question of place and placemaking and the role of infrastructure in the production of place.

THE DEVELOPMENT OF THINKING ON PLACEMAKING

The post-modern criticism of modernism's seeming lack of interest in 'place' as a design concern began in the 1960s.[4] Many urban practitioners and commentators of this period, such as Jane Jacobs, Kenneth Frampton, Yi Fu Tuan, Norberg-Schulz, Jan Gehl and Kevin Lynch, were deeply interested in understanding placemaking.[5] Influenced by their training and/or interests in philosophy and sociology, they introduced ideas such as historical reference, environmental contextualization, and bodily experience into the understanding of place, as discussed below.

Contemporary practitioners, such as Bureau E.A.S.T, emphasize the need to understand the culture of place as a means of designing successful infrastructure.[6] This understanding has historically been developed by philosophers and sociologists who have elucidated how social aspects of place are understood. The cultural significance of infrastructure is noted in philosophical thought, where it functions metaphorically to illuminate the relationship of human beings to the physical and social world. A well-known example is Heidegger's conception of placemaking in terms of infrastructure, in his illustration, a bridge. Heidegger's writing on phenomenology intensified an interest in the experiential aspects of the built environment in design discourse, particularly after the publication of his 1954 essay, "Building, Dwelling, Thinking"; in this, Heidegger specifically discusses the relationship of the idea of the bridge to human experience. Although his writings have been extensively analyzed and interpreted in nuanced ways, we are interested in his use of the bridge as an element through which to explain the phenomenological significance of built structures in the landscape and their symbiotic production of meaning that is both existential and cultural (that is, embedded in language). Heidegger uses the bridge as an example within a larger discussion to explain how humans relate to built form and place. Heidegger proposes that a bridge is not only a useful built object but, more importantly, also a facilitator of a mental connection and association with place:

> The location is not already there before the bridge is. Before the bridge stands, there are of course many spots along the stream that can be occupied by something. One of them proves to be a

> everyday, of real and valued practices, the geographical source of meaning, vital to hold on to as 'the global' spins its ever more powerful and alienating webs. For others 'a retreat to place' represents a protective pulling-up of drawbridges and a building of walls against the new invasions. Place, on this reading, is the locus of denial, of attempted withdrawal from invasion/difference. It is a politically conservative haven, an essentializing (and in the end unviable) basis for a response; one that fails to address the real forces at work.[12]

Massey cautions us on a too limited or pre-determined notion of place; it is instead to be understood as inclusive. And, as Massey also states:

> This is certainly not to argue against 'the distinctiveness of the place-based' nor – and most particularly – is it to declare that 'there is nothing special about place after all' (Dirluk, 2001, pp.21 and 22). Quite to the contrary: but what is special about place is not some romance of a pre-given collective identity or the eternity of the hills. Rather what is special about place is precisely that throwntogetherness, the unavoidable challenge of negotiating a 'here-and-now' (itself drawing on a history and a geography of thens and theres); and a negotiation that must take place within and between both human and nonhuman [...] This is the event of place in part in the simple sense of the coming together of the previously unrelated, a constellation of processes rather than a thing. This is place as open and as internally multiple. Not capturable as a slice through time in the sense of an essential section. Not intrinsically coherent."[13]

But what does a sense of place mean, and how do we design for a sense of place? There are a plethora of approaches to choose from when designing for place. Even more fundamentally, is designing for a sense of place even the right question? Massey herself raises this point: "The question I want to pose to this is: does it have to be place? Does it have to be territorial at all? Perhaps it is not 'place' that is missing, but grounded, practised, connectedness."[14] While connectedness is often the literal function of infrastructure, it can, via a more socially and culturally inclusive notion of function, also facilitate the creation of a sense of place. To this end we can elucidate that the value of designing for a 'sense of place' is just good design practice: that someone deeply considers the place for which they are designing and makes a sensitive assessment of what it means to be in such a place for the people who live there, play there, work there or even just pass through. Only once this assessment has been made is it then possible to design according to this intention of creating social connectedness. Other designers will have other intentions and through a heterogeneity of approaches, the sense of what place is, was and could be will emerge.

CONTEXTUALIZATION IN FORM AND MATERIALS

Designers contextualize their projects in many ways. At its most basic, contextualization of built form can be formal, temporal or typological. Formal aspects include use of or reference to materials, details, proportion and massing. Temporal aspects are references to historical function and iconic features. Typological contextualization results from the study and classification of built form or space based on specific categories of shared formal characteristics such as building height or the relationship of building to street. As architect, and historian Kenneth Frampton remarks in his seminal essay from 1983, architecture should take a position which "distances itself equally from the Enlightenment myth of progress and from a reactionary, unrealistic impulse to return to the architectonic forms of the preindustrial past."[15] Of his particular approach to place as a critical regionalism, he states:

> The fundamental strategy... is to mediate the impact of universal civilization with elements derived indirectly from the peculiarities of a particular place... It may find its governing inspiration in such things as the range and quality of the local light, or in a tectonic derived from a peculiar structural mode, or in the topography of a given site.[16]

This implies a complex and rigorous study of local ways of knowing and making and was and is one of many respected approaches to placemaking.

Aspects contributing to contextualization and a continuity in place establishment include reference or response to existing materiality and

4:1 Pechet and Robb art and architecture with PWL Partnership Landscape Architects. Granville Street Lighting (2010), Vancouver, Canada. Photo: Clayton Perry.

its configuration, scales of buildings and facades and the configuration of street furniture. For example, in Vancouver, Canada, the use of neon signage has been identified as a historic characteristic of some key shopping streets and districts, such as Granville Street and Chinatown. This history became a point of departure for the design of newer lighting and streetscapes introduced as part of the revitalization of Granville Street by Pechet Studio (Figure 4:1). While the historic neon signs were not imitated, the new lighting replicated the illuminated street edge. As principal Bill Pechet explains,

> [O]ver the years we had lost a lot of amazing signage on the street. It was a chance to kind of produce an after image of what the signage might have looked like, but in a very simple way, a repeating set of LED tubes that could coexist with the remaining blade signs that were still existing on the street and also to reinforce connectivity of the entire ten blocks. The vortex, the visual vortex of them draws you down in both directions.[17]

Here the contextualization of the design was formal, temporal and typological. It was formal in the harmonizing of pattern of vertical light fixtures with the existing blade signs. It was temporal in recalling the former presence of neon lighting and typological in the extension of the tube form of neon fixtures into the LED tubes. It also gave to this now formally unified 10-block stretch of street an identity and imbued it with a distinctiveness, of place.

DESIGNING FOR PLACE: CONTEXTUALIZATION FOR THE ENVIRONMENT

Designing with a sense of place allows designers to customize the environment to social and cultural aspects of the site. Designing comfortable environments is one such strategy. This is far from a new innovation; ancient Romans, whether in Rome or their other hot-climate colonies, designed public spaces such as forums with various climatically considered spaces—rooms, galleries, arcades and porches. Different forums served different functions, such as markets dedicated to fish, cattle or flowers, and they could be adapted to new purposes. The Roman Forum began as a market, but by 170 BCE had become an administrative centre and given monumental form to serve a variety of government functions. Here, sun protection and ventilation were provided by substantial roofs elevated on elaborate columns as well as porticos around the perimeter which allowed shaded places for meeting or work. Some centuries later in southern Spain (960 CE to 1400 CE), cities such as Cordoba and Granada needed streets shaded from the very strong sun. Thick exterior walls and carefully dimensioned interior courtyards, surrounded by two or three storeys, kept interiors cool by limiting sun penetration. Flat roofs offered cool sleeping spaces in the evening. This courtyard housing typology also served the mainly Muslim culture by shielding women from outside view as well as offering rooftop socializing spaces. In some southern Swiss towns, sidewalks have traditionally been covered since the early modern period (1700-1900), providing shelter from the sun for pedestrians and shoppers. Today in Vancouver, which is on the edge of a rainforest, canopies are generally provided outside stores to protect window displays from sun and rain and to shelter passing pedestrians as well. The characteristics of how streets are made, what environmental control is provided, and where seating is located, are all responses to climate, social interactions and cultural norms. Designing for these aspects requires observing the typologies and materials of design that have been established and incorporating and re-interpreting them thoughtfully into new design. This work contributes to a sense of place which comes from considering infrastructure, such as streets and sidewalks, as more than merely practical elements for the ordered movement of vehicular or foot traffic and in fact as an integral part of the social fabric of a location.

A less pragmatic, but perhaps more spiritually enriching approach, has been elucidated by scholars Knut Knutsen and Christian Norberg Schulz in the Norwegian school of architectural thought. These designers and theorists focus on approaches to place as the primary influence on architectural design decisions. As Knutsen wrote, "Respect and reverence for a landscape must be prevailing values. Respect is not just a matter of making buildings subordinate to the landscape, but also to emphasize it, develop it—maybe even create new nature."[18]

DESIGNING FOR PLACE: HISTORICAL CONTEXTUALIZATION

HISTORICAL CONTEXTUALIZATION

A design strategy relevant to much of the urbanized world is that of historic contextualization: the previous uses and functions of sites, including cultural ones, are often important to the design of new elements. When successful, this strategy respects the past use of place and integrates meaningful social and cultural knowledge of place to the redeveloped site. However, one of the critical questions in the case of historic contextualization is exactly how to refer to social and cultural contexts of the past while designing with the language and within the social and technological context of the present. The simple reproduction of past elements is often censored by the design community as 'inauthentic', and true to neither use, form nor materiality. From these considerations arises the question of authenticity and what authenticity means, both generally and to designers specifically.

How, then, can historic context be used as a generator of design capital in a way that is authentic? Furthermore, can design capital successfully integrate history and express it without being derivative or anachronistic? This issue can refer to authenticity of form in relation to history, technique, structure or materials; it can also encompass considerations around historic preservation, including whether or not this should be done at all. Mrinalini Rajagopalan discusses authenticity in the context of architectural theory, writing, "The etymology of the word authenticity can be traced to the Greek root 'authentes', meaning author, and the earliest uses of the concept of authenticity were linked to evaluating objects and artifacts as original and genuine as opposed to counterfeits or reproductions."[19] This raises obvious issues regarding how to design or build with historic materials or in historic contexts; according to Rajagopalan's argument, the replication of historic building forms would create a 'counterfeit' of the original fabric. While this seems at first glance relatively straightforward, the issue is more complex. Rajagopalan goes on to point out that the idea of authenticity gained popularity as "the laying of claims to a particular set of 'authentic' histories and traditions that would differentiate modern individuals from premodern societies [...] The urgency to preserve historic monuments as 'authentic' documents of the past, was a product of modernization rather than a reaction to it."[20] As such, she argues, the idea of preservation "has always been embedded within and fashioned by distinctly global processes such as colonialism, capital networks of trade and cultural exchange and nationalist narratives."[21] Rajagopalan supports this argument by citing the example of the Nara Document on Authenticity (1994), which was introduced as a response to globalization.[22] The Nara Document on Authenticity is a 1994 UNESCO World Heritage text that articulates the need for an enlarged understanding of cultural diversity and cultural heritage in conservation practices; its aim is to encourage a more objective evaluation of the value and authenticity of cultural property.[23]

Authenticity is also a much-debated term in the context of global mass tourism and the industries that service it. Among philosophers, anthropologists and ethnographers it may be understood as a quest for an existence untainted by modern industry and commerce; for tourists it may mean something else entirely. John Urry, for example, has identified different types of tourist based on their attitudes to the tourist experience: romantic, collective and post-tourist.[24] Each has different expectations of what Urry calls the "staged authenticity" of the tourist site. Erick Cohen also makes several insightful points about what authenticity might mean for tourists. He argues that while many tourists are seeking something "other" or outside the everyday, be it landscapes, architecture or culture, they are still doing so within a commoditized context and points out that "authenticity is a socially constructed concept."[25, 26] It is a "negotiable concept,"[27] and for tourists it is partly determined by the type of tourist experience to which they aspire. New cultural values may achieve "a patina of authenticity over time," or what Cohen terms "emergent authenticity."[28] Cohen concludes that "commoditization does not necessarily destroy the meaning of cultural objects either for locals nor for the tourists, although it may do under certain circumstances."[29] Finally, Cohen suggests that the commoditization of tourism does not necessarily create meaninglessness for locals or inauthentic experiences for tourists. From the tourist's perspective, the authenticity of the experiences will be determined by their expectations. As can be seen from this discussion, it is not a simple thing to address historic preservation or contemporary design within the context of the historic. Nevertheless, it is critical to (and desired by) societies to reflect their cultural or social context and history, and interpretation of place within the context of the past is part of this discussion. Questions of authenticity are complex and will inevitably arise in the process of evaluating infrastructure which takes on historic aspects as part of its design approach. As such it is important for designers and decision makers to engage with the topic so that the outcome achieves the intention of all parties.

LEARNING FROM EXAMPLES: THE TOURIST DISTRICT

In *City-Spaces: Tourist Places*, the authors refer to the use of cultural capital to refashion cities to better serve the tourist economy. It is, they argue, "[d]riven by the negative consequences of de-industrialization, decentralization and globalization, [and]many cities have utilized these culturally based planning initiatives as a means to reposition themselves in a rapidly changing economic environment and/or to reaffirm their standing in an evolving metropolitan hierarchy."[30] One manifestation, the tourist district, is especially pertinent to the discussion of infrastructure and the deliberate use of culture and place as an economic tool; it is also of interest because of the questions of authenticity that it raises.

Claims to authenticity are complicated by tourist expectations, economic objectives and the needs of the local community and often criticisms of gentrification. Tourist districts are places where design quality is prioritized; the authorities with jurisdiction over these areas have committed resources to develop them in anticipation of a positive outcome for a city or region. Tourist districts themselves are not necessarily a model of how to approach all aspects of city design, but they are a source of strategies for giving identity to an area through investment in design, especially if their design draws on cultural and social ideas specific to a place and used in evaluating its economic efficacy.

The tourist precinct has also been the focus of scholars wishing to address the issue of cultural differentiation and appropriation of place. In City Spaces-Tourist Places (2005), Hayllar, Griffin and Edwards describe the clear benefits to cities in differentiating themselves from each other and creating qualities of place. The authors define a tourist precinct as:

> A distinctive geographic area within a larger urban area, characterized by a concentration of tourist-related land uses, activities and visitation, with fairly definable boundaries. Such precincts generally possess a distinctive character by virtue of their mixture of activities and land uses, such as restaurants, attractions and nightlife, their physical or architectural fabric, especially the dominance of historic buildings, or their connection to a particular cultural or ethnic group within the city. Such characteristics also exist in combination.[31]

Although there is little available economic analysis to validate the investment in these spaces, several studies are referenced that indicate significant benefits to cities in terms of job creation and increased economic activity.[32] There is also widespread adoption of the approach of regenerating areas for touristic purposes, which would indicate that cities are seeing relatively significant benefits even if they are not explicitly quantifying them. From our perspective, this is an important example of cities seeing value in design and investing in it for a future economic gain.

Any analysis of the intangible benefit of tourist districts to the city must also consider that benefits are not only enjoyed by tourists but by locals as well, and it can be difficult to differentiate between these benefits. In fact, the presence of a local population is deemed important in contributing to the success of the tourist experience within a city: the tourist wants an authentic local experience in order to connect with the city and understand it.[33] One of the recognized hallmarks of authenticity is local inhabitants and ways of life, and therefore the tourist district needs to attract local residents who will also participate in and enjoy the spaces and amenities created. As such, the tourist district needs to become an integrated part of the city. In the context of today's need to compete to attract not only tourists but also international talent and investment, the city as a whole can learn from the tourist district, and the strict demarcation between a 'tourist district' and a successful city may become more and more blurred.

The external or place-connecting functions are fundamentally about helping the tourist relate to, appreciate or comprehend the place they are visiting. In this context ' the place' is the broader destination of the city, or even country, rather than just the precinct per se. The contention here is that the tourist does not visit the city to experience the precinct but rather, that visiting the precinct is an important part of experiencing the city. In a sense, the precinct acts as an intermediary, which enhances the tourist's feelings of connection to or experience of the place, in particular its people, history, way of life and spirit.[34]

And while business centres of modern city centres may seem indistinguishable from one another, the tourism precincts of those cities, "would appear to be important markers of place distinctiveness. They thereby provide the tourist with strong memories of the city and may validate pre-conceived notions of the city's character and special qualities." [35]

Many of the evaluation tools that are used in the tourist district can be applied to infrastructure: infrastructure too is able to act as agent in building cultural, community and economic assets. Like a tourist district, infrastructure can aggregate related services around it, producing a precinct with particular spatial, social, cultural and economic attributes. Like architecture, a bridge or other infrastructure can be a form of "objectified cultural capital," its "physical form, as defined by architecture, aestheticizes spaces with recognizable markers that forge a particular sense of place, 'pulling' visitors to precincts."[36]

This discussion is not intended to promote the development of tourist districts or say that a city should be designed in the same way that tourist districts have been in the past, but rather to examine the interest from governments in developing 'tourist districts' and the willingness to acknowledge the value they bring to the city. The tourist district, by definition, must focus on highlighting the cultural and social qualities of the place—either by using historical aspects of the place or by creating new interpretations of what the city or place would like to express.

CONCLUSION

It is because of the power of infrastructure design to influence the development of neighbourhoods that the outcome can have such positive outcomes or potentially negative effects such as dislocating social groups and even changing the fabric of cities. As such, this power should be wielded carefully and thoughtfully. Design capital plays a role as it can participate in empowering particular portions of society by placemaking which at minimum is welcoming and at best will enriche communities and lives through its presence. In order to achieve this aim, the design intention must focus on how it is to be accomplished. As discussed, the primary question here must be 'who is this infrastructure built for?' Once this is decided, the power of design and infrastructure can be wielded accordingly.

NOTES

1. Ruth Glass, "Introduction: Aspects of change," in Centre for Urban Studies (ed.) *London: Aspects of Change* (London: MacKibbon and Kee, 1964).
2. This is evident in the massive Frankfort and Stuttgart housing projects of Ernst May in the mid 1920s and the CIAM conferences on The Minimum Dwelling in 1929. The need for mass housing was essential not only to workers but also their employers and with the housing shortages caused by WWI across Europe, mass housing was also a political issue. Many of the avant-garde housing proposals, such as those built for the Weissenhof Seidlung Exhibition in Stuttgart in 1927 proved too expensive for the working class and as many had maid's rooms that were more attractive economically and culturally to the middle class.
3. A. Tallon, *Urban Regeneration in the UK* (London: Routledge, Routledge, 2010), 248.
4. Kenneth Frampton, "Towards a Critical Regionalism," in *The Anti-Aesthetic: Essays on Postmodern Culture,* ed. Hal Foster, 1st ed. (Port Townsend, Wash: Bay Press, 1983), 16.
5. Jane Jacobs, *Death and Life of Great American Cities* (New York: Random House, 1961); Christian Norberg-Schulz, *Genius Loci: Toward a Phenomenology of Architecture* (New York: Rizzoli, 1980); Jan Gehl, *Cities for People* (Washington and London: Island Press, 2010); Kevin Lynch, *The Image of the City* (Cambridge, MA: The MIT Press, 1960).
6. Bureau E.A.S.T, (Aziza Chaoun), https://www.daniels.utoronto.ca/news/2009/09/08/aziza-chaounis-bureau-east-fez-river-project-world-touring-exhibition .
7. Martin Heidegger, *Poetry Language, Thought*, trans. Albert Hofstader (New York: Perennial, 1971), 151-52.
8. Heidegger, *Poetry, Language, Thought*, 152.
9. Yi-Fu Tuan, *Space and place: The perspective of experience* (Minneapolis: U of Minnesota Press, 1977), 6.
10. Yi-Fu Tuan, "Sense of Place," in *Space and Place: The Perspective of Experience* (Minnesota: Minnesota Press, 1976, 2001). See also, for example, Henri Lefebvre, *The Production of Space* (1974), trans. Donald Nicholson-Smith (Malden, MA and Oxford: Blackwell, 1991) and Edward Relph, "The Paradox of Place and the Evolution of Placelessness" (1976), in *Place and Placelessness,* ed. Robert Freestone and Edgar Liu (New York and Abington: Routledge, 2010).
11. We use the term, appropriate, here in the sense that Lefebvre intended as the right to occupy already-produced urban space, or the right to produce urban space so that it meets the needs of inhabitants; appropriation gives inhabitants the right to 'full and complete usage' of urban space in the course of everyday life. Lefebvre, *Production of Space.*
12. Doreen Massey, *For Space* (London, England: Sage Publications Ltd., 2005), 5.
13. Massey, *For Space*, 140.
14. Massey, *For Space*, 187.
15. Frampton, "Towards a Critical Regionalism," 20. This could be understood as a critique of both modernism (progress) and post-modernism (return to the past).
16. Frampton, "Towards a Critical Regionalsim," 21.
17. Bill Pechet, Design Capital Interview with Bill Pechet, August 5, 2020, http://blogs.ubc.ca/meyboom/.
18. Knut Knutsen, quoted in Iván I. Ricón Borrego, "Landscape Architectures in Norway: The Influence of AHO Masters on the National Tourist Routes of Norway," *Cuaderno de Notas* 20 (2019): 91.
19. Mrinalini Rajagopalan, "Preservation and Modernity: Competing Perspectives, Contested Histories and the Question of Authenticity," in *The Sage Handbook of Architectural Theory* (Los Angeles; London; New Delhi ; Singapore ; Washington DC: SAGE Publications, 2012), 308.

20. Rajagopalan, "Preservation and Modernity," 309.
21. Rajagopalan, "Preservation and Modernity,"321.
22. Rajagopalan, Preservation and Modernity," 319.
23. It is an update of the previous Venice Charter of 1964 which had focused on the restoration of historic monuments and the recognition of value of cultural properties.
24. John Urry, "The Consumption of Tourism," *Sociology* 24, no.1 (Feb. 1990): 23-35.
25. Erik Cohen, "Authenticity and Commoditization in Tourism," *Annals of Tourism Research* 15 (1988): 372.
26. Cohen, "Authenticity and Commoditization," 374.
27. Cohen, "Authenticity and Commoditization," 372.
28. Cohen, "Authenticity and Commoditization," 379-380.
29. Cohen, "Authenticity and Commoditization," 383.
30. Bruce Hayllar, Tony Griffin, and Deborah Edwards, *City Spaces-Tourist Places* (New York and London: Routledge, 2010), 21.
31. Hayllar, Griffin, and Edwards, *City Spaces*, 517.
32. Leslie Sklair, "Iconic architecture and capitalist globalization," *City* 10, no. 01 (2006): 21-47.
33. Hayllar, Griffin, and Edwards, *City Spaces*, 57.
34. Hayllar, Griffen, and Edwards, *City Spaces*, 50.
35. Hayllar, Griffin, and Edwards, *City Spaces*, 50.
36. Moira Scerri, Deborah Edwards, and Carmel Foley, "The economic impact of architecture to tourism" [online], in: *CAUTHE 2016: The Changing Landscape of Tourism and Hospitality: The Impact of Emerging Markets and Emerging Destinations*, ed. Madalyn Scerri and Lee Ker Hui (Sydney: Blue Mountains International Hotel Management School, 2016): 437-458.

5

THE ECONOMICS OF DESIGN CAPITAL

INTRODUCTION

The decision whether to build any type of infrastructure must consider the costs of building and the benefits that it brings. Because costs are, in many cases, largely covered by the public purse, the project analyses that government agencies carry out must hold up to intense public scrutiny. A good, comprehensive economic analysis of any project will compare all the costs with all the benefits to ascertain whether or not it is a good decision to go ahead with the project. However, if any of the benefits or costs are overlooked, the process will produce skewed results. This chapter argues that such is the case with many infrastructural decisions, where neither the costs of poor design nor the benefits of good design are fully considered. Consequently, decisions regarding the allocation of costs for the design of infrastructure are fundamentally flawed. Economists call this 'market failure', where the market neglects to take into account the true costs associated with the production or consumption of an item. For example, environmental, air and water pollution are factors that are often overlooked when carrying out an economic analysis of goods. These oversights eventually lead to market failure with regard to the true cost of products.[1]

In the context of well-designed infrastructure, these overlooked factors—or externalities in the language of economics—include basic tangible economic elements such as local job growth, increased services, higher property values, and increased business income and tourism to the area. More intangible benefits include those that are of social value such as improved quality of life, improved feelings of safety in the area, and heightened visibility for the region; cultural values such as reflection of identity, the expression of cultural attributes or even heightened attention to cultural norms or taboos (in the case of infrastructure that extends into the realm of public art) are other intangible benefits. While in this discussion we are referring to these items as benefits, the way extrinsic factors are commonly discussed in economics are losses or harm to another party in some form (such as the environment). If we frame it in this way, we can say that these benefits are *not* included in poorly designed infrastructure, thereby creating a loss to society. There are current methods from other disciplines, particularly environmental economics, that are applicable to assessing future benefits and losses that can, and should, be used by public authorities to help them make decisions on infrastructure spending. However, there is a resistance to assigning design quality a value—similar to attitudes to environmental considerations, people are concerned that to give an economic value to something so incalculable will cheapen it. However, as Jason Scorse points out in *What Environmentalists Need to Know about Economics*[2] this is a misperception because "if attempts are not made to assign monetary value to the environment, the default value is zero or close to zero."[3] To ignore these values, which reflect important social factors, when making decisions about infrastructure is not only shortchanging ourselves but also future generations of the potential benefit from these public investments.

The field of economics has long analyzed these often-overlooked costs and benefits. These were first identified in 1924 by A.C. Pigou, who posited that when party 'A' provides a service to party 'B' for which payment is made, party 'A' may, in the course of providing that service, injure parties 'C', 'D' and 'E'. But the cost of this injury is not included in the economic transaction due to difficulties in measuring and facilitating such transactions.[4] These other costs are considered "extrinsic factors." This argument also applies to positive influences such as increased access to property that would result in benefits to a landowner when new transportation infrastructure is built. In the case of infrastructure, the extrinsic factors could be costs to society or they could be benefits, depending on how the design of the infrastructure is considered. The specified design priorities determine which social priorities are considered and designed for and, as such, they may or may not include aspects of extrinsic factors: for example, is a pedestrian crossing or bicycle route prioritized at an interchange? If not, then the final solution will likely be tacked-on afterward and consequently be substandard for those transport modes. The extrinsic factors of benefits to public health and sustainable transportation will be lost but it is likely a more economic and efficient design for cars and trucks will result since that was prioritized. Dealing with environmental, visual, or social and cultural impacts are even more difficult discussions than those prioritizing other more tangible factors.

What is clear from the engineering literature and project methodologies is that the estimate of the benefits of any design improvement is not regularly undertaken and there is hesitation about how it might be carried out:

> The challenge of maximizing the visual performance benefits of transportation projects may add to the final cost of the transportation facility ... The benefits of visual performance improvements may not be readily quantifiable in monetary terms. Where tourism is involved, increased revenue could be used as a proxy for benefits. In other cases, the increase in community well-being due to enhanced aesthetics may be difficult to measure in monetary terms, but an attempt could be made using the willingness-to-pay approach, where residents, road users, and pedestrians are asked how much they are willing to pay to see a specific improvement in the visual performance of the transportation facility and its immediate environment.[5]

The major deterrent in reporting and assessing the aesthetic benefits of infrastructure is the difficulty for engineers who are running the projects in ascertaining the value of these intangible benefits. However, economists, transportation planners and sociologists have many tools at their disposal for valuing intangible benefits. The question then becomes: what are the unaccounted benefits and how are these tools to be applied to assess them? This chapter begins to explore this issue with the intention of giving decision makers better tools to evaluate the benefits of well-designed infrastructure. This is not to suggest that we are experts in economically valuing extrinsic factors; rather, we are pointing out some of the well-known methodologies with the intention of starting the discussion of how this is done and how these approaches could be applied to the design of infrastructure or, for that matter, anything designed in the public realm.

INTANGIBLE BENEFITS AND EXTRINSIC FACTORS

Economists recognized the need to value environmental goods that are not bought and sold in marketplaces decades ago. The seminal finding of J. Krutilla[6] (1967) was that people value natural wonders simply because they exist: although their enjoyment can be assigned an economic value, it is not one set by the standards of the marketplace. Krutilla argues that people are willing to pay for the maintenance of a natural wonder, although they cannot buy or sell it. This is often termed a 'passive use value,' and without including passive use values in an analysis of public goods, it is almost impossible to assign them any economic value.

'Public goods' are those that are enjoyed by the public, equally. A public good is one where "one person's use of the good does not inhibit another's use of the good (nonrival) and where once the good is provided to one it is by definition provided to all (nonexcludable)."[7] Examples include things such as air quality, national defence, and remote wilderness areas. Purely public goods are generally provided or protected by government bodies. Without the inclusion of these types of economic values, however, items of public good are given no value and so an economic evaluation of any type of decision related to them is partial and thus flawed.

In economic theory, goods are not priced when either no markets exist for them or because the markets that exist do not work to value the factors sufficiently. This is the case for infrastructure design. As such, it is fitting to look to environmental economics—where the environmental effects have no public market—as a precedent. Similarly, design aspects of infrastructure are a public good as they have no market in which to evaluate value.[8]

PRICING PUBLIC GOOD

In order to properly value environmental good, public good and other extrinsic factors, economists study monetary valuation methods which try to assign economic value to these extrinsic factors. These approaches include hedonic pricing as well as contingent valuation methods and other questionnaire-based methods such as the Conjoint Measurement Method, the Welfare Evaluation Method and the Wellbeing Evaluation Method. These will be further explained and discussed below.

HEDONIC PRICING

In 1856, Fredrick Law Olmsted convinced the City of New York that the purchase, financing, construction and maintenance of Central Park could be paid for by the taxes on the increased property values that would occur as a consequence of the construction of the park. Shortly after Central Park was built, he provided an analysis that supported his position.[9] His was the first analysis of what has now been demonstrated in many other studies. In John Crompton's 2001 paper, "The Impact of Parks on Property Values: A Review of Empirical Evidence,"[10] he observes that many people are willing to pay more for a house near a park and that this willingness to pay more provides "capitalization" of the park. This concept is termed the "proximate principle."[11] Similar to struggles that government agencies have with securing funding for infrastructure, parks are also seen as a public good which is costly—in this case, costing includes not only the construction and maintenance of the park facility but also the lost revenue from the lack of development on that site. Whereas infrastructure may have other uses, a park is purely for recreation and so provides a good comparison for the benefit of an "extraneous aspect" of a bridge or piece of infrastructure.

Conceptually, the value of any property on the open market should reflect the increase in value to the purchasers of the proximity to the public good (in the case discussed above, the park); this relationship can be revealed by analysis of hedonic pricing. Hedonic pricing, in essence, tries to deconstruct the observed price of a house, an automobile, an office building, etc., into component attributes. It was first used for automobiles when trying to develop a price index that accounted for changes in the attributes that cars included as new but standard features from one year to the next. The idea was that merely observing the increased prices of automobiles was an inaccurate representation of their actual value; in fact, more and more features (attributes) were included as standard each year so that in many cases vehicle prices were not increasing at all when one applied a like-for-like comparison of 'apples to apples' or 'attributes to attributes.'[12] In many advanced applications today, hedonic pricing goes further and uses the process to estimate the value of a non-market resource based on the prices of goods that are actually circulating in a market.[13] In the case of land, its price reflects the characteristics of any property built on it, characteristics of the location (including its global position) and characteristics of the environment. To calculate the impact of parks on land values, hedonic pricing uses regression analysis to correlate the presence of the park with increased property values in accordance with the relative distance from the park to the property. If property values are increased by the presence of the park, the question would then be whether there is sufficient capitalization to make up for the capital, maintenance and lost revenue. As found in studies by Crompton et al., this increase in property value is estimated to be approximately 20% for adjacency to the park and to decrease as distance from the park increases.[14] Their analysis supports the general finding that parks are self-financing and can be funded by the capitalization afforded by the proximate principle.

However, parks are not automatically beneficial to property values or neighbourhoods.[15] Flat parks which mainly contain sports fields—considered "active parks"—are not highly beneficial to adjacent neighbours due to noise and traffic congestion.[16] This difference in benefit to a neighbourhood and thus in proximate capitalization is dependent on factors such as neighbourhood characteristics and, of course, design quality.[17]

More recently there has been increased attention given to the externalities on property prices (Des Rosiers, Bolduc and Thérialt, 1999). One relevant study, completed by François et al. used hedonic methods to analyze the impact of landscaping such as hedges, trees, curbside landscaping and porches on property values. The study found tree cover in the surrounds has a positive impact on property values, and even more so if the residents are mainly retired. A higher percentage of ground cover also has a positive effect on property values while a lower one has a negative effect. Above average vegetation, however, can have a negative effect. More specifically, the study finds that the property premium is between 3.6% to 3.9% for a hedge, 12.4% for a patio and 4.4% for landscaped curbs.[18]

From this analysis of parks and landscape design, we can see a well-defined pattern of property value impact, which, over time, leads to an ability to predict the consequences of the decision to build a park or change landscaping on the value of property around it. It should therefore, with enough analysis of similar types of infrastructure, be possible to estimate impacts on property values around an infrastructure.

CONTINGENT VALUATION METHOD

As discussed in the introduction, the recent study of the Erasmus Bridge in Rotterdam, completed by TU Delft and using the Contingent Valuation Method, estimated the Willingness to Pay (WTP) of the population of the Netherlands for this piece of infrastructure. The bridge was designed by the architects UN Studio and was completed as part of a regeneration of the old port in Rotterdam. It is now a significant attraction and a landmark for the city. The TU Delft study found the public's willingness to pay for the increased costs of the enhanced design instead of the most economic bridge to be significantly more than the cost of the bridge by a factor of four to five.[19] The additional cost of the increased design quality as compared to the base cost of the most economic bridge design was 18 million euros; however, it is worth highlighting, the public was willing to pay between 69.7 million and 95.7 million euros above the base price of the bridge. Using a method such as this, then, can reveal the value to the public of well-designed infrastructure.

Contingent valuation methodology uses survey methods to understand people's preference for public goods and what they would be willing to pay for improvement in these goods. Leading economists, such as Nobel Prize winners Kenneth Arrow and Robert Solow, argue that contingent valuation methodology is the most promising approach for determining prices for the extrinsic factor of goods or potential impacts on the environment.[20,21] This approach has been used for over 45 years to estimate the worth of public goods, such as natural features, in thousands of circumstances and there are well-established discussions with regard to its methodology and accuracy.[22] The main debate about this methodology is the potential for unintended influencing of the willingness to pay responses in the surveys undertaken, which would invalidate the findings. However, since 1970, contingent valuation methods have been used by economists in over 1600 studies in 40 countries to value aspects as diverse as recreation, hunting, water quality improvements, air quality improvements, decreased mortality risks from nuclear reactor improvements, and toxic waste dumps. In terms of aesthetics, there have been more recent studies on iconic bridges[23] and bridge lighting improvements.[24] There is, therefore, significant research on how to set up investigations of extrinsic values and achieve the most accurate results.

IMPORTANT METHODOLOGICAL FACTORS

An issue that arises from the use of the contingency valuation method is that members of the public have difficulty in assessing personal value if they have no prior experience with what they are trying to evaluate. In other words, people have a better ability to value things with which they have experience. The Erasmus Bridge study assessed the willingness to pay of the public once the bridge was built; that is, after the public had experienced it and understood the implications of the bridge in situ. It would be more difficult to have the public imagine and assess the implications of a large piece of infrastructure that does not yet exist. Detailed illustrations and descriptions of impacts on businesses, tourism, and local life would have to be included if using this methodology.

Formatting of the questions is also critical to the accuracy of the responses. Until the mid 1980s, contingent valuation methods generally asked open-ended questions, such as ‘How much would you pay for...?’ In 1992, the National Oceanic and Atmospheric Administration produced an extensive report on the contingent valuation method which suggested that, "[t]he simplest way to approach the valuation problem, is to consider a contingent valuation survey as essentially a self-contained referendum in which respondents vote to tax themselves for a particular purpose."[25] Since then, contingent valuation methods have generally asked questions such as: ‘If it cost $x would you be willing to pay for it?’, with different questionnaires asking different prices. The results from this style of survey provide a cumulative distribution function of percentage willingness to pay versus dollar amount, known as the dichotomous choice method.

Other requirements to ensure the survey produces meaningful results include providing sufficient, accurate information; ensuring the survey is balanced and impartial; insulating the topic from any general dislike of big business; reminding respondents of the availability of substitutes, and of their budget constraints; facilitating "don't know" responses; and providing an opportunity for respondents to reconsider at the end of the interview.[26]

LONG-TERM POTENTIAL

Contingent valuation research could therefore be carried out with meaningful graphics and a good description of the benefits to business, tourism and public life in the area, which would perhaps give a sufficient idea of the benefits to the public; nevertheless, one could hypothesize that an underestimation by the public will be made in these early cases because of the difficulties in imagining the impact of the infrastructure. To obtain more certainty, studies of contingent valuation, ideally conducted before and after an infrastructure is built, should be made. However, since infrastructure planning, design and construction take a long time, one must allow sufficient years after the infrastructure is built to understand the true impacts; these studies would have to be in the order of 15 years apart.[27] One of the advantages of dealing with infrastructure is that it is a large investment and so the research to assess its value to the public would be a relatively minor part of the whole cost. Similar to an environmental assessment, a social and cultural assessment would result in a more thorough understanding of the social and cultural costs and benefits of relative design decisions.

In the longer term, with a series of studies undertaken on infrastructure that is already in place, a solid body of data and expertise should be developed. From the data obtained, patterns could be identified that could lend credence to estimates done on precedents that share similar characteristics. This would allow prior studies to inform government policy for upcoming work and to simplify the process.

COMPARISON OF HEDONIC PRICING AND CONTINGENT VALUATION METHODS

Hedonic pricing and contingent valuation methods are commonly used and well-documented methods for determining economic values for public goods. Contingent valuation is often employed where hedonic methods are not available for the public good that is being evaluated—for example, this would occur when no relevant economic pricing data is available. Ideally, using both would provide complementary methods and valuable analytic information for each infrastructural decision.

In past research, these methods have been proven to be internally consistent but have produced variable outcomes when the results of each are compared. Several authors, including W. Michael Hanemann,[28] Peter A. Diamond and Jerry A. Hausman,[29] John Loomis et al.,[30] David S. Brookshire et al.,[31] and Richard C. Bishop and Thomas A.Heberlein[32] have completed studies on the accuracy of contingent valuation in comparison with hedonic methods. Results are not straightforward but indicate that while not perfect, the methodology is very valuable and in many cases quite accurate. Improvements in survey methodologies and understanding of bias and other response factors have improved the outcomes significantly over the years and continue to do so.[33]

Brookshire et al. (1982) examined the relationship between hedonic and contingent valuation methods to evaluate the relationship between the two methods using pollution and the Los Angeles housing market as a test case.[34] They studied the expressed willingness to pay for an improvement in air quality and compared it to rents in different areas through the established hedonic method developed by Rosen[35] and later by A. Myrick Freeman.[36] Their results show that willingness to pay is consistently below the differential in rents due to air pollution. The willingness to pay stated by participants was in fact up to 50% lower than the actual differential when all other factors are excluded. This is consistent with another study about willingness to pay, in this case for goose hunting licences. Bishop and Heberlein (1979) concluded that the willingness to pay was more than 50% underestimated.[37] Other studies have indicated the opposite.[38][39] In general, however, it has been argued by Hanemann that flawed survey methodologies produce the major inaccuracies and that the results from surveys without these inaccuracies are sound.[40] This is supported by the vast numbers of surveys carried out throughout the world to value public goods.

VALUE OF THE SYDNEY OPERA HOUSE AS AN EXAMPLE OF EXTRINSIC VALUATION OF AN URBAN INVESTMENT

While the societal value of architecturally significant buildings has been talked about in different ways, including among scholars such as Cristina

Garduño Freeman in terms of social value,[41] at times consulting firms are asked to try to place economic values on them. A 2013 Deloitte report on the value of the Sydney Opera House demonstrates the brand value of places and symbols: in this case as a significant economic contribution over and above the costs of bricks and mortar. The report valued the Sydney Opera house to be worth $4.6 billion dollars to Australia and to contribute $775 million to the Australian economy annually, supporting 8, 439 jobs directly and indirectly. This example begins to outline the intangible contributions of architecture to fields like tourism, city economies and the value of national symbols in the context of trade and investment.[42]

The Deloitte report gives us a clear example of the benefits of architecture to a city above and beyond the basic shelter function of a building. As shown in the simplified flowchart below by scholars Scerri et al.[43] (Figure 5:1), there are many factors across several areas that are influenced and interrelated in a large-scale investment. In their study of the Sydney Opera House, Deloitte points out all the extrinsic factors that need to be considered in the analysis of the benefits to society deriving from this building—and these benefits are accrued annually. In this scenario, such benefits as increased tourism, cultural brand issues (such as differentiation, relevance, esteem and knowledge of place), and a valuable digital footprint are all considered significant.

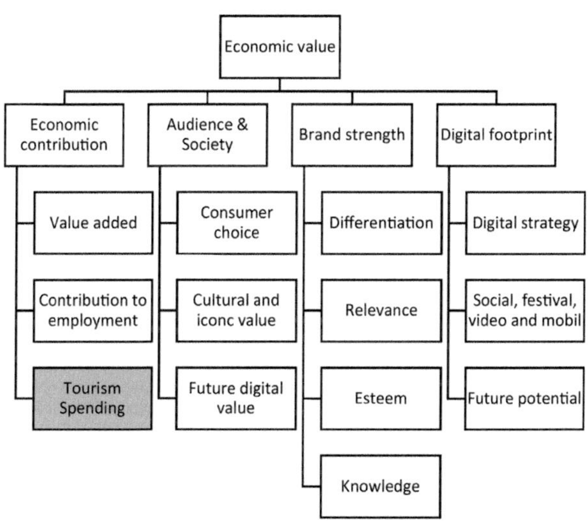

5:1 Diagram: Method of economic estimation of the value of the Sydney Opera House, by Scerri, Edwards, Foley based on 2013 Deloitte study.

The extension of these factors to major urban infrastructure can easily be made: such an analysis could be completed for any major bridge, building or square in an urban area. The intention of such an analysis would be to provide a more accurate economic analysis of the project so that better decisions can be made in the future and that investments in infrastructure can be freed from merely considering the 'lowest common denominator' of financing. In other words, it becomes possible to give a real value to design quality and for infrastructure to be properly evaluated.

From this discussion, we demonstrate that there is a clear value brought to a place via infrastructure that offers aesthetic qualities to space and defines place. And, notwithstanding valid concerns around gentrification, this value will be lost if it is not recognized and used for the benefit of the local residents. There is more at stake than simply economic considerations of construction cost and functionality in building infrastructure.

While we have examined methods of determining the value of infrastructure to the general public, there are multiple overlapping benefits that can be evaluated. If we assess value to the public through contingent valuation, how does this relate to an economic analysis of the extrinsic value of increased tourism, for example, or the increase in business in an area? One would not want these factors to be double counted but they must definitely be included. Through careful, transparent and precise work, this type of undertaking is possible.

EVALUATION OVER TIME AND SPACE

In addition to the challenges of attempting the valuation of infrastructure in a particular geographic region at a particular time, another challenge is that its impact is not limited to the current timeframe or geographic region. For example, the benefits of Parisian bridges are not limited to the era in which they were built. Arguably, with the number of visitors to Paris increasing alongside the rise in world travel and an increase in people with disposable income, the value of those bridges—to Paris, to France as a whole, and even to people outside the country—is much higher now than when they were originally built. This brings a conundrum—how do we ask people in the future whether they value a place conceived of in the present? Should we even include this value in a decision-making process? Is trying to predict future preferences important or even valid in the decision-making environment that currently exists?

To consider this argument about geographic boundaries from the other side, would someone say that the Golden Gate Bridge has no value to them because they do not live in the United States? The UNESCO World Heritage Foundation looks at elements worldwide that are valuable to humanity; the benefit brought to a society may not have boundaries that are defined by geopolitical borders.

These questions are valid and worth considering, but in the context of a world where the case for design value to society is so poorly made, it makes sense to first focus on assessing accurate current value. Future or extra-geographic value considerations may occur at a time when we have become better at valuing extrinsic factors in these types of decision-making processes.

CONCLUSION

As happens so often, what seems to be common sense needs to be validated economically in order to make a case for doing it. In the case of building high-quality infrastructure that is intended to participate socially and culturally in its location, there has, to date, been no serious effort to regularly and routinely take into account all societal benefits for an infrastructure project. Because of this failure, our infrastructure has been built with a false economic model, which discounts the importance of social and cultural aspects in its design. This chapter has proposed several methodologies for the evaluation of societal willingness to pay for, as well as to put an economic price on, such improvements. Furthermore, our analysis demonstrates the potential to fund such design improvements through methods already in practice today in other applications. It is hoped that using these economic methods to put real prices on the benefits brought by good design will help make the case for high-quality design that incorporates social design aspects as a primary intention.

NOTES

1. Jason Scorse, *What Environmentalists Need to Know about Economics* (New York: Springer, 2010), 8.
2. Scorse, *Envirommentalists*, 40.
3. Scorse, *Environmentalists*, 40.
4. A. C. Pigou, *The economics of welfare, 2nd edition* (London: MacMillan and Co., 1924), 161.
5. Jeffrey Brown, review of *Transportation Decision Making: Principles of Project Evaluation and Programming by Kumares C. Sinha and Samuel Labi* (Hoboken, NJ: John Wiley & Sons, 2007), 375, *Journal of American Planning Association* 75, no.1 (2008): 94-95 (Taylor & Francis, 2008).
6. John V. Krutilla, "Conservation Reconsidered," *The American Economic Review* 57, no. 4 (1967): 777.
7. Scorse, *Environmentalists*, 15.
8. It is worth mentioning Coase's work on extrinsic factors commonly referred to as Coase Theorum. (John Black, Nigar Hashimzade, Gareth Myles, 2012). Coase theorem. In *A Dictionary of Economics* 4th ed., (2012) (Oxford: Oxford University Press), accessed June 27, 2017, http://www.oxfordreference.com.ezproxy.library.ubc.ca/view/10.1093/acref/9780199696321.001.0001/acref-9780199696321-e-437.) This theorem states that in the presence of an externality, an outcome will be economically efficient no matter how property rights are allocated as long as the transaction cost is minimal. This is because bargaining will take place to resolve the problem regardless of the property rights involved. However, Coase also points out that the theory very rarely holds in practice because the transaction costs (costs of bargaining and information gathering) often lead to inefficient bargaining. In the case of infrastructure, the costs will involve multi-jurisdictional government bargaining with landowners and public decision makers and so the transaction costs are extremely high. Thus, the outcome of well-designed infrastructure will not occur without significant intent.
9. John L. Crompton, "The impact of parks on property values: A review of the empirical evidence," *Journal of leisure research* 33, no.1 (2001): 7.
10. Crompton, "The impact of parks," 1.
11. Crompton, "The impact of parks," 1.
12. Zvi Griliches, "Hedonic price indexes for automobiles: An econometric of quality change," *The Price Statistics of the Federal Government*. NBER Books (National Bureau of Economic Research Inc, 1961): 173-196.
13. Sherwin Rosen, "Hedonic prices and implicit markets: product differentiation in pure competition," *Journal of political economy* 82, no.1 (1974): 34-55.
14. John L. Crompton, "The impact of parks on property values: empirical evidence from the past two decades in the United States," *Managing Leisure* 10.4 (2005): 203-218.
15. John Tibbetts and Charles J Fausold, *Open Space Conservation* (Lincoln Institute of Land Policy, 1998), 9.
16. John L Crompton, "The Impact of Parks on Property Values: A Review of the Empirical Evidence," *Journal of Leisure Research* 33, no. 1 (2001): 29.
17. For further information see, William H. Whyte, *The Social Life of Small Urban Spaces* (Washington DC: The Conservation Foundation, 1988). Whyte spends a lot of time deconstructing when open spaces (parks, plazas, etc.) are valued or not.
18. Francois Des Rosiers et al., "Landscaping and House Values: An Empirical Investigation," *Journal of Real Estate Research* 23, no. 1–2 (January 1, 2002): 159, https://doi.org/10.1080/10835547.2002.12091072., https://www.tandfonline.com/action/showCitFormats?doi=10.1080%2F10835547.2002.12091072.
19. Roy Heijnsdijk, "The Iconic Value of Infrastructure Projects: A case study to the iconic value of the Erasmus Bridge" (Dissertation. TU Delft, Delft University of Technology, 2015).
20. Kenneth Arrow et al., "Report of the NOAA Panel on Contingent Valuation," *Federal Register* 58, no. 10 (1993): 43.

21. Richard T. Carson et al., "Was the Noaa Panel Correct About Contingent Valuation?," SSRN Scholarly Paper (Rochester, NY: Social Science Research Network, 1996), 4, https://doi.org/10.2139/ssrn.31992.
22. Examples include, Robert Cameron Mitchell and Richard T. Carson, *Using surveys to value public goods: the contingent valuation method.* Resources for the Future, 1989; R. G. Cummings, D.S. Brookshire and W.D. Schulze, *Valuing Environmental Goods: An Assessment of the Contingent Valuation Method* (Rowman & Allanheld, 1986).
23. Heijnsdijk, "Iconic Value of Infrastructure."
24. Seungmin Nam, Sae-eun Park, and Hong-Chul Shin, "Accessing the Economic Value of Night View of Bridge Using Contingent Valuation Method: The Case of South Korea's Han-River Bridge," *International Journal of Culture, Tourism and Hospitality Research,* 2015, 360.
25. Kenneth Arrow, et al., *"Report of the NOAA panel on contingent valuation." Federal register 58.10 (1993): 4601-4614, 23.*
26. Michael W. *Hanemann*, "Valuing the envi ronment through contingent valuation," *The journal of economic perspectives* 8, no.4 (1994): 19-43.
27. For example - planning and approvals (2 years), designing (1.5 years), tendering and construction (3 years) and then a period to examine the effect of the infrastructure (8 years).
28. Hanemann,"Valuing the environment," 19-43.
29. Peter A. Diamond and Jerry A. Hausman, "Contingent valuation: Is some number better than no number?" *The Journal of economic perspectives* 8, no.4 (1994): 45-64.
30. John Loomis, et al., "Evaluating the validity of the dichotomous choice question format in contingent valuation," *Environmental and resource economics* 10, no. 2 (1997): 109-123.
31. David S. Brookshire, et al., "Valuing public goods: a comparison of survey and hedonic approaches," *The American Economic Review* 72, no. 1 (1982): 165-177.
32. Richard C. Bishop and Thomas A. Heberlein, "Measuring Values of Extramarket Goods: Are Indirect Measures Biased?", *American Journal of Agricultural Economics* 61, no. 5 (December 1979): 926-30.
33. John Loomis et al., "Evaluating the Validity of the Dichotomous Choice Question Format in Contingent Valuation," *Environmental and Resource Economics* 10, no. 2 (September 1, 1997): 109, https://doi.org/10.1023/A:1026403916622.
34. David S. Brookshire et al. "Valuing public goods," 165-177.
35. Sherwin Rosen, "Hedonic prices and implicit markets: product differentiation in pure competition," *Journal of political economy* 82, no. 1 (1974): 34-55.
36. A Myrick Freeman III, "Hedonic Prices, Property Values and Measuring Environmental Benefits: A Survey of the Issues," *Scandinavian Journal of Economics* 81 (1979): 154-173.
37. Bishop and Heberlein, "Measuring Values," 926-30.
38. Kealy, M. J., J. Dovidio, and M. Rockel (1988), "Accuracy in Valuation Is a Matter of Degree," *Land Economics* 64, no.2 (1988): 158–171.
39. T. Brown, P. Champ, R. Bishop, and D. McCollum (1996), "Which Response Format Reveals the Truth About Donations to a Public Good," *Land Economics* 72, no. 2, 152–166.
40. W. Michael Hanemann, "Valuing the environment," 19-43.
41. "Social value is defined as the attachment that people and communities have for places, which is expressed through people's interactions and engagements with each other and with the place itself. Iconic works of architecture hold special symbolic and aesthetic associations for specific groups of people. Typically, they are famous landmarks that are used to represent places or countries at a global level." Cristina Garduño Freeman, *Participatory Culture and the Social Value of an Architectural Icon: Sydney Opera House* (Routledge, 2018).
42. Deloitte, "How do you value an Icon; The Sydney Opera House Economic, Cultural and Digital Value, 2013".
43. Moira Scerri, Deborah Edwards, and Carmel Foley, "The Value of Architecture to Tourism," in *Proceedings of 26th Annual CAUTHE Conference,* 2016, 7.

6

CREATING DESIGN CAPITAL

Once the idea of design capital is defined, the question becomes how do we design something with design capital? At this point it should be mentioned that since design capital is bestowed by society at large, we can only design something which has potential to accrue design capital. Since design is valued through its social impact—people developing an affinity toward it, or assessing it as valuable to them or significant to them or their society in some way, then designing for design capital entails designing for our societies. As such, our proposed solution is to design infrastructure as a social and cultural object as well as a functional one, and to incorporate aspects of social and cultural desirability within design. As D'Hooghe argues:

> One can look at infrastructures of mobility as a system, or one can look at it as a series of artifacts.[...][R]ather than a system of transportation planning and engineering, we may read infrastructures as objects of cultural production with a spatial content not unlike that of architecture or sculpture.[1]

This expanded notion of infrastructure is an idea currently prevalent in conference themes and recently established educational programmes, like MIT's Advanced Urbanism School. While historically, precedents for architects as designers of infrastructure exist—Palladio designed bridges and water systems in Venice and the Veneto in the 16th century, for example—through the late 18th and 19th centuries the bifurcation of the production of buildings and infrastructure into architecture and engineering lessened architecture's perceived role in the construction of infrastructure, although it did not entirely negate it, as the megastructures of the 1960s attest.[2]

While the relationship of architecture to culture has been debated at least since the Renaissance, when it was established as a fine art rather than a mechanical art,[3] architecture can broadly be thought of as the transformation of culture into built form. While this may be a somewhat abstract way of expressing what architects do, this is a common assumption. For example, in the early 20th century, architect and founder of the revolutionary design school, the Bauhaus, Walter Gropius, stated: "Good architecture I conceive to be both a science and an art. As a science it analyzes human relationships; as an art it coordinates human activities into a cultural synthesis."[4] Later in the century Ralph Rapson, architect and one time Dean of Minnesota's School of Architecture, asserted, "It is this insistence upon a properly understood moral and social program, honestly employing the science and technology of today, that is one of the keys of significant architecture.[5]

In architecture, as in other disciplines, there are different criteria for assessing the value of a design, and judgements may vary. Some will prioritize formal and others functional considerations; however, what we have identified as very effective in the translation of culture into built form is the focus on concept (Lawson 1994) or underlying idea, referred to variously as "image" (Alexander), "primary generator" (Darke 1978), or "organizing principle" (Rowe 1987) or most commonly "parti", from parti pris, meaning a decision taken (Leupen et al. 1997).[6] The concept or parti will in most cases be derived from the site or program, the client or community vision, singularly or in combination.[7] Contemporary architectural projects that have been judged successful by professional and public audiences in almost all cases have a clearly articulated underlying idea or 'design intention.' This design intention is often where social and cultural concerns are brought to the project and integrated into the design; it is usually included in the architect's published project description. With more prominent architecture firms, the cultural and social preoccupations of the firm are often published in writings by the principals or in books about the firm. The connection of theoretical frameworks with the more celebrated design firms gives credence to the idea that a cultural and social theory is important to architecture, and may contribute to the professional and public status of these firms. It is an indication that these design firms have been concerned with interpreting the cultural context of their projects and translating it into a built form. Design intention is clearly elucidated and foregrounded in most of the professionally and often more generally esteemed contemporary architectural projects. Intention is referenced to explain to a lay public how social and cultural concerns were brought to the project and integrated into the design. The success of this consideration is demonstrated by awards won, press endorsements and expressions of public enjoyment.

Much can be learned in this regard from studying the curricula and pedagogy of architecture schools. The training of an architect today develops in several stages, taking approximately nine years overall. This training includes an overall general education (bachelor's degree), followed by formal architectural training in an architecture school (bachelor's or master's degree level). In North America, this section of training is mandatory and usually lasts three years—other places have varying systems but all have this component of training. The current curriculum of architecture schools includes the design studio, the largest component, as well as a significant number of courses in the history and theory of design, classes in building systems (mechanical, energy, and structural), as well as courses in design media (drawing and representation), law and professional practice. Finally, a formal apprenticeship or practice portion is undertaken which takes two to three years. This lengthy training period is deemed necessary to acquire the breadth of social, cultural and technical knowledge that is required, as well as the skill in synthesizing various knowledge and procedural requirements. The act of mediating between material form and cultural ideas is not an easy one and there are many approaches; however, this mediation is necessary for the results to successfully accrue design capital.

In contrast, engineering curricula include foundational courses in mathematics, physics, graphics, electrical engineering, heat and thermodynamics, statistics and English, as well as courses specific to the different engineering disciplines. A law and ethics course is also required. Much of the emphasis is on analysis and understanding physical laws and applications. There are usually a few liberal arts electives for engineering students and they are generally free to pick anything that interests them. Engineering is a four to five-year bachelor's degree followed by three years of practice and an ethics exam required upon completion of an accredited degree. As such, there is very little focus on social or cultural issues. That said, it should be noted that problem solving around social issues is an increasingly important focus of innovative engineering schools and is generally introduced to the curricula through the method of capstone projects. However, once the social problem is identified, the focus shifts to solving the technical problem at hand. Analysis and problem solving around technical matters is the primary educational focus of an engineering education, with efficiency and safety the key motivations imparted to the students.

PEDAGOGY OF THE ARCHITECTURE SCHOOL

In architectural education, pedagogy has varied across time and within different cultures and institutions. Techniques used in architectural education include courses (lecture or seminar format), workshops and studios. The other major teaching areas where public values are discussed and incorporated are the history and theory courses where an academic pedagogy is developed and transformed into design concerns and vocabulary. These concerns and vocabulary are then applied in the design studio. Currently "the design studio is still the core of curricular structure in schools of architecture worldwide, and considered the norm for architectural design practice."[8] What is relevant to the discussion of design capital is the overall relationship of pedagogical approaches to the larger set of public values of the time. Studio teaching is key to constructing this relationship, and two aspects of the studio format are critical. Firstly, teaching occurs via clearly defined design projects with iterative design attempts by the student; this is usually undertaken in a space and format that in many ways mimics the professional design office. The second aspect is the critique of the project which involves mentors, faculty members and, periodically, external reviewers.

The design studio is a recurring focus of scrutiny and evaluation as witnessed in the countless articles devoted to it in an array of contemporary design journals.[9] The design studio is understood to be "an important process, which aims to shape the architectural sensitivities of students and to develop their communicative abilities as well as their problem-solving skills."[10] The studio is not only understood to be the core of architectural education, it is also deemed to be the site of adaptation to meet the new social needs, as well as technical and production requirements, of the profession.[11] The design studio is also where new knowledge is produced and disseminated and social relations of design are established "according to changing social and political forces."[12]

> Characteristics of the architecture studio include: project-based work on complex and open-ended problems, very rapid iteration of design solutions, frequent formal and informal critique, consideration of a heterogeneous range of issues, the use of precedent and thinking about the whole, the creative use of constraints, and the central importance of design media.[13]

This is where architecture students practise design and the area where most student effort is focused. Studio courses are typically semester-long projects, respond to open-ended problems and are allotted the most time in the curriculum, often approximately 25 hours a week and generally three times the dedicated time and credits of a single class. The studio is usually taught with a small student-to-faculty ratio usually 1:12 or 1:15—so that individual tutoring, considered to be the most effective type of instruction in student design development and the acquisition of judgement, can be implemented.[14]

Students are exposed to a number of viewpoints and design methodologies via the variety of professors encountered in a mandated number of studios (usually a minimum of six). The pedagogical aim is that students begin to develop their own design methodology. Although studio does integrate the technical aspects of design, in that students work with a variety of materials (steel, concrete, earth, cladding materials, glass, assemblies ,etc.), the main focus of design studio is on the development of design intent and judgement and its manifestation in built form. This design intent is usually concerned with addressing the social and cultural concerns of both the building user and the individual, corporate or public client for whom the student and architect is designing. The architect designs for the client and, ideally, within a determined social context as well; in design studio, the social context is very definitely a component of design. As architectural educator Anders Bergstrom argues: "The studio is not just a dominant feature of the curriculum, but often provides the epistemological foundation for architecture as an academic discipline."[15] The conceptual framework for how we think about designing our built environment forms the foundation of architecture as an academic discipline. The conceptual framework is thus a large and important field of study for academics and architectural critics and it is then demonstrated in practice in architectural projects.

It is a general belief within architectural education that "[t]he ability to apply acquired knowledge with imagination and judgment is fundamentally necessary to every creative architect. Creative synthesis is pre-eminently the life blood of architectural education and architectural practice."[16] It is this creative synthesis, in conjunction with the development of a sound conceptual framework, that is the goal of studio teaching. In the studio context, "students must be able to think at a high level of abstraction about the overall problem ('What is a community? What fosters community?') but also be able to shift focus to detailed design."[17] This is accommodated by an iterative approach to design.

Other aspects of studio teaching which develop skills that could potentially contribute to the creation of design capital include frequent formal and informal critical reviews from peers, faculty and visiting experts.[18] These can take the form of discussions among studio colleagues, 'desk crits' with faculty, and 'pin ups' of collective discussion. These various critiques offer a variety of opportunities for informal knowledge exchange where social and cultural assumptions and values can be conveyed and tested. The use of precedents is also important in the acquisition of knowledge about design in the context of the social and cultural values of the immediate and distant past. Given the temporal and spatial differences between the precedent and the studio project, imagination is needed to bridge those differences and social and cultural awareness to assess them. The studio is also a site for socialization, and it is where habits of thought are absorbed and an ethos of common purpose is established.[19]

Courses augment studio education. The history and theory classes in design education also expose students, however abstractly, to the complex manner in which culture and social structures influence design and its reception, and to a critical perspective on architectural representations. Design media classes, which teach drawing, rendering and representation, and often include video media and parametric design tools, play a significant role in architectural education and are essential in the various stages of design development. They range from the personal exploratory pencil sketch to the highly conventionalized construction drawings essential to the translation of design into built form. Renderings and, more recently, sophisticated computer and 3-D virtual constructions are used to convey design conceptions to clients and larger public audiences. As architects and others in the design professions produce representations that others translate into actual form, design media are an integral part of studio culture.

The process of design involves the synthesis of many, sometimes competing, requirements into a whole which satisfies all the technical and functional requirements of the brief while imbuing the project with social and cultural meaning. Design is an iterative, usually non-linear, process and should involve the designer questioning the assumptions under which he or she is operating. A good designer will question every constraint and supposition while formulating a design solution:

> Design is partly a kind of intuitive skill that makes brilliant syntheses and partly a matter of good critical sense. The critical sense needed is the self-examination that makes it possible for the designer to reject some of his most spontaneous conceptions, conceptions that were often compelling to the conceiver at the moment but which his later critical faculty will discard as meretricious or inappropriate.[20]

As in other disciplines, the final design often appears simple and clear but in actuality it has taken many attempts and many revisions to come to a successful, defensible design resolution.

HISTORICAL DEVELOPMENT OF STUDIO TEACHING

To understand how architectural training evolves with culture and society it is worth looking at the history of this mode of teaching. Studio teaching in the academic form we find it now is an early modern development. This more academically influenced studio over time replaced the guild system of education of the master mason in the late 15th and early 16th centuries. The guild system was augmented and then replaced with a more intellectual education that culminated in the academies of the 17th century, especially the influential French Academy of Architecture founded in 1671. Since then, design has been 'taught' in some form of master's studio, atelier, or more recently, the creative design studio. Architecture as intellectual pursuit, artistic practice and autonomous discipline relies on these studios to foster personal creativity through individual student design, rather than students working on the designs of a master or established practitioner. As individual creativity came to be privileged over received traditions and craft conventions in the early 20th century, the studio became the venue in which this individuality could be nurtured and assessed.

Another legacy of the shift from guild to studio is the emphasis on the design intent or 'concept', "the basic general scheme of an architectural design."[21] While the concepts altered over time according to changes in social, political and cultural context, the studio and the importance of design intent survived. Also persisting is the importance given to the 'parti' or concept conveyed via an esquisse (sketch)[22] as an expression of the student's talent or individuality. The process from parti through design development and resolution was intended to demonstrate judgement and presentation skills (both visual and verbal) in the final atelier and école presentations. The final project was evaluated on how well it represented the parti esquisse."[23]

> The importance of this procedure cannot be over-stressed. The production of the esquisse was the student's own creative act; and the resulting document was to constitute a guarantee of the originality and genuineness of his idea against any outside influence, whether it be criticism from a strong-willed patron or sarcasm from fellow students.[24]

The importance of individual creativity, proof of the ability to transform concept into form and space in programmatic resolution, as well as the demonstration of representational skills able to communicate this ability are consistent with learning objectives in architectural education today. However, as expected, there are significant differences between the 17th and 21st centuries. There are now professional accreditation bodies that monitor professional practice and scrutinize the different design schools for competence across a number of areas, including law, servicing infrastructure and structural factors. The kinds of projects students undertake have changed according to social concerns and the influences of the professional press and, more recently, mass and social media. Nevertheless, the parti continues in the 21st century as in the 17th: "a strong idea clearly stated, simply presented and well indicated, a solution which was easy to read, in other words, provided the firm basis upon which a jury's support could be built."[25] While the studio continues "to provide the epistemological foundation,"[26] for the discipline, the epistemology has altered over time as has the audience whose support is courted. In the 17th century the "public" for the architecture of the Academy was the monarch and aristocracy. This public gradually increased through the 18th century until in the 21st century it has become both more diffuse and fragmented. The design professions have, however, since the 18th century been educated to best present their individual creative response[27] to their respective audience, and according to their social and political context. [28]

THE BAUHAUS

Architectural education responded to the social, political and cultural upheavals of the early 20th century by introducing a new and innovative curriculum and pedagogy. This occurred in the wake of the Russian Revolution in 1917 and in the immediate aftermath of World War I. The epicentre of this innovation was the Bauhaus, founded in 1918 and based on initiatives to reform artistic and architectural education in Germany.[29] In response to World War I, and its associated social and cultural turmoil, assembled artists, architects and educators insisted on a new basis for design based on aesthetic principles, the machine, industrial mass production and socialist thought. The inaugural 1918 Bauhaus curriculum was initiated by an introductory course exploring individual expression and then divided into making and theory, the former based on materials and the latter on aesthetic, formal explorations via painting, sculpture and photography. Making occurred initially in a workshop setting, rather than a studio. The objective was to balance thinking and feeling; that is, of maintaining individual creativity in the context of industrial production: "the principles of modern art guided the technical production of architecture toward a new aesthetic."[30] The attention given to contemporary avant-garde art and to industrial production wed architecture and design to contemporary social and cultural developments. The Bauhaus forced design—and especially architecture — to respond to the social and cultural context that included a newly conceived mass public. The latter was addressed through an ambitious programme of publications and exhibitions.

Prior to 1927, there was no explicit architecture instruction; selected students took classes in construction and engineering in a neighbouring Institute for the Building Trades and served apprenticeships in the director's office.[31] However, in 1927, an architecture programme was initiated which was centred on a studio format, supported by classes on mathematics, statics, strength of materials, and steel and reinforced concrete taught by a construction engineer.[32] What was considered essential—and therefore taught in-house—was the study of 'design for living' which was intended to encourage the incorporation of consideration of the social context of any project.[33] In 1930, the Bauhaus became a School of Architecture and Interior Design with a focus on specialization and professionalism, and architecture became primarily a spatial and aesthetic proposal.[34] It was this idea of architecture that Bauhaus members took with them to North America when they fled Germany with the rise of fascism. Arriving in Chicago in 1933 to assume the post of director of the School of Architecture at the Amour Institute (renamed IIT in 1947), Mies van der Rohe felt he had finally "reunited Architecture with building in the studio."[35] Although the Bauhaus émigrés to the US were not initially as influential as promoters of European modernism as some have proposed, the idea of a reformed architectural education focused on the studio and responsiveness to local cultural traditions and vernaculars as well as efficiency, functionalism, inexpensive construction and industrial production was adopted.[36]

The studio remains the focus of architectural education, although what is deemed relevant in terms of the technical, social and aesthetic issues explored has evolved over time.

POSTMODERNISM

Architecture education underwent another major shift with the onset of postmodernism.[37] While postmodernism was broadly based on social and cultural criticism, it took specific forms in the architecture and design disciplines. Postmodernism offered critiques of the modern movement that ranged from its aesthetic and technical preoccupations, to its inattentiveness to history or cultural diversity. New forms of knowledge were deemed necessary for architectural education in response in to societal changes, including the incorporation of sociology and linguistics to the curriculum. More comprehensive and diversified histories of modern and historical architecture appeared that emphasized the social, historical and often political contexts of projects. These histories established a critical attitude to architecture and encouraged multiple discourses on the relationship of design to societal developments.[38]

With the rapid increase in the number of academic programmes offering doctoral degrees in architecture in the 1970s, a new importance was given to theoretical and historical knowledge. Theoretical developments in philosophy-semiology, phenomenology, structuralism and post-structuralism were grafted onto architectural issues and pervaded the curriculum. Semiotic studies of meaning in architecture proposed that architecture could be understood as a language with the power to convey cultural meaning.[39] Semiology's concern was with language, in particular how meaning is created and communicated via signs and symbols. The transmission of 'meaning' led to interests in reception of signs and how they are interpreted by different audiences, and the conventions of communication.[40] The structuralist philosophy of Michel Foucault gave new methods of conducting research into institutions and building types.[41] The thinking of post-structuralist philosophers, such as Jacques Derrida, formed the basis for design research that tested the rules by which design is created and evaluated.[42] These various theoretical explorations are ways that the design professions gain societal and cultural knowledge and develop critical skills regarding this knowledge.

Another line of philosophical reasoning that came to dominate academic architectural thought over the same period was phenomenology. Phenomenology proposed the active participation of individuals in constructing the world around them. It was consulted as an alternative, pre-conscious way to understand how meaningful places are created and provided an alternative to the exploration of *techne*, a concrete experience of making, as a basis for expressive technology.

Theory, as it appears in the curriculum and pedagogy of architecture schools, can be understood as a means of engaging with the pressing issues of the day; by its very nature, it is itself under constant critique and revision. The abstract and speculative nature of much postmodern theory has led to attempts to rebalance design with a re-engagement with its operative, technical capacity and/or more pragmatic approaches to building. Postmodern critics sought the "revitalization of theory by making it more relevant to contemporary problems, more closely linked to a global agenda capable of addressing the complexity of contemporary practice in a global context."[43] This serves to highlight just how embedded architecture, landscape architecture and the design professions are in their cultural and social contexts. These debates are disseminated in studios and seminars via academic texts, exhibitions, and discourse and inform curricula and influence pedagogy. Such theoretical investigations influence professional practice, give practitioners insight into contemporary social and cultural concerns and provide a shared set of parameters by which design is judged and valued.

HISTORY AND THEORY COURSES

Next to studio, history and theory courses are the most influential in the acquisition of knowledge pertaining to society and culture offered in an architecture school. These courses offer not only precedents, a catalogue of built forms and landscapes, but also the cultural and social contexts and theoretical assumptions that informed their design. Histories are constructed and theories developed in response to the issues of the era in which they are written.

Architecture, at least post-Renaissance, has been concerned to some degree with not only an object but also with the object's perception, both physiologically and culturally.[44] In the Renaissance, idealized proportions were marked out with decorative details and attributed with religious significance. In the modern period, more scientific notions of perception and the theorization of the subjective and cultural contingencies of aesthetic judgement were influential. By the early 20th century, psychological and physiological aspects of vision and hence the fine arts were paramount in architectural theory and education, as exemplified in the Bauhaus. Postmodern architecture explored the cultural and linguistic bases of reception and meaning-making.

Debates on the role of history in architecture school curricula tend to coincide with larger changes and pressures within architecture education as a whole. History as design veneer or source of practical knowledge erupted in the debates on architecture as profession or art in the 1890s in Great Britain, which was resolved by the "principle that architecture is the interpretation of construction into form of aesthetic value."[45] Writing about history from within the modern movement and its specific preoccupations, Sigfried Giedion pointed out that history's "purpose is to give the students a greater oversight into the nature of the problem and the ways it has been tackled in the past, so that they can approach it with a wider outlook and be less seduced to imitate the latest fashionable examples in the current magazines."[46] History should be "liberating but not inhibiting [the student's] spatial imagination" and afford an opportunity to question the conventional so as to respond to the unprecedented developments of the 20th century.[47 48] The position of the discipline of architecture as science or art, technical course or humanities subject has often shifted with larger societal change. How the discipline is perceived has also influenced the standing of both the studio and of history within the curriculum. Optimism about post-war reconstruction in 1940s Great Britain led to an emphasis on science, and post-war ideological shifts led to alterations in architectural education: functionalism prevailed and history and cultural considerations were marginalized.[49] However, as the British architect and educator Blundell-Jones countered, culture "should be central and all pervasive, running into the most technical areas, for architectural values are reflected through technical means. There is hardly any technical decision in the design of a building which is not also a value decision and therefore a cultural statement."[50] It is the studio that preserves these architectural and cultural values: "Studio tuition, has mitigated against the fragmentative effects of elsewhere. Studio teaching is inevitably integrative, in that all aspects of the discipline, technical or cultural, have to be engaged and understood in relation to each other."[51]

History and theory were also implicated in the later debates about postmodernism. Their use of historical precedent and semiological theory to debunk narrow modernist notions of functionalism, were seen as glib or obtuse.[52] Currently, architecture is understood as part of cultural production and its history and contemporary criticism are greatly influenced by current cultural theories that operate within an educational paradigm of interdisciplinarity. The role of history in design education is tied to the complex teaching objectives of schools of architecture which must accommodate professional accreditation boards and institutional academic criteria. At present, there is pressure for "the education of architects to be based on knowledge rather than skills, [... l] ike architectural design, architectural history should be about useful and reflective knowledge, not just techniques and facts."[53]

History has served architectural education as a source of precedents, not only of architectural form, but also of the context and varied social and cultural forces producing them. Of course, history also allows students to see the consequences of decisions that were made. The courses in theory of design serve to allow analysis of the cultural and social claims made on behalf of specific projects and, more generally, the reception and uses of architecture by society at large. As Giedion remarks, "History is not static but dynamic, that history is an ever-changing process, depending upon the point of view of each succeeding generation."[54]

Today we see this process continues, with the constant evolution of what is considered and analyzed in history and theory classes. Sustainability, post-colonialism and more recently the Black Lives Matter and Black, Indigenous and Peoples of Colour (BIPOC) movements have challenged the typically Eurocentric and paternalistic history/theory pedagogy inherited from early 20th-century architecture schools. As such, we can anticipate significant changes in design concerns in the near future. The curriculum and pedagogy of architecture and landscape architecture will undoubtedly respond to these larger social and cultural shifts so as to prepare its graduates to better serve communities by expressing those values in their design.

NOTES

1. Alexander D'Hooghe, "The Objectification of Infrastructure: Elements of a Different Space and Aesthetic for Suburban America," *PROJECTIONS* 10, 2011, 85.
2. Examples are the work of the Metabolists in Japan, archigram in the UK and specific projects of the 1960s and 70s globally. See: Reyner Banham, *Megastructures: Urban Futures of the Recent Past* (New York: Harper and Row, 1976).
3. See, Kevin Harrington, "Changing Ideas on Architecture in the "Encyclopédie," 1750-1776 (Ann Arbor, 1985) and Sylvia Lanvin, "Re: Reading the Encyclopedia: Architectural Theory and the Formation of the Public in Late-Eighteenth-Century France," *Journal of the Society of Architectural Historians* 53, no. 2 (June 1994), 184-192.
4. Ralph Rapson, (1959) quoting Walter Gropius in "Objectives of Architectural Education," Journal of Architectural Education 14 no. 2, 21, DOI: 10.1080/10464883.1959.11102411 http:dx.org/10.1080/1046883.1959.11102411.
5. Rapson, "Objectives," 21.
6. Ann Heylighten and Genvieve Martin, "That Elusive Concept of Concept in Architecture," *Design Computing and Congnition'04*, ed. J.S. Gero (Dordrecht: Kluwer Academic Publishers, 2004), 58.
7. Heylighen and Martin, "That Elusive Concept," 58.
8. Burkay Pasin, "Rethinking the Design Studio-Centered Architectural Education: A Case Study at Schools of Architecture in Turkey," *The Design Journal: An International Journal for All Aspects of Design 20,* sup.1 (2017), *https://doi.org/10.1080/14606925.2017.1352656.*
9. For example, *Journal of Architecture and Planning Research (Autumn 2007); The International Journal of Architectural Research* (July 2017); *The International Journal of Art and Design Education* (June 2010); *The Design Journal: An International Journal for All Aspects of Design* (2017); *The Journal of Architectural Education* (Autumn 1987).
10. Lyla Y. Tokman and Rusen Yamacli, "Reality-Based Design Studio in Architectural Education," *Journal of Architecture and Planning Research* 24, no. 3 (Autumn 2007): 245.
11. Marta Masdin and Josep Fuses, "Reconceptualizing the design studio in architectural education: Distance learning and blended learning as transformation factors," *International Journal of Architectural Research* 11, no. 2 (July 2017): 6-23.
12. Thomas A Dutton, "Design Studio Pedagogy," *Journal of Architectural Education* 41, no. 1 (Autumn 1987): 16.
13. Sarah Kuhn, "Learning from the Architecture Studio: Implications for Project-Based Pedagogy," *International Journal of Engineering Education* 17, no. 4/5 (2001): 349.
14. This can be contrasted with engineering education, which is generally imparting physical laws that do not require reiterative application or discernment processes, or a studio setting.
15. Anders Bergström, "Architecture and the Rise of Practice in Education," *Architectural Theory Review* 19, no. 1 (2014): 18, https://www.tandfonline.com/doi/abs/10.1080/13264826.2014.894604.
16. Rapson, "Objectives," 23.
17. Kuhn, "Learning from the Architecture Studio," 351.
18. Kuhn, "Learning from the Architecture Studio," 350.
19. Dana Cuff, *Architecture: The Story of Practice* (Cambridge, Mass: MIT Press, 1991), 65–66. Joan Ockman and Rebecca Williamson, eds., *Architecture School: Three Centuries of Educating Architects in North America* (Cambridge, Mass. : Washington, D.C: MIT Press ; Association of Collegiate Schools of Architecture, 2012), 64.
20. John E. Burchard, "Some keys to Pandora's Jug," *Journal of Architectural Education (1947-74)* 14, no. 2 (2015): 14, ACSA-AIA Seminar: the Teaching of Architecture (Autumn, 1959), 19-21, accessed February 14, 2020, https://www.jstor.org/stable/1424014.

21. *Webster's Third New International Dictionary,* 1971. For example, the Renaissance architectural theorist Leon Battista Alberti wrote in his 1471 *de re architectura* that architecture was "Idea Building," meaning that it was concerned with conveying a concept.
22. "The esquisse was a sketch produced within a maximum of 12 hours, by each student, isolated within the confines of the Ecole in a private alcove or loge. It embodied his interpretation of a programme sprung upon him on a given morning, and constituted a record of his very own concept of the plan, section and elevation of the building (or group of buildings) required to fulfil its requirements. Keeping a copy of his esquisse, the student returned to his atelier when he was given six weeks or so to develop further his original idea." Jean-Paul Carlhian, "The Ecole des Beaux-Arts: Modes and Manners," *Journal of Architectural Education* 33, no. 2 (1979), 10, published online January 2, 2014, https://doi.org/10.1080/10464883.1979.10748615.
23. Carlhian, "The Ecole des Beaux-Arts," 14.
24. Carlhian, "The Ecole des Beaux-Arts," 10.
25. Carlhian, "The Ecole des Beaux-Arts," 14.
26. Bergström, "Architecture and the Rise of Practice," 18.
27. The initial Bauhaus manifesto of 1918 speaks of crafts and the fine arts with a certain ring of the Arts and Crafts Movement. It also has certain elements of the Werkbund with its concern to engage with machine production. It was not entirely unprecedented nor consistent across the fifteen years of its existence, before its closure by the Fascists.
28. This could be contrasted with the development of engineering education which was in the 19th century divided from architecture in its own school in France. There were debates about the split or rationalized, engineering approaches (Viollette le Duc and Duran in France and Schinkel in Germany) and architecture approaches (the Ecole des Beaux Arts in France and the Bauacademie in Germany).
29. The initial Bauhaus manifesto of 1918 speaks of crafts and the fine arts with a certain ring of the Arts and Crafts Movement. It also has certain elements of the Werkbund with its concern to engage with machine production. It was not entirely unprecedented nor consistent across the fifteen years of its existence, before its closure by the Fascists.
30. Ockman and Williamson, *Architecture Schools*, 336.
31. Walter Gropius was the first director of the Bauhaus 1918-1927. Wallis Miller, "Architecture, Building and the Bauhaus," *Bauhaus Culture: From Weimar to the Cold War,* Kathleen James-Chakrabarty ed. (Minneapolis and London: University of Minnesota Press, 2006), 165.
32. The architecture programme was initiated by Hannes Meyer when he became the second director of the Bauhaus. Miller, "Architecture," 82.
33. Miller, "Architecture," 83.
34. This change occurred with the arrival of Mies van der Rohe as the third director of the Bauhaus in 1930.
35. Miller, "Architecture," 88.
36. See, Kathleen James-Chakrabarty, "From Isolationism to Internationalism: American Acceptance of the Bauhaus, *Bauhaus Culture: From Weimar to the Cold War,* ed. Kathleen James-Chakrabarty (Minneapolis and London: University of Minnesota Press, 2006), 153-170; 225-228.
37. Post modernism was a controversial term when first formulated, some commentators, critics and academics preferring other terms, such as after modernism or late modernism. It was initially used in architecture history and criticism, most noticeably by Charles Jencks in his influential *The Language of Postmodern Architecture (1977).* Postmodernism developed different meanings in different disciplines.
38. Two examples of such histories are Leonardo Benevelo, *History of Modern Architecture.* 2 vols. (Cambridge MA: The MIT Press, 1977) and Manfredo Tafuri, *Architecture and Utopia* (Cambridge MA: The MIT Press, 1977).
39. Ockman and Williamson, *Architecture Schools,* 342. Interest in semiology also produced a radical theory among academically trained architects, such as Peter Eisenman, who conceived "form as a language totally independent of programmatic and technological requirements." Ockman and Williamson, *Architecture Schools*.

40. Examples of architectural interest in semiotics are: Robert Venturi, Denis Scott Brown and Steven Izenour, *Learning from Las Vegas* (Cambridge MA: The MIT Press, 1977) and Robert Venturi and Denise Scott Brown, *Architecture as Signs and Symbols: for a Mannerist Time* (Princeton: Harvard University Press, 2004).
41. The work of Bernard Tschumi is often engaged with the philosophy of Foucault. See for example. Gordana Fontana-Giusti, *Foucault for Architects* (London and New York: Routledge, 2004).
42. The collaboration between architect and philosopher is demonstrated in, Anthony Vidler, Bernard Tschumi and Jaques Derrida, *Tschumi Parc de la Villette* (London: Artifice 2004).
43. Ockman and Williamson, *Architecture Schools.*
44. These interests are also evident in earlier times. For example, in classical Greece, this was quite literal: the entasis and cant of columns, as well as the curve of the stylobate, were all in aid of correcting the distortion of human perception of geometric form.
45. Alan Powers, "Teaching History in Schools of Architecture in the Age of Eclecticism," *Architectural History and the Studio*, eds. Adam Hardy and Necdet Teymur (London: ?uestion Press, 1996), 20.
46. Sigfried Giedion, (1957), "History and the Architect," *Journal of Architectural Education* 12 no. 2, 16, published on line June 2, 2015, DOI:10.1080/10464883.1957.1102375, hppt://dx.doi.org/1080/10464883.1957.1102375.
47. Giedion, "History," 16.
48. Sigfried Giedion, "History and the Architect," Journal of Architectural Education, no. 12:2 (1957): 16.
49. Peter Blundell-Jones, "Implicit and Explicit," in *Architectural History and the Studio,* eds. Hardy and Teymur, 67. Blundell goes on to state: "Everything was to be measured and calculated in a literal expansion of the programme devised by Hannes Meyer for the Bauhaus in 1928."
50. Blundell-Jones, "Implicit and Explicit," 71.
51. Blundell-Jones, "Implicit and Explicit," 71.
52. An early example of postmodern architecture writing, see: Charles Jencks, *The Language of Post Modern Architecture,* 1978 and ed. Richard Blunt, Geoffrey Broadbent and Charles Jencks, *Signs, Symbols and Architecture,* 1980.
53. Iain Borden, "Architecture, Not," in *Architectural History and the Studio,* eds. Hardy and Teymur, 145.
54. Giedion, "History," 15.

7

CREATING DESIGN CAPITAL: LEARNING FROM ARCHITECTURE

THEORY IN PRACTICE

Design theory, which elucidates design methodologies and approaches, does not remain solely in the academy. By necessity it must be put into practise, making architectural practice highly relevant to the discussion here. Many firms such as Diller Scofidio + Renfro, Patkau Architects, Steven Holl Architects, and SANAA (Kazuyo Sejima and Ryue Nishizawa) are small practices with well-developed theoretical positions and now practice all over the world with large commissions. They, as well as many well-known architecture firms such as Office of Metropolitan Architects (OMA), Morphosis, and Bjarke Ingels Groups (BIG), have principals that teach as well as practise, bringing concepts and theories from the academy to their projects and vice versa. The discourse about their projects is sophisticated and grounded in contemporary social and cultural considerations which they articulate in their writings and discussion of their projects.

The influence of the pedagogical and curricular objectives of an architectural education is also evident in larger firms, including those involved in infrastructure projects. Here, too, social and cultural objectives are expressed alongside those of technical and practical considerations. It is helpful to understand how the theory discussed in the previous chapter gets put into practice; there is neither a right nor wrong way to go about design and each designer has their own approach. The validity of the approach is in the reception of the project by both peers as well as the public. As illustrative examples we discuss here four projects in terms of their engagement with contemporary social and cultural issues: The World Arab Institute by Jean Nouvel, Seabird School by Patkau Architects, Petronas Towers by Cesar Pelli Architects, and Yokohama Terminal by Foreign Office Architects (FOA).

7:1 Jean Nouvel, Gilbert Lézénès, Pierre Soria, Architecture Studio. Institut du Monde Arabe, (1981-87), Paris, France. Photo : Auguste Fischer.

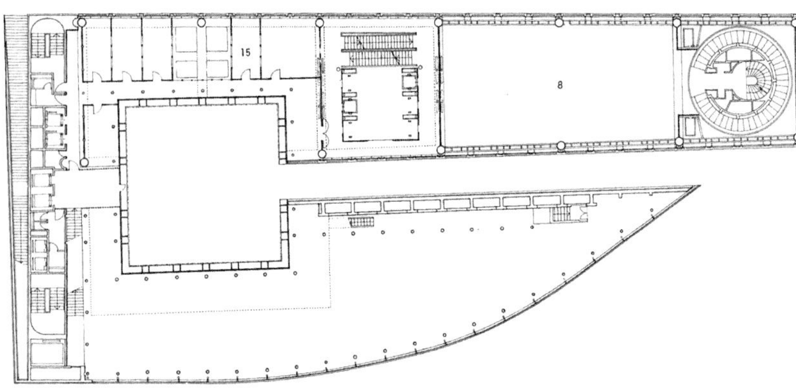

7:2 Jean Nouvel, Gilbert Lézénès,Pierre Soria, Architecture Studio, Institut du Monde Arabe, (1981-87), Paris France.

WORLD ARAB INSTITUTE (INSTITUT DU MONDE ARABE): PARIS, 1981-87. JEAN NOUVEL AND ARCHITECTURE-STUDIO

The World Arab Institute was first proposed under the government of Giscard d'Estaing in 1974 with the objective of emphasizing the connection of France, and Europe, with the Arab world, and to highlight their shared experience of the Mediterranean. (Figure 7:1) Importantly, there was enthusiasm for such a project in the Arab world. When the act founding the Institute was signed by the Minister of Foreign Affairs in 1980, 19 Arab states had joined in this shared cultural and financial commitment.[1] The Institute subsequently became one of the grand projects of President François Mitterrand when he assumed office in 1981.

The architects, Jean Nouvel and Architecture-Studio,[2] interpreted the project as follows: "[a] place of cultural mediation, the institute is situated at the intersection of two worlds in tension, of two cultural groups who are attracted to and repulsed by each other, who are fascinated by and reject each other."[3] This verbal description of the project suggests the beginning of a translation of an intellectual concept into a design concept, or parti. The concept of duality and the negotiated relationship between the divided can be recognized in the two contrasting volumes of the design, a curved form referencing the arc of the Seine to the north and a rectilinear form whose exterior cladding recalls the screened windows of Arab or Middle Eastern buildings. (Figure 7:2) This juxtaposition of cultural references is restated in the viewing deck that looks onto Notre Dame and the sequestered courtyard, typical of traditional Middle Eastern urban fabric, that forms the interstitial space between the two major volumes.

The Ateliers Jean Nouvel website emphasizes the centrality of the cultural dimension to their design:

> A cultural position in architecture is a necessity. This involves refusing ready-made or facile solutions in favor of an approach that is both global and specific. The Arab World Institute is a showcase for the Arab World in Paris. It is therefore not an Arab building but an occidental one.[4]

The website also acknowledges that the Arab state members of the commission were surprised by the design, but noted that they did appreciate the symbolic elements. One such element was the "moucharabiehs," screens of mechanically-operated apertures:

> [These] polygons of varying shapes and sizes create a geometric effect recalling the Alhambra. From an urban point of view the Institute is a hinge between two cultures and two histories. If the south side of the building, with its motorized diaphragms, is a contemporary expression of eastern culture, the north side is a literal mirror of western culture: images of the Parisian cityscape across the Seine are enamelled on the exterior glass, like chemicals over a photographic plate. These patterns of lines and markings on the same façade are an echo of contemporary art.[5]

Heylighen and Martin use the World Arab Institute as an example of how a parti is successfully manifested in architecture. They comment on the south façade and its merging of references to both tradition (the moucharabieh) and modernity (the diaphragm of the camera lens) via their shared function of controlling illumination:

> While in actuality the façade functions differently from its precedents and is of an entirely different scale, it allows the ideas of a high-tech building and traditional Islamic architecture to be held simultaneously. [...] This resulted in a gigantic Islamic pierced screen, which makes this modem high-tech building a permanent reference to traditional Islamic architecture.[6]

It is the success of this cultural referencing via architectural form that has garnered praise and begun the acquisition of design capital. The cultural acumen expressed in the Institute's design won it an Aka Khan architectural award. The jury described the building as forming "a successful bridge between French and Arab cultures."[7]

This was the first in a long list of international prizes and awards that Jean Nouvel Ateliers would accumulate in the following decades.[8] These recognize his ability to resolve the social and cultural issues of a project's urban context as well as to solve technical issues with originality. Nouvel's attention to social and cultural issues could be attributed to the critical and reforming critiques of institutional architectural education in Paris in the late 1960s. Nouvel was a student at the Sorbonne in Paris during the May '68 political demonstrations that began with student protests against social injustice and traditional institutions in France and he engaged with international currents of this tumultuous time. Upon graduation in 1971, Nouvel became assistant architect to Claude Parent, an anti-establishment figure, and was a founding member of two anti-establishment groups: the "Mars 1976" movement and the Syndicat de l'Architecture, France's labour union for architects.[9] Nouvel states that his work is the result of "a quest to create a unique concept for a singular combination of people, place and time."[10] The World Arab Institute benefits from this contextual approach in its consideration of not only its urban site but also the specificities of place that are shaped by local as well as global forces.

SEABIRD ISLAND COMMUNITY SCHOOL / LAME'IWESAWTEXW: AGASSIZ, CANADA, 1988-1991. PATKAU ARCHITECTS

Seabird Island Community School was commissioned by the Seabird Island Band, a member of the Stó:lō Tribal Council and a largely agricultural community settled on the Fraser River delta, some 120 km from the Pacific Coast.[11] (Figure 7:3) The new school was to serve two broad and interrelated functions, one practical and the other philosophical.

Programmatically, the school was commissioned to replace a former Federal Day School (c.1916), which had reverted to band control in 1978, two portable classrooms as well as offices and a gymnasium dispersed to the Seabird Island Band Office Building and the Seabird Island Band Hall respectively. It was to provide modern classrooms, a gymnasium and staff quarters to accommodate K-12 students. It was also to serve as a community building; its design supported a community-based education and community events such as feasts and gatherings in non-school hours. In addition, the building was to be built by local band members with no previous experience of the required construction technology. Most importantly, the design had to register the culture of the Seabird Island Band as vital and contemporary.

Philosophically, the new school was intended to fulfil the educational goals initiated in 1978 in providing "an environment where [Stó:lō] identity and culture will flourish."[12] It was to advance the pedagogical objectives of the community which were largely influenced by Indigenous culture, and

7:3 Patkau Architects. Seabird Island School (1988-91), Agassiz, Canada.

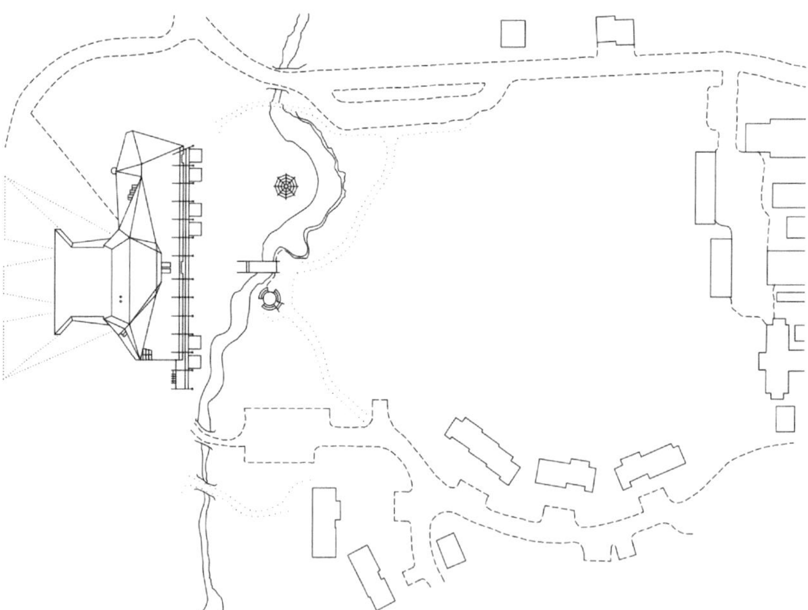

7:4 Patkau Architects. Seabird Island School (1988-91), Agassiz, Canada.

included the teaching of traditional skills by elders and community members. It was critical that the building avoid any resemblance to residential schools with their painful associations of family separation, isolation, loss of language and cultural identity, and Eurocentric regimes of learning. Therefore, parents and community were to be included in the education of students. Traditions and the Stó:lō language were integrated into the curriculum and the building was to give the sense of "being at home."[13]

The envisioned building was the result of decades-long overhaul of Indigenous education in Canada and British Columbia marked by the Indian Control of Indian Education Act (1973) that returned education to local bands. The Seabird Island Band began implementing that Act with the establishment of the Seabird Island Community School in 1978. This led to the Seabird Island Planning Study of 1984 that proposed a new school, purpose-built for the innovative band-led pedagogy and curriculum and to further the philosophy, values and objectives of the Seabird Island Band. Its objectives included the integration of mainstream Canadian education and Stó:lō traditions and culture to instil pride and identity in students, while providing them with the skills to thrive both within their own community and a multicultural world. The school was intended to equip students for modern life and be "an agent for the maintenance of cultural values, belief and norms of the Stó:lō community."[14] Central to that philosophy is the geographical and ecological system in which the community resides: a site defined by mountains to the north/ northeast, housing against the surrounding forest and an arc of community buildings facing a grass commons to the south, and a river to the east.

The Seabird Island School by Patkau Architects was commissioned in 1988 and opened in September 1991. The Patkau project accommodated conventional Western educational practices—nine classrooms plus kindergarten, a gymnasium/ community hall, library, reading rooms, home economics room/kitchen, offices and reception, washrooms and service areas. It included in its design open access to classrooms and adjacent exterior learning spaces. In addition, classrooms were augmented with aspects supportive of Indigenous educational aims: a large south-facing porch that opened onto teaching gardens and articulated the building with tectonic form and roof planes that recognized a disposition toward relating form to legendary zoomorphic characters, such as a bird, which it often recalls for band members. The building's orientation responds both to environmental factors and social circumstances: it is closed to the north winds and opened to southern sun exposure and it engages the community buildings across the commons. (Figure 7:4)

There was much in the education and experience of the principals of Patkau Architects that prepared them for the success of this building. They were schooled, formally or informally, in both Western and Indigenous ideas about site and tectonics. Not long after the opening of the school, John Patkau wrote: "When presented with a commission, our intuitive starting point is to seek those things that are particular to the project and to center our architectural response around them."They "search for 'found potential'—those aspects of site, climate, or local culture—that facilitate the development of an architectural order evocative of circumstance."[15] Of the Seabird Island School in particular, he goes on to say, "Potential was found in the site and the client studies." From the study of the latter, he notes the suffering imposed by European culture, and the need not for an institution but a design to enable the "passing on knowledge within an expanded family." In response to this need, the porch was conceived as a public space, with teaching gardens immediately adjacent to classrooms and fish-drying racks that frame the porch's eastern extremity. The interior space was consciously planned to be open and figured "like a landscape" in order to avoid any semblance of the hierarchical spaces of residential schools with their barriers between students and family or community. Also influential was Patkau Architects' understanding of tectonics that encouraged their timber forms to be imbued with the memory of traditional post-and-beam structures. The provision of a framing model allowed local band members to build the school and thus develop capacity and skills within the Stó:lō community. The resulting school could be both contemporary and yet maintain Stó:lō cultural beliefs.

Its "discreetly tectonic" architecture also allowed the school to participate in international architectural discourse.[16] The complex timber framework and sweeping shingled roof are relatable to autochthonous practices, serving as totemic, mythic elements but also reference Western architectural theory. The eminent American historian and theorist, Kenneth Frampton, notes of the building:

> the totemic, mythic elements of the project emerge here at a more rooted level where they express themselves as a kind of Semperian

roof work rising up on an alpine metaphor in response to mountain backdrop then tapering out in a mid-distance silhouette to evoke the animistic imagery of the Pacific Northwest and to discretely suggest the great totemic houses of a lost Oceanic culture.[17]

In referring to the 19th century German architect and theorist Gottfried Semper, Frampton is referencing a theory of architectural style which posited that architectural form arose from basic ways of making in response to materials at hand and essential human need. This is something he finds appropriately recalled in the contemporary design of Seabird School.

Seabird Island School was successful among the architectural community and the specific Indigenous population for which it was built. This success has in part been attributed to the ability of the conceptual and tectonic language of the building to resonate with contemporary architectural theory and with the Indigenous community's cultural expectations and habits of engaging with built form. Both architectural theory and Indigenous practice acquired new cultural relevance and esteem in this cross-cultural exchange. The differentiation of façade orientation, relation of building to site and the choice of materials were sensitive to traditional Indigenous practices while also referencing contemporary discourse on the particularities of place and region. The forms given to roof, porch supports and massing in response to orientation, site and materials also allowed a metaphoric and animistic reading of them.[18] The school has been celebrated by both the professional and local community and has won several design awards including the Canadian Architect Award of Excellence (1989), and in 1992, the Canadian Wood Council Honour Award, the Lieutenant Governor's Medal in Architecture and the Governor General's Medal.[19]

The school is consequently in the process of accruing design capital. This was in part assisted by Marie-Odile Marceau, who was appointed regional director of the Federal BC Native Schools Program in 1985. Marceau had declared as its mandate not only a collaborative design process but also excellence in design.[20] This involved a rigorous competition process that began with a request for proposals issued jointly by the bands and the regional director of the BC Native Schools Program. Interviews, shortlisting and the final decision were all made jointly.[21] The Seabird Island Community School was the first completed of the twelve schools commissioned and among the award winners.[22] While the professional press would conclude that these schools had a significant impact on levels of pride and self-esteem in the communities, they cannot alone solve all the educational and social issues facing rural Indigenous communities; they have perhaps served as a resource in ameliorating these issues.[23]

Design capital was invested not only in the expressive aspects of the project but also in the actual construction technology: the construction model fabricated to assist local Seabird Island residents to build the school also instructed them in contemporary timber construction and these amateur builders have gone on not only to build five other schools of the BC Native School Program, but also to become an enduring contemporary construction management company.[24] The Seabird Island Community School project is an inspiring example of how design capital can accrue through a commitment to design excellence by the client, the collaborative design process with the Stó:lō community and the comprehensive design knowledge of the architects.

PETRONAS TWIN TOWERS, KUALA LUMPUR, MALAYSIA, 1994-97. CESAR PELLI AND ASSOCIATES

The Petronas Twin Towers, Kuala Lumpur, began as an unspecified office tower in an urban development project intent on capturing the Asian real estate market in 1990; however, it became an intentionally symbolic building in 1994-98 when it was finally designed by Cesar Pelli.[25] (Figure 7.:5) The building was intended to be an example of what Prime Minister Mahathir Mohamad called wawasan (Vision 2020): "A blueprint for the country's development, a variety of large infrastructure projects."[26] It was deliberately built "for symbolic as well as functional reasons."[27] While the development was initiated by the Malaysian government,[28] it was not until the nationally-owned Petronas petroleum company decided to occupy the site in January 1991 that the national government became directly involved.[29] In April 1991, Cesar Pelli Associates won an invited international competition for the north-west portion of the site.[30] The selection committee's objectives were an "extraordinary" design and one that "complied with the masterplan, was functional and efficient, and expressed the qualities and heritage of Malaysia."[31] According to Abduk Rahim Naim, chief operating officer of Kuala Lumpur City Centre (KLCC)

7:5 César Pelli. Petronas Twin Towers (1998), Kuala Lumpur.
Photo: Marcin Konsek.

Holdings Berhad, "That is what Mr. Pelli gave us. His design has elements of Islamic architecture identifiable with our country. The other architects' designs looked as if they could be built anywhere. Mr. Pelli's could be in no other place but Kuala Lumpur."[32] Discussion during the competition included not only technical and economic issues but also aesthetic and philosophical concerns.[33]

Pelli was equipped to comply with the brief and to give expression to Malaysian heritage and qualities via his education, professional experience and design skill. Pelli had academic and professional credentials which gave him considerable social capital and visibility in the field of high-rise design. He holds architecture degrees from Argentina (1949) and the US (IIT, 1954), had taught at UCLA (1960s) and was Dean of Yale School of Architecture (1977-84). Prior to establishing Cesar Pelli Associates in 1977, he had worked in esteemed architecture offices such as those of Eero Saarinen and Victor Gruen. At the time of the invited competition for the Petronas Towers, the American Institute of Architects named Pelli one of the ten most influential living American architects (in 1995 it awarded him the AIA Gold Medal). He had also designed several towers. Thus, by April 1991, Pelli had accrued considerable social and cultural capital via his education and professional experience.

Pelli's design methodology was acquired through his education and experience and assisted in his response to the question of what a modern Malaysian architecture would look like. He endeavoured to "rethink the character of the traditional skyscraper and to unburden it of American or European connotation."[34] One of his initial steps was to study Islamic tradition where he found repetitive geometries an underlying constant feature[35] and where geometric patterns carry greater symbolic weight than in Western culture."[36] This was also one aspect of Islamic design that was abstract enough to accommodate modern design sensibilities, as both shared a preference for abstract, geometric form. However, the original suggestion of a twelve-point geometric star as the basis of a floor plate of very useable floor space was jettisoned on the suggestion of the Prime Minister of Malaysia for an 8-point star (created by two rotated squares) which, while evoking more closely traditional Islamic motifs, also produced less useable floor space.[37] In response, Pelli compensated for the functional loss by designing curved bays that would alternate between the eight points of the star. Here, symbolic function was prioritized by the client and made functionally optimal by the architect's design skill. The curved bays also added an additional echo of Islamic 'arabesque' to the design. According to Pelli, "Such complex geometries were a way of linking the building to Islamic design tradition without resorting to 'cultural pastiche,"[38]

Two other aspects of Pelli's design contributed to the social and cultural ambitions of the stakeholders. These were the figurative and place-defining aspects of the building's composition. The symmetrically-aligned towers produce a void which, with the skybridge connecting them at the 41st and 42nd floors, forms a gateway that frames the civic space beyond and creates a landmark that outlines the city of Kuala Lumpur. This was intentionally "a design that is unabashedly symbolic. That announces its presence as a landmark, as a gateway to an important development."[39] It was Pelli's thinking that: "Because they [the dual towers] will appear for the first time in Kuala Lumpur, they will be forever identified with the place—in the same way the Eiffel Tower is identified with Paris, although its structure and form were not derived from Parisian or French architecture."[40] Pelli also attributes this landmark status to the gap between the two buildings which he considers "unlike any Western skyscraper" but also "not derived from Malaysian tradition."[41] Interestingly, Pelli refers to the philosophy of Lao Tzu about the importance of the void over the object defining it, and hence makes perceptible a notion from Chinese culture, a major demographic in Malaysia.[42] Place is expressed in the more functional aspects of the building: its primarily concrete construction, the sunshades that are integral with the window detailing on the entire façade, and the linen finish given to the steel that diffuses the strong sunlight. Place and culture are also conveyed in the small floor plates that are common to Malaysia and by the prayer hall located in the skybridge.

The geometry, exploitation of the aesthetic potentials of a building envelope, and the relating of a building to civic space are also aspects of Pelli's architecture prior to the Petronas Towers commission. It is a product of the firm's approach, which has the objective "to create architecture possessing an articulate relationship to its particular place, the function it serves, and its social and civic context, expressed in an aesthetic language consistent with contemporary construction technology."[43] For Pelli, "Petronas Towers demonstrates that a tall building can be designed to closely tie in with the culture, history, and climate of its place—a regional skyscraper of global structure."[44] Here, design value is estimated to result from "site-specific architecture that responds to the place where it is built—not just the physical site, but also the cultural, social, political and historical context."[45] The architects attribute this design value to an approach that is very much modelled on the design studio of architectural school.[46]

Petronas Towers can also be examined from the perspective of stakeholders' desire to create a building with a significant cultural and social message, one which symbolically represented the modernizing aspirations of a developing Asian country through both a very advanced representation of technology and a reflection of the historic culture and social fabric. The challenge, in short, was to include "conceptions of 'Malaysianness'" (what it means to be Malaysian) and "progress" (an appropriate national form of cultural and socioeconomic development) and manifest them in a single artefact.[47] The role of the building was not only to symbolize an aspirational identity, but also to influence how the Malaysian population viewed itself: "The Petronas Tower's role in national development is not merely aesthetic, envisioning a state conception of Malaysian urbanity: the building also promotes new "ways of seeing" among citizens."[48] That is, the Towers create and shape perspectives, both literal (the framing of the cityscape) and figurative (national and cultural identity).

The use of the high-rise as a symbol of progress is not a new or original idea; by itself, it could not carry the full weight of representation as high-rise buildings have been a feature of Kuala Lumpur for at least the last two and a half decades.[49] The originality here is the architect's expression of cultural significance through a traditional geometry associated with a particular culture while integrating it with an extruded shape which would give visual identity and environmental benefit. The architect had determined where abstraction should be most effectively situated to convey cultural identity. Cesar Pelli Associates also had to provide a distinctive language that would be inclusive to the numerous cultures within Malaysia so that the building 'belonged' to everyone. Hence the importance of its geometric elements, the void, and the presence of technologically modern and unprecedented form that could be assigned new, collective meanings.

Like most high-rise developments in dense urban locations, Petronas Towers has been criticized for its functional drawbacks. The local press predicted it would be unhelpful to the everyday lives of Malaysians and increase pollution and traffic congestion in the area.[50] Nevertheless, Petronas Towers was praised after its completion by both the professional and official press releases; the development was "understood as part of a broader attempt to make the national capital into a 'world city'"[51] and was viewed as successful by the government of the day. Petronas Towers continues to be referred to frequently in the context of the cultural identity of Kuala Lumpur and Malaysia. Today, it is rated as the number one attraction in Kuala Lumpur since visitors can go up to the bridge and observation deck.[52] Here, we see the accrual of design capital in action as this function was not specified by the stakeholders but was provided for by the design allowing the building to garner uses that allow public engagement in unanticipated ways.

YOKOHAMA INTERNATIONAL PASSENGER TERMINAL, 2002. YOKOHAMA, JAPAN. FOREIGN OFFICE ARCHITECTS (FOA)

Yokohama International Passenger Terminal, completed in 2002, is the result of an international competition held in 1994 for the redevelopment of the Osanbashi pier along the harbour front and adjacent to recent industrial harbour developments to the south and east of Yokohama Bay. (Figure 7:6) In mounting this competition, the city of Yokohama recognized the importance of design and also the publicity a globally mounted search would invite: the competition attracted over 600 entrants.[53]

The winners, Foreign Office Architects (FOA), brought to the project their social capital as recent graduates of the Harvard Graduate School of Design and the Bartlett School of Architecture (University College London) where they had imbibed the most current theoretical thinking regarding form-making, combining the philosophy of Gilles Deleuze with digital technology. They had also worked in the vanguard offices of Office of Metropolitan Architects (OMA) and circulated within the architectural intellectual elite of the time; they had acquired Bourdieu's "social capital." The Yokohama International Passenger Terminal was consequently featured in major design publications. It was published in AA Files while still in project form (1995), and within a year of completion in Architectural Review (2003). It continues to be an often-cited project more than a decade after its unveiling, appearing in AD Classics twice (2014; 2018), Architecture Daily (2018), and CICA (Comité International des Critiques d'Architecture

7:6 Foreign Office Architects (FOA). Yokohama Passenger Terminal (2002), Yokohama, Japan. Courtesy of Tony Wu.

/ International Committee of Architectural Critic), (2019). It also appears in at least two books, The Digital Turn in Architecture 1992-2012, where the project's initiation in 1995 identifies it as an early example of the "digital turn" and Yokohama International Port Terminal.[54] Its continued presence within the design world contributed to the fact that, "well before its completion in 2002, the Yokohama International Port Terminal was acclaimed as one of the most meaningful architectural achievements of the digital age, but its authors never mentioned here [in their 1996 account] either computers or digital technology."[55] This omission also contributed to its elevated status within the design profession. In not dwelling on the digital aspects of its design, the architects were able to focus attention not on the tools of its design but its concept.

The brief required a repurposing of the existing 750-metre pier for an international passenger terminal, a garden of 500 square metres, public spaces, "a great symbol"[56]/ an iconic building[57] and an expression of "ni-wa-minato"[58] (which has been given various interpretations: for example, "very bright with skylight"[59] and which the architects interpreted as "a mediation between garden and harbour"[60]). The brief and the dimensions of the pier established certain parameters of the design. A five-metre height limit, the height required for accessing the ships, was imposed on the horizontal layer between aprons and roof plaza, and the 6% gradient of the access drive and the area required for the traffic plaza determined the position of the main entrance along the 750m length of the pier.[61] The Osanbashi pier was roughly aligned with Osanbashi Avenue and Yokohama Park with its World-Cup-calibre stadium; therefore, the pier was also connected to the city fabric via a significant artery. The International Port Terminal development also occurred within the context of growing concerns among residents that they were losing their waterfront to large-scale port infrastructure of vast container terminals. Yokohama had undertaken a determined transformation of the port into a premier hub port able to compete globally with other Asian harbours.[62] By offering park-like amenities and connecting the pier to the city's parks and avenues, FOA were able to allay the concerns of residents.

FOA's initial concept for the project was that of a landform building offering seamless connection between programmatic spaces, which was consistently realized on several levels: structurally, programmatically and metaphorically. Structurally, the use of folded steel plates allowed the terminal to be configured as a low-profile, three-storey structure maintaining unobstructed views to the inland waterfront. Its flanking timber pedestrian ways and undulating surfaces were able to suggest a public space continuum with Yamashita and Akarenga Parks.[63] In addition, the structure provided spaces unencumbered by columns and, in conjunction with the raised flooring, offered concealment for mechanical systems and luggage-handling units.[64] This openness of design was consistently adhered to in the programme and its list of required spaces and functions, with the lateral extensions (aprons) creating parallel pedestrian routes that, together with the open and flexibly configured space, allowed for differentiated loops of pedestrian and passenger traffic. The fact that circulation is accommodated by ramps further reinforced the concept of movement and accessibility, and the seamless transition from interior to exterior. Flexible furniture, such as mobile kiosks used in border control checks, could be removed to allow non-restricted use of space. The envisioned landform also enlarged the requirements from a 500m garden with public spaces and amenities to an 1800m park with commensurate public viewing decks and a civic hall. The concept of a seamless milieu (in terms of movement, structure, material) offered flexible boundaries and spaces to the facility.

The philosophical and digital currency of the project is visible in both form and commentary. The Deleuzian philosophical notion of "fold," made visible in FOA's folded/bent steel structure, gave the project philosophical and technical significance.[65] The concept of "seamless connection," expressed through the continuity of movement and material, was also in keeping with the philosophical notions of the unlimited, open-ended aspect of Deleuzian thought.[66] It was this, rather than computer technology, that the architects emphasized in their initial presentations. The engineer for the project, Kunio Watunabe, noted that "the design of the structure had by convention been the responsibility of the engineers, it was now led by the feeling of the architects."[67]

The project garnered success not only due to its status among an influential group of practitioners working within the elite academies of the US and UK, but also owing to the project's ability to capture the approval of the stakeholders represented by the jury of architects,[68] the Yokohama Port Bureau and politicians. Within architectural discourse the terminal "represented an emergent typology of transportation infrastructure. Its radical, hyper-technological design explored new frontiers of architectural form and simultaneously provoked a powerful discourse on the social responsibility of large-scale projects to enrich shared urban spaces."[69]

From these examples we can see that the education of the architects, both formally and informally, enabled them to assess competition briefs in a manner that allowed them to capture both the programmatic requirements of the building but also its wider cultural and social aspects. Each of these buildings offered both stakeholders and the public opportunities to engage with the building and the immediate context it created. All were award winning, demonstrating that they have acquired cultural value. These awards and prizes also bestow social capital upon the architects and enhance the value of their architecture. This accounts for the ability of these buildings to acquire cultural capital.

However, it is society at large that determines the durability of this cultural capital and the eventual design capital accrued by the buildings. Society and values change, and the durability of the cultural and design capital may be affected: Jean Nouvel, alongside allies in the World Arab Institute, is currently defending the contextual integrity of the building, which is threatened by development along the edge of its south court.[70] Seabird Island Community School retains its esteem among the Stó:lō and the wider community, but other schools of the B.C. Native School Program have not fared so well, even those that are award winning and by celebrated architects.[71] Pelli's Petronas Towers continue to appeal; however, criticism of the larger urban development in which it sits and a dimming of enthusiasm for globalization may come to influence its popularity.[72] Despite these contextual issues, though, the buildings have garnered public support and remain as important cultural and social markers of place.

These examples demonstrate how architectural methodology works to embed social and cultural meaning into design. Each of these examples is very different in its context, and its building programme and all the architects have very different approaches. Nevertheless, they share a methodological stance which ensures that cultural and social issues are deliberately considered. The architects then interpret these considerations into a built form that is meaningful to the society in which—and for which— they are designing.

NOTES

1. Nineteen Arab states joined France in the initial establishing of the Arab World Institute by an Act of government signed by the Minister of Foreign Affairs in February 1980. Three more Arab states had joined by 1989. Thierry Fabre, "L'institut du monde arabe: entre deux rives," *Vingtième siècle*: *Revue d'histoire* no. 32 (October- December 1991): 77, accessed September 6, 2020, http://www.jstor.com/stable/3770000.
2. Architects are Jean Nouvel (lead architect), Gilbert Lézénès, Pierre Soria, Architecture Studio. Architecture-Studio is an international collaborative and interdisciplinary group of architects and designers founded in 1973 with offices currently in Paris, Italy and Shanghai.
3. Fabre, "L'institute du monde arabe," 75. Lieu de médiation culturelle, l'Institut est place a l'intersection de deux mondes en tension, de deux ensembles culturels qui s'attirent et se repoussent, qui se fascinent et se rejettent. D'où les contradictions qui le traversent et les périls qui le menacent.
4. Ateliers Jean Nouvel, text by Jean Nouvel,accessed September 25, 2020, https://www.jeannouvel.com/projects/institut-du-monde-arabe-ima.
5. Jean Nouvel, Ateliers Jean Nouvel, https://www.jeannouvel.com/en/projects/institut-du-monde-arabe
6. Ann Heylighen and Genviève Martin, "The Elusive Concept of Concept in Architecture. A First Snapshot During Design," in *Computing and Cogmitiomn'04*, ed. J.S. Gero (Dordrecht: Kluwer Publishers, 2004), 58.
7. Aga Khan Award for Architecture (1987-89 Cycle),accessed Seotember 9, 2020, https://www.akdn.org/architecture/project/institut-du-monde-arabe.
8. Awards include: The Lion d'Or of the Venice Biennale, 2000; the Gold Medal of the RIBA and the Borromini Prize in 2001, the Wolf Prize in 2005, the Pritzker Prize in 2008 and a Gold Medal and 2 Equerres d'Argent from the French Academy of Architecture as well as the National Grand Prize for Architecture. He also has several international Honorary Awards. https://www.jeannovel.com/en/jean-nouvel/.
9. Jean Nouvel, https://www.jeannouvel.com/en/jean-nouvel/.
10. Jean Nouvel, https://www.jeannouvel.com/en/jean-nouvel/.
11. The Seabird Island Band is of Stó:lō culture and heritage, and has been a member of various organizations that emerged in response to the Trudeau government's Liberal Indian Policy, a Federal Government White Paper in 1969. In 1994 it was a member of the organization formed of the unification of Stó:lō Nation Canada and the Stó:lō Tribal Council which represented an area from roughly Yale, on the Fraser River to the Salish Sea. In 2004-05 eight bands left the Stó:lō Nation to reconstitute the Stó:lō Tribal Council—the Seabird Island Band was one of them. See, Stó:lō, accessed March 20, 2021, https://www.stolonation.bc.ca.
12. Ethel Bernie Gardner, "Seabird Island community school: unique features of an Indian Band School," Master of Education, University of British Columbia, 1986, 35.
13. Gardner, "Seabird Island," 39.
14. Gardner, "Seabird Island," 57.
15. John Patkau, "Patkau Architects Investigations into the Particular," *The Journal of the International Institute* 3 no. 2 (Winter 1996),https://quod.lib.umich.edu/j/jii/4750978.0003.2*?/-patkau-architects-investigation-into-the-particular.
16. Kenneth Frampton, "Patricia and John Patkau. Tecto-Totemic," *Perspecta* 28 Architects. Process. Inspiration. (1997): 180-89, quote 180.
17. Frampton, "Patricia and John Patkau," 180.
18. For a fuller discussion of this and the relationship of form-shifting of the Seabird Island School (understood as a bird, fish, canoe, shell, longhouse) and Indigenous traditions of masks with their production of "paradoxes of perception,"

see Michael Milojovic, "An Architecture of Difference: Some New Places of Learning for British Columbia's First Nations," *Australian-Canadian Studies* 15, no. 1 (1997): 85-89, https://www.acsanz.org.au/archives/1997-15-1-4milojevicarticle.pdf.

19. Patkau Architects,accessed October 3, 2020, https://patkau.ca.
20. Royal Architectural Institute of Canada College of Fellows 2011, 42, https://raic.org/sites/raic.org/files/raic/documents/2011fellows.pdf.
21. Milojovic, "Architecture of Difference," 84.
22. At the completion of the programme, a total of fifteen major national awards were won by the twelve schools.
23. See the revisiting of the schools of the commission of the B.C. Native Schools Program in 2009 by Adele Weder, "Architecture of Hope Revisited," *the Tyee* (February 27, 2009), https://thetyee.ca/Photo/2009/02/27/ArchHope/print.html .
24. The Newhaven Projects Ltd, established in 1988 features an image of Seabird Island School on its website. See also, Milojevic, "Architecture of Difference," 84.
25. Clifford A. Pearson, "Other than their status as the world's tallest buildings, what else do Cesar Pelli's Petronas Towers have..." *Architectural Record* (January1999): 92, accessed November 4, 2020, https://www.archrecord.com.
26. Cesar Pelli, Charles Thornton and Leonard Joseph, "The World's Tallest Building: Malaysian Petronas Twin Towers serve as both a cultural and economic symbol," *Scientific America* 277, no. 6 (December 1977): 94.
27. Tim Bunnell, "Views from Above and Below: The Petronas Twin Towers AND/IN Contesting Visions of Development in Contemporary Malaysia," *Singapore Journal of Tropical Geography* 20, no.1 (1999): 4.
28. The development was on the site of the colonial-era race course adjacent to the commercial centre of Kuala Lumpur and was managed by Kuala Lumpur City Centre Holdings Berhad in 1990. An international competition for a masterplan for the site was held in 1990, with building competitions to follow.
29. The Petronas company also became a major stakeholder in the in KLCC Holdingsm Sendrian Berhad, the investment holding company for the development. Pearson, "Petronas Towers."
30. The other firms invited were: Murphy/Jahn, Aldo Rossi, John Burgee, Kohn Pedersen Fox and KKS (of Japan). Pearson, "Petronas Towers.".
31. Abdul Rahim Naim, chief operating officer of KLCC Holdings Berhad quoted in Pearson., "Petronas Towers."
32. Pearson, "Petronas Towers."
33. Pelli, Thornton and Joseph, "The World's Tallest Building," 94.
34. Pelli, Thornton, Joseph,"The World's Tallest Buildng," 96.
35. Pearson, "Petronas Towers."
36. Pelli, Thornton and Joseph, "The World's Tallest Building," 96.
37. Pelli, Thornton and Joseph, "The World's Tallest Building," 96.
38. Pelli quoted in Pearson, "Petronas Towers."
39. Pelli quoted in Pearson, "Petronas Towers."
40. Pelli quoted in Pearson, "Petronas Towers."
41. Pelli, Thornton and Joseph, "The World's Tallest Towers." 99.
42. Pelli, Thornton and Jospeh, "The World's Tallest Towers," 99. Lao Tzu is a Chinese philosopher of about 500 BCE and founder of Taoism. Ethnic Chinese account for about 20% of the population.
43. Michael Crosbie and Pelli Clarke Pelli Associates, *Pelli Clarke Pelli Architects* (Berlin: Birkhauser, 2013), 17.
44. Crosbie and Pelli Clarke Pelli Associates, *Pelli, Clarke, Pelli*, 30.
45. Crosbie and Pelli Clarke Pelli Associates, *Pelli, Clarke Pelli*, 32.
46. Crosbie and Pelli Clarke Pelli Associates, *Pelli, Clarke Pelli*, 32.
47. Bunnell, "Views," 5.
48. Bunnell, "Views," 6.
49. Ken Yeang, *The Architecture of Malaysia* (Amsterdam: Pepin Press, 1992), ref. in Bunnell, "Views," 7.
50. *The New Straits Times*, Kuala Lumpur, July 5, 1996, ref. in Bunnell, "Views,"16.
51. Bunnell, Views," 7. He cites the following on the concept of "world city": J. Friedmann, "The world city hypothesis," *Development and Change* 17 no. 1 (1986): 69-83 and J. Douglas "World city formation on the Asia Pacific Rim:

Poverty, "everyday forms of civil society and environmental management," in *Cities For Citizens* ed. M. Douglass & J.Friedmann, (Chichester: Wiley), 107-38. Cf. Bunnell , "Views" 7.

52. Petronas Twin Towers (Kuala Lumpur) - All You Need to Know BEFORE You Go - Updated 2020 (Kuala Lumpur, Malaysia)," accessed October 4, 2020,https://www.tripadvisor.ca/Attraction_Review-g298570-d2373838-Reviews-Kuala_Lumpur_City_Gallery-Kuala_Lumpur_Wilayah_Persekutuan.html.
53. Those given honourable mention and the four other finalists shared many characteristics: iconic form, inventive circulation paths, and reference to waterfront parks with gardens. See, "Yokohama International Port Terminal/ 4 competition entries by AA Members, *AA Files* no. 29 (Summer 1995): 22-38. https://www-jstor-org-ezproxy.library.ubc.ca/. The finalists presented "a Japanese sword," a "glass box with Japanese roof," and the "back of a whale;" only with FOA did "no symbol come to mind." See Irénée Scalbert, "Y.I.P.T.," CICA (Comité International des Critiques d'Architecture / International Committee of Architectural Critic) 2019, https://cicarchitecture.org/2019/07/25/the-yokohama-international-port-terminal/.
54. Greg Lynn and Farshid Moussavi, *Yokohama International Port Terminal* (Montreal: Canadian Centre for Architecture, 2018). This publication plots the development of the project from brief to conclusion.
55. Mario Carpa points this out in his introduction to the FOA excerpt in *The Digital Turn in Architecture 1992-2012* (Chichester: John Wiley and Sons Ltd., 2013), 57.
56. Scalbert, "Y.I.P.T."
57. MoMA, Foreign Office Architects (FOA), London, Farshid Moussavi, Alejandro Zaero-Polo, Yokohama International Port Terminal, 2000, https://www.moma.org/collection/works/95092.
58. "Yokohama International Port Terminal/ 4 Competition entries by AA Members," *AA Files* no. 29 (Summer 1995): 22-38, https://www-jstor-org-ezproxy.library.ubc.ca.
59. Scalbert, "Y.I.P.T."
60. Foreign Office Architects, "Yokohama International Port Terminal," *Architectural Design* (July-August,1996), reprinted in Carpa, *The Digital Turn*, 61.
61. Scalbert, "Y.I.P.T."
62. Scalbert, "Y.I.P.T."
63. David Langdon, "AD Classics: Yokohama International Passenger Terminal/ Foreign Office Architects (FOA)," *ArchDaily*, (2014), accessed September 23, 2020, https://www.archdaily.com/554132'ad-classics-yokohama-international-passenger-terminal-foreign-office-architects.
64. Farshid Moussavi Architecture, "Yokohama International Port Terminal," accessed September 23, 2020, https://www.farshimoussavi.com/node/15#yokohama_international_port_terminal_yokohama_japan.
65. Gilles Deleuze, *The Fold,* trans. Tom Conley (Minneapolis: University of Minnesota Press, 1992).
66. Scalbert, "Y.I.P.T."
67. Scalbert, "Y.I.P.T."
68. The judges included Irata Isozaka (vice-chairman) and Rem Koolhaas.
69. Langdon, "Yokoham International Passsenger Terminal."
70. "Le Blog de l'IMA 13 Janvier 2020, Jean Nouvel et Jack Lang au JDD : l'institut du monde arabe est agressé," accessed March 10, 2020, https://www.imarabe.org/fr/blog/2020/01/jean-nouvel-et-jack-lang-au-jdd-l-institut-du-monde-arabe-est-agresseé.
71. See, Weder, "Architecture of Hope."
72. See, Bunnell, "Views."

8

CASE STUDIES: SMALL SCALE

INTRODUCTION

The purpose of the next three chapters is to discuss significant examples of infrastructure with documented or potential design capital to give the reader an idea of how design capital emerges. These chapters are also attentive to historic context because the value of design may accrue over time. Here, we provide examples of what is meant by design capital and also offer a 'forensic analysis' of how this design capital came to be by interrogating questions such as what conditions are necessary in the nascent phases of a project's inception for design capital to arise. This provides a more in-depth understanding of how to design a project so that it delivers more than a singular pragmatic function but also offers beneficial social and cultural outcomes.

Within these chapters, the discussion focuses on at least three aspects of each case study. Firstly, we identify the intentions of the 'owner' or initiating stakeholders at the initiation of the project. It is the thesis of this book that successful design for the public realm does not happen by chance, but is instead planned from the outset by all the parties involved in the project and its subsequent modifications. This starts with the owner or initiating stakeholder—in the case of infrastructure it could be a government agency or municipality, for example—generally, any authority having jurisdiction in the case of infrastructure in the public realm. Secondly, each case study assesses the architect or project designer's approach—the cultural or social aspects they emphasized or explored and brought to the fore. How did they intervene at the site, or in the district or location? We distil this by looking at what the designers said about the project, either in person or in publications. Thirdly, we examine the implications of the design over time: what value did the design bring to the street, to the block, or to the district? How did it contribute to or influence the social fabric of the place? A historic lens is invaluable in examining the impact of design over a long period of time. In more contemporary projects, we scrutinize the more short-term effects while still looking for proof of the significance of the design's impact.

We begin with smaller-scale designs because they are less dependent on the full range of complexities associated with urban contexts and the mosaic of urban factors influencing the realization of design capital in larger scales of infrastructure. We can isolate elements: examine the approach of the owners/project instigators, examine the approach of the designers and look at local effects as a result of the design. In this chapter, we look at the small-scale infrastructures—street furniture and fountains, rest stops and entryways. They are designed moments of delight and respite while also fulfilling the infrastructural task that they have been assigned. These infrastructures often function as part of a network or form a series along a route; so, although we consider them singly, we also acknowledge their participation in larger systems.

FOUNTAINS

Historical and contemporary fountains are a delightful example of small-scale urban infrastructure. They often serve multiple public functions and, with few exceptions, are deemed a public good. Many fountains provide an essential service as a sanitary source of drinking water and are also markers of space and sources of neighbourhood identity. They can be modest or elaborate, but for most fountains, design is a consideration in the evaluation of not only the specific fountain but also of the space it occupies. They are also culturally-imbued infrastructure: the symbolic celebration of water has been identified with shaped stone basins fed by natural aquifers in settlements of some 4000 years ago. Early fountains were fed by simple pumps drawing water from meagre sources; use was rationed to essential human need and ceremonial use only. Rome, for example, had developed a complex hierarchy of public fountains ranging from monumental structures to simple basins by the 6th century BCE. The investment in fountains was understood as essential to public life. Although the city was built along the Tiber River, its waters were unpotable, creating the need for an infrastructure of aqueducts and fountains to ensure clean drinking water. By the Renaissance, the inundation of the Tiber was a significant problem for health, urban order and institutionalized power, that is, to public life. Fountains were understood to not only offer a rationalized release of water but also to instil civic order, while their control and expressive vocabulary legitimized political and social power structures. By the late 16th century fountains were also seen as symbols of progress. Fountains, and the systems of aqueducts, underground passages and conduits that enabled them, promised to bring order to the unpredictable and dynamic flow of the Tiber with a more controlled, rational output.[1] The stakeholders formed a "collusive interrelationship between private wealth, civic claims and papal authority that mediated access to water."[2] Fountains gave visibility to the technical feats that brought water to neighbourhoods: control over natural forces, the difficulties overcome in connecting the various parts of the full expanse of a single aqueduct, the multiplicity of conduits used, and the restoration of the ruined foundations of the ancient infrastructure. The physical improvement to the city that resulted was seen as rational and modern. Contemporary commentators noted of the fountains that, "all are not only useful and necessary, but beautiful."[3] Fountains were understood to be essential urban infrastructure, but also a civic enhancement of everyday life. Competitions were held for major fountains and many were a public/private partnership. These partnerships frequently involved local aristocratic families, who would often agree to the maintenance of the fountain and piazza in exchange for some control over the distribution of its water.

CEREMONIAL FOUNTAINS

THE TREVI FOUNTAIN, ROME, 1732-1762. NICOLA SALVI

The Trevi Fountain is an example of diverse stakeholders (popes, influential families and civic officials) recognizing the social and cultural value of augmenting a simple terminus to an ancient aqueduct, the Aqua Virgo.[4] (Figure 8.1) The aqueduct itself was influential in the urban development of the surrounding low-lying area in the 1st century CE. The first fountain on the site appeared some eight centuries later. The Trevi Fountain of today continues to mark the 9th century terminus of the Aqua Virgo, although it assumes a more complexly expressive role than the modest wall fountain that marked its medieval site.[5] The presence of the fountain has influenced the street patterns, building form and social geography of the neighbourhood and the symbolic topography of the city as a whole. The fountain's social significance was leveraged by successive popes to claim spiritual power and by civic governments to assert their secular authority.

The Trevi Fountain as seen today resulted from a design competition initiated by Pope Clement XII in 1730, and the taxes he levied to pay for it. It was intended to be a new, more spectacular fountain than its predecessor. The fountain's redesign afforded an opportunity for the display of civic pride, public expression of papal power and pastoral care, and to provide greater accessibility to water. Its design was also a response to recent site alterations: the enlargement of abutting palaces, embellishment of churches on the piazza and nearby, the enlarging of roads leading into the piazza, and the remnants of an abandoned project from the previous century.

The architect, Nicola Salvi, built upon the foundations of the earlier project using the greater dimensions of its northern position to orchestrate a monumental, elaborately sculpted back wall and to exploit the enlarged basin to affect more exuberant water jets and cascades. (Figure 8. 2) His design was practical in that it overcame the hydraulic limitation of the site: the water flow was gravity-fed and the elevation of the site minimal, not much below that of the incoming water. Salvi's solution was to sink the fountain in order to maximize the height at which water could be drawn and then made to cascade to the basin below, introducing a dynamic rush of water, spray and sound.[6] The excavation of the basin allowed not only for a more dynamic and dramatic display of water, it also provided a space for the public to gather along the fountain's perimeter, accessed by stairs and withdrawn from the street above.

The design of the Trevi Fountain was both pragmatic and political in its response to recent changes to its urban context. It is, essentially, an elaborate wall fountain; the wall to which it abuts belongs to a palace of mediocre design that had been recently extended. The architect's solution was to envelop the existing façade with a veneer of giant Corinthian columns, a central Roman triumphal arch and an elaborate didactic sculptural narrative, featuring the deities of water, abundance and health. These symbols of the benefits of water bestowed social significance on the functional presence of water. The wall and its symbols were also political

8:1 Nicola Salvi. Trevi Fountain, (1762) Rome.
Photo: David Liff.

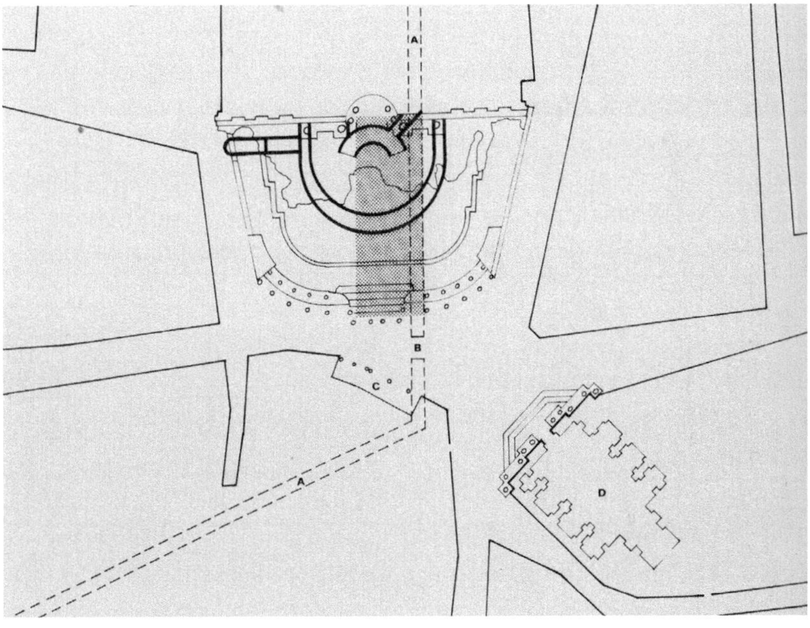

8:2 Trevi Fountain Site Plan. (A) Aqua Virgo; (c) medieval portico; Stippled area: Alberti , 1453-1643; thick outline: Bernini, 1643-1732; thin outline: Slavi, 1732-1762. Drawing: A. Ceen.

in that it dissociated the fountain from the wall of the private palace and powerful family to which it belonged and associated it instead with the public institution of the papacy. At the very summit of the wall, the papal coat of arms of Pope Clement XII asserted the beneficence of his power. Its larger cultural import was conveyed via sculpture that made historical references to the antiquity of the aqueduct from which its water flows.

The Trevi Fountain served not only to provide local residents with drinking water but also to humidify the surrounding microclimate.[7] The functional aspects and narrative design of the fountain recognized the dual audience for which it was built: entertaining locals while exalting papal supremacy to visitors. As a popular image in the print culture of 18th century Rome, it served a nascent tourist audience where its secondary functions of visual delight and entertainment were highlighted.

The Trevi Fountain no longer performs its original function of providing safe, publicly accessible drinking water, and its references to classical mythology and the nuances of papal and secular power of the past may be obscure to present-day audiences. However, it continues to serve locals in improving the microclimate and as a marker of place, giving identity to a neighbourhood and the city of Rome. The Trevi Fountain has acquired value as one of the more popular tourist sites in Rome and its iconic function has been transferred to cinema (Three Coins in the Fountain, 1954) and architecture (Charles Moore's Piazza d'Italia in New Orleans, 1978). As a post-modern architectural stage-set, the Piazza d'Italia sought to serve an Italian diaspora with a recognizable spatial presence and cultural reference. The architects of both the 18th and 20th century, through their training and social standing, have been able to imbue the fountain with not only cultural capital but also design capital.

QUOTIDIAN WATER FOUNTAINS

Quotidian drinking water fountains were envisioned for individuals moving through the city, rather than for home or work use, and conceived as part of a city-wide network. They were an innovation of the mid-19th century and the new urban environment and social life that emerged in major metropolises at that time.[8] Large cities such as Paris, London, Rome and New York installed them as a public service for reasons of sanitation and health and, in London especially, to combat cholera and drunkenness. Rome's nasoni (noses), initiated in 1872, were composed of a simple column of cast-iron, stone or occasionally travertine marble, a metal spout at mid-height and a drain beneath. (Figure 8:3) They are still recognizable across Rome, and are considered a symbol of the city and a "precious historical and social heritage."[9] In London, fountains of the 19th century ranged from simple spigot, basin and attached metal cup to marble monuments replete with commemorative or moralizing inscriptions. In the 21st century many of these fountains have also been repaired, replaced with copies or relocated so as to preserve their service and civic as well as historic presence. Their durable materials, craftsmanship, visibility and supplementary association with important events and ideas (such as the commemoration of jubilees and the emancipation of slaves) endowed the provision of water with social as well as utilitarian value.[10] Many cities have currently initiated the installation of public drinking fountains in response to a contemporary problem—to curb the use of disposable plastic bottles associated with bottled water consumption.

WALLACE FOUNTAINS, PARIS, 1872. CHARLES-AUGUSTE LEBOURG

The urban redevelopment of Paris by its chief municipal official, Georges-Eugène Haussmann, in the mid-19th century saw the opening up of the dense fabric of the city with straight thoroughfares, parks, squares, and an underground water and sewage system. This required a distribution of space and water to be put in place to allow for a system of public drinking water fountains, in addition to the more ceremonial, storied and entertainment-focused water features to be found in the city. Haussmann had proposed a modern city in which clean, aqueduct-fed water would be pumped to individual buildings, thus replacing the dependence on expensive water sellers and the heavily polluted River Seine. Although clean, safe drinking water was understood as an essential municipal service and amenity, and fountains were recognized as a public good, potable water was still not available to all in the 19th century.

The Wallace fountains were introduced to Paris in 1872 as a solution to the difficulty of accessing drinking water during, but also in the aftermath of, the 1871 Franco-Prussian War and subsequent uprising of the

8:3 Nasone, Via Casilina, (ca. 1870s-), Rome, Italy.
Photo: Martin Koppenhöfer (dieterdreist).

8:4 Charles-August Lebourg. Wallace Fountain in Montmartre (1872), Paris France.
Photo: Martin Robson.

Paris Commune. (Figure 8:4) These political and social upheavals had disabled public infrastructure as well as destroying buildings. Stakeholders included municipal authorities and the philanthropic community. The Wallace fountains were a public / private partnership between the British philanthropist Sir Richard Wallace (who provided the fountains) and the city, who furnished the plumbing and installation and determined their location. They were distributed throughout Paris to offer free, publicly accessible drinking water. The manufacture and design of the fountains were decided on by Wallace: they were cast-iron, offered in freestanding and wall models and, because they were industrially fabricated, could be produced quickly and in quantity. As mass-produced objects they could be easily inserted into Paris's newly organized boulevards and squares with their accompanying 'invisible' underground water pipes and conduits.

The drinking fountains were functional urban elements. Materials were chosen for their practicality: iron for its suitability to the casting process and reproducibility which made it inexpensive relative to alternatives, and paint which assisted in maintenance and protected the fountains from the elements. Continually running water was thought to deter bacterial growth and attached metal cups, stored in the water-filled basin, assisted both the imbibing of water and the cleanliness of the cups. The design also took its urban setting into account—the height of the basin prevented dogs from drinking from it while the sculptural figures that encircled the basin functioned like vertical bars to prevent horses from doing the same. The fountains provided free drinking water to those who could not afford to buy it from water sellers or as an amenity of their accommodation; it also provided an alternative to alcoholic beverages.

For Richard Wallace, though, the fountains were more than mere utilitarian fixtures. They were carefully designed by the French sculptor Charles-Auguste Lebourg who was commissioned to add beauty and allegorical meaning to their practical design.[11] They were painted green to blend with Haussmann's new tree-lined streetscapes and, at nine feet tall, the free-standing "grand" model was visible from a distance and so served as a spatial marker. The grand model was also endowed with allegorical enhancement: four caryatids, representing virtues (one being sobriety), support a dome from which water flows into an elevated basin. In 1872, 40 free-standing and ten wall-mounted fountains were installed in Paris.

Proving popular, a further ten were added in 1876 and another ten fountains just three years later. Eventually two additional models were introduced.

There are still 103 Wallace fountains in operation in Paris, dispensing free, clean drinking water. They are among the approximately 1200 water points currently within the city. Their enduring use and popularity have ensured their continued urban presence, and because of their skilful design they can be moved to different sites where they might be more useful. They have also been retrofitted with a small stainless steel push-button to save water and make them more hygienic. Their longevity demonstrates that the fountains have design capital: they are saved and re-used as they are considered valuable to society, as opposed to being discarded. They now participate in the city's environmental initiatives as an important incentive to the abandoning of plastic bottled water,[12] and two Wallace fountains have been given historic preservation protection.[13] They are regularly maintained and repaired and periodically restored. Their design capital has accrued from an appreciation of their design functionality, visual characteristics, public service and popularity.

CONTEMPORARY FOUNTAIN REVIVAL

While providing safe drinking water to urban populations was rarely a major priority for fountain design in the mid-20th century, fountains continued to have significant functions, among them noise dampening, microclimate enhancement and providing place identity.[14] Currently, a new round of public drinking fountains offering free, clean drinking water has been initiated in both Rome and London; both of these initiatives involve public-private entities. Rome has reconceived the nasoni as a "House of Water," a ten-foot-tall kiosk offering free tap or sparkling water, information to tourists and charging points for mobile devices. These were installed in 2015 by Acea, the company responsible for maintaining the city's water supply.[15] In London, Thames Water and the Mayor's Office announced in 2019 a new design for water fountains in the city.[16]

The significance of drinking fountains in the civic realm is currently being recognized in the public-service sector, among city officials, water providers, hardware producers and environmental activists. It is also being recognized by the design community where the importance of design in the re-establishment of drinking fountains as a significant urban amenity is championed. In 2014, the online architecture journal Dezeen reported on London fountain proposals designed by celebrated architects, such as Zaha Hadid.[17]

Just as the proposal of free public drinking fountains was sparked by the public health issue of contaminated water, particularly cholera outbreaks, in the 19th century, so the resurgence in support for free public drinking fountains in the 21st century is the result of a public emergency—the over-use of single-use plastics and the environmental damage that it causes. And stakeholders in both the 19th and 21st centuries sought solutions in well-designed structures.

FLEET FOUNTAIN, LONDON 2018.
MICHAEL ANATASSIADES

Design professionals and non-governmental organizations have initiated fountain design in aid of ending the dependence on bottled water. One example is the collaboration between a design studio (Jane Withers Studio) and arts community figure (publisher/ curator/ collector Charles Asprey) to found The London Fountain Company, which has garnered sponsorship from institutions, charities and cultural events.[18] Their aim is to reinstate the drinking fountain as an urban feature and "to commission a beautiful and functional fountain that would become a loved feature of the city such as the Wallace Fountains in Paris and the Nasone in Rome."[19] The industrial designer Michael Anatassiades was commissioned to design their first fountain. His Fleet drinking fountain was unveiled at the London Design Festival in 2018. (Figure 8:5) Anatassiades' fountain is a polished cast-bronze faceted column with a concave upper surface cut with a crevice through which water both appears and disappears. Activated by sensors, the water arcs to allow both touchless drinking and bottle filling. Its intentionally small footprint contributes to an uncluttered urban realm, while its bronze surface will form a patina over time. According to the designer, "[i]t needed to be more of an experience than just a place to stop and fill a bottle. It needed to blend into the environment and not scream for attention. The simple shape reveals nothing of its inner workings and responds to the demands of being within the public domain."[20]

8:5 Michael Anastassiades for Fountain London. Fleet Fountain (2018), London, UK. Photo: Andy Stagg.

8:6 Pechet and Robb Art and Architecture. Seating at the Burrard Shipyards Pier (2010), North Vancouver, Canada.

A Fleet fountain was permanently installed at South Kensington Tube station where it continues to function as part of the #OneLess foundation's mission to stop the use of single-use plastic bottles. The London Fountain Company envisions more Fleet fountains, with both wall-mounted and free-standing editions made from a variety of materials including stone, cast-iron and the original bronze.[21] The design community, at least, understands that "the drinking fountain is, in its way, a symbol of the civilized city, a generous public gesture that makes the metropolis liveable."[22]

STREET FURNITURE, URBAN CONTEXT AND HISTORIC INTEGRATION

Fountains are just one specific form of small-scale street infrastructure. Today, street furniture functions as a form of small-scale infrastructure as it must augment the public realm functionally and meaningfully, often in conjunction with historical urban fabric.

THE BURRARD PIER, VANCOUVER , CANADA, 1999-2019. BILL PECHET WITH DURANTE KREUK LTD, LANDSCAPE ARCHITECTS

A contemporary case study of small-scale infrastructure is a public realm enhancement consisting of the redevelopment of the historic shipyards in North Vancouver, Canada in 1999 to 2019. The stakeholders for the redevelopment of the area were real estate developer and builder Pinnacle International, Inc. and the City of North Vancouver who negotiated public amenities for greater density and height allowances.[23] Architect and university lecturer, Bill Pechet of Pechet and Robb, was involved in the design of the public amenities in collaboration with project coordinators Durante Kreuk, landscape architects. The design mandate was to transform an early 20th century dry dock for ship construction into a an early 21st century public pier with waterfront plazas. This project is a particularly good example of how to integrate historic content within a redevelopment to create design capital.

The Burrard Pier, a historic bridge pier in North Vancouver, is a remnant of the ship-building industry which has almost, but not quite, disappeared from the area. Pechet and his partner in the early stages of the project,

Stephanie Robb, were responsible for the street furniture and railings for the public space of the pier. (Figure 8:6) Design interventions in historic building fabric often risk a preoccupation with replicating more recognizable references to the original building. Pechet and Robb, however, sought to avoid this, thinking instead about the logic of the materials evident in the pier's construction and their adaptation by the shipbuilders themselves. Pechet describes the design approach:

> [T]here was a culture in the shipyards where they were very resourceful and so, if they didn't have a light fixture, they would just grab something that was hanging around and mis-use found objects to make, for example, a light fixture out of something like a hose. There was just this improvisational thing that they were doing because they kept having to rebuild buildings depending on what ships they were producing.... So we use those two things, materials — in the process of becoming things — and also the idea of improvising with objects.[24]

This improvisation can be seen in the design of the pier's light fixtures; once the trash cans created for the pier, they are now inverted and suspended as lighting. While still "recognizably trash cans when illuminated, they are also something else."[25]

STREET FURNITURE AND LIGHTING

Granville Street, Vancouver, Canada, 2010, Pechet and Rob art and architecture and Pechet Studio, both with PWL Partnership Landscape Architects Inc.

Another example of a small-scale infrastructural intervention is Pechet's street furniture designs along Granville Street in 2010. Granville Street was a major commercial artery in early 20th century Vancouver and a major entertainment district in the city, an aspect which remains to this day (Figure 4:1). The stakeholders for this project were the City of Vancouver and the Business Improvement Associations; their aim was to revitalize Granville Street and upgrade its image with the addition of ceremonial lights, benches, and other street furniture. The project was a collaboration with PWL Landscape Architects and Pechet and Robb.

8:7 PECHET Studio with PWL Partnership Landscape Architects Inc. Granville Street Bollards (2012), Vancouver, Canada. Photo: PECHET Studio.

The project was attentive to its important historical role in the city and especially its function as an entertainment area. Pechet notes:

> [O]ne of the things that came along with that was this incredible signage and it was the place for everybody in the Lower Mainland to come to and be entertained. ... over the years we had lost a lot of amazing signage on the street. It was a chance to kind of produce an after image of what the signage might have looked like, but in a very simple way, a repeating set of LED tubes that could coexist with the remaining blade signs that were still existing on the street and also to reinforce connectivity of the entire ten blocks.[26]

These approaches demonstrate a way to work from the historical precedent that does not slavishly replicate its form but instead draws on it for its design cues.

With regard to other aspects of the Granville streetscape and its design intervention, there is an approach to the street furniture that participates in the social role of the street as a place of entertainment and public gathering. (Figure 8:7) The numerous benches and chairs along the street differ in their styles and clustering to allow for a variety of social relationships. They were designed to be an invitation to sociability, as Pechet comments:

> We designed the benches in such a way that people can share them and have a choice about whether they want to address each other or not. People can face different directions if they're occupying the same thing. If you look at their placement, some of them are very playful, like two chairs that are far away from each other so that you have to yell to talk to your friend.... or text them! There are other placements that are clustered in subtle but unusual ways that can lead to alternative body postures and conversation nexus.[27]

Another delightful approach to small-scale infrastructure is to consider it as an event—such as Heatherwick Studio did with the Rolling Bridge, completed in 2004. (Figure 8:8) It was one of many projects realized by developers and the Paddington Partnership, in the development of Paddington Basin of the Grand Union Canal development. A developers' consortium, partnering with the Canal and River Trust and the Padding-

8:8 Heatherwick Studio. Rolling Bridge (2004) London.
Photo: Steve Speller.

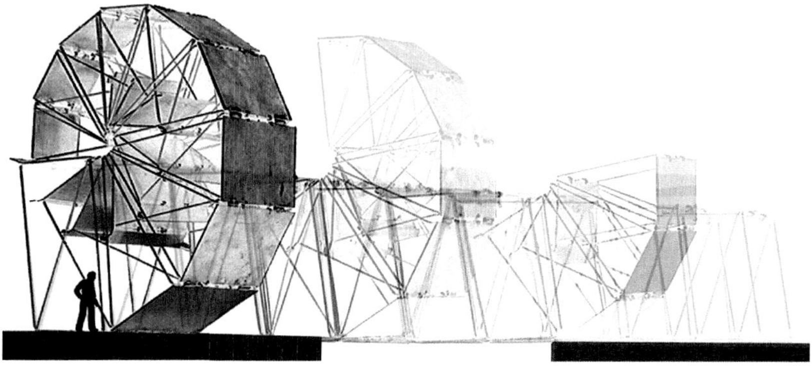

8:9 Heatherwick Studio. Rolling Bridge. Rolling Bridge (2004) London.

ton Trust, aimed to create a number of activities at the former disused industrial site in order to attract new people and global leaseholders for the many projected residential and office buildings. The Rolling Bridge, operated by Merchant Square and organized by European Land and Property, was one of those site activators. The Union Canal developers recognized the historical infrastructure of the canal (1820s) and the contemporary infrastructure of the Heathrow Express to Paddington Station (1998) as assets and amenity for the conversion of the site into a globally attractive commercial, office and residential area.[28] The Rolling Bridge was one of the earlier interventions in the Grand Union Canal development. Heatherwick's intention was to offer a refreshed view of the retracting bridge type: it would "get out of the way" but not "break apart"; it would be a self-contained structure, sculptural, as well as steel and wood machine, and surprisingly quiet—something unexpected in an industrial site. (Figure 8:9) Activation of the bridge happens only periodically during the week so its stilled sculptural form is a major consideration. The Rolling Bridge has become a tourist attraction as well as a functioning foot bridge.[29] It won a 37th Structural Steel Design Award in 2005 and was awarded High Commendation in the Architectural Design Emerging Architecture Awards in December of the same year. The latter noted that it was not only "a showpiece feat of engineering" but also "delightfully conceived, resolved, detailed and made."[30] The Rolling Bridge has entertained people with its clever movement—simple yet surprising in its nature. As architecture critic, Paul Goldberger, writes for The New Yorker:

> [Heatherwick] hatched the idea of a normal-looking bridge that would reveal its secret only when it began to open, and he figured out a hydraulic system that could be embedded in the railings, so that the bridge would have no visible cables or piers. The Rolling Bridge opens silently, and the whole process seems almost magical, as if the bridge were initiating the movement itself. So many people want to see the bridge in action that its operators now oblige every Friday at noon, whether or not any boats need to pass.[31]

GUY'S HOSPITAL, LONDON, 2006-07.
HEATHERWICK STUDIO

Heatherwick Studio again demonstrates that a project of apparently small scale can have significant impact in its design of an entrance to Guy's Hospital, London. (Figure 8:10) In 2002 Heatherwick was commissioned by the Guy's and St. Thomas' NHS Foundation Trust to improve the entrance to Guy's Hospital including a number of improvements to wayfinding, access and appearance, for patients, staff and visitors.[32] A significant component of the commission was the reimagining of the entrance to its harsh, modern complex and in particular the Boiler House that abutted the main entrance. As Heatherwick explained to The New Yorker, he started by: "thinking about what it would be like to be an old lady who is ill and being driven to the hospital by her grandson." This led him to reorganize the flow of traffic at the hospital's entrance, move a parking area, change the lighting and signage, and, finally, to wrap the boiler house with huge, undulating panels of woven, stainless-steel braid, which when illuminated at night acted as a beacon, indicating the entrance to the hospital. Termed the Boiler Suit', this second façade not only improved the public space defined by its exterior but also provided solar modification on the south façade while allowing venting of interior boilers.[33] Heatherwick did not see fixing the traffic as the practical side of the job and decorating the façade as the aesthetic part. For him, getting the grandmother closer to the front door and making her eyes light up as she saw the kinetic façade were part of the same process."[34] Such approaches are instigated by the designer's ability to think of function in multiple ways and to invent responses that make a better public realm and enrich the public space of

8:10 Heatherwick Studio. Boiler Suit, Guy's Hospital (2007), London, UK.
Photo: Steven Speller.

the city. Heatherwick's attention to the intimate aspects of the function of form and space in part explains his success. As Goldberger observes: "The popularity of Heatherwick's designs is a testament to his drive to make his work comprehensible to people who don't know the first thing about design."[35] In 2007, the Boiler House won a Building Better Healthcare Award for Public Space, and the design industry FX Magazine 's Judge's Special Award, suggesting that not only the lay public but also health and design professionals recognized the value of design.

In both of these projects by Heatherwick Studio, the clients recognized the importance of design to the realization of their development or service goals. The design team interpreted the larger social and cultural requirements of a bridge and a wayfinding system. Both Rolling Bridge and Boiler Suit function as inventive enhancements of public life and, as demonstrated by the design awards as well as their celebration by the public, have accrued some design capital and have the potential to accrue more in the future.

SCENIC ROUTES PROGRAM, NORWAY, 2005-2025

Norway's National Scenic Routes Program is an insightful example of infrastructure where design has been considered essential from the very inception of the project. Between 2005 and the present, this comprehensive programme of augmented road building has realized 120 affiliated projects, with 240 envisioned by 2030. Infrastructure includes not only roads but also viewpoints, pathways, lookouts, stairways, laybys, picnic areas, toilets, information stations, memorial structures and art installations. A significant functional, and consequentially design, requirement is the provision of both dramatic views via extraordinary structures and intimate contact with the landscape via restrained insertions.

These infrastructure projects are a government initiative and the expansion of the programme was blessed by the Norwegian Parliament.[36] It is funded and supported by various government departments, including the Ministry of Foreign Affairs among other Ministries and agencies, such as Innovation Norway. The infrastructure is considered to participate in several social and cultural realms in addition to those of transport and to have both national and local importance, culturally as well as economically.[37] It is understood to enable an enduring set of social practices and

8:11 Reiulf Ramstad Arkitekter. Trollstigen Visitor Cente (2012), More og Romsdal, Norway.
Photo: Chell Hill, CC BY-SA 3.0, via Wikimedia Commons.

relationships and to celebrate a national conception of landscape and the notion of allemennstretten (public access to nature), and long-established viewing practices. The social and cultural values embedded in these roadside amenities are expressed through design. The values of good design are also evident; the projects are of durable materials, structurally sound, responsive to local geological and climatic conditions, consider sustainability,[38] address social concerns, express cultural values and are innovative.

The value of the programme and its various projects has been recognized in the variety of awards it has amassed from the architecture community, construction and tourism industries, and heritage groups, all of which are publicized on the official website of Norway's National Tourism Office.[39] The role of government support for design has also been acknowledged with the Topos Jubilee Award from the German landscape architecture magazine in 2012, which recognized "the State's active role in promoting and commissioning architecture in the development of the Norway Scenic Routes attraction."[40]

The active role of Norway has included the ongoing marketing of the scenic routes, their natural settings and their amenities; they have been promoted at World's Fairs, embassies, national and international museums, in film, websites and travelling exhibitions (notably Detour which toured North America, Asia and Europe in four periodically revised editions from 2006.)[41] The National Scenic Routes of Norway Program was a concerted effort to facilitate nature, heritage and design tourism and served not only nation-building and economic growth but also accomplished global visibility and competitiveness. Design was central to this effort.

While the scenic routes trace the topography of Norway and give controlled access to fjords, mountains, coastlines and geological novelties via contemporary design, they also provide access to national cultural heritage and UNESCO world heritage sites. Remnants of earlier roads and structures have been retained and remain visible in stone walls, bridges and road paving, and thus place encounters with contemporary architecture in the context of a history of engagement with the landscape. Contemporary viewing platforms and other structures update a cultural tradition of nature pursuits; they reinscribe and preserve the intangible heritage of 19th century tourism, including its way of "seeing the landscape at a distance."[42] The contemporary interpretation of social, cultural and historical aspects of the programme is essential to its success and hence the initial heavy investment in architecture and landscape architecture design. As one Norwegian academic argues, the National Scenic Routes Program provides "infrastructural scenery""— scenery produced by infrastructure.[43]

Function is complexly considered by the stakeholders: the coordinated installations are intended to combine and balance the varied demands of tourism, nature preservation, heritage practices, contemporary design and economic development. The Scenic Routes Program aims not only to encourage the economic development of marginalized settlements, the reassertion of the national and cultural importance of nature and the distinctive features of Norway's landscape—the fjords, mountains and waterfalls—but also to promote innovative younger Norwegian architecture and architecture landscape practices. While the projects tend to participate in a global aesthetic of extravagant form enabled by steel and concrete, they also reference a tradition in Norway's modern architecture where buildings are configured by the landscape, as exemplified in the modernist work of Sverre Fehn.

The programme involves over 50 architects, landscape architects, designers and artists who have been commissioned in open and invited competitions while arts-oriented councils and juries guide decision-making. Spokesperson for the project, press manager Per Ritzler, comments: "Our scenic routes are unique...They are about the landscape of course, but also about the architecture."[44] The establishment of an Art Council, whose membership includes an architect and a landscape architect, ensures that good design is as much part of the evaluation as economic factors in the vetting of projects. Clearly, design mattered and was funded beyond the cost of a simple replacement of the wooden sheds and meagre structures that preceded them. It is exemplified in both astounding structures and modest installations.

Videfossen Waterfalls Viewing Platform (1997) by Jenson and Skodvin Architects is an example of an astonishing structure replacing a pre-existing simple construction adjacent to a historic tourist route, Gamel Strynefjellsvegen (Old Strynefjell Mountain Road). The contemporary viewing platform offers an immersive experience of cascading water, deafening sound and icy spray from a concrete and reinforced steel plate structure anchored to the rock, its levelled surface all that remains of an earlier structure on the site. It affords pedestrians a safe overlook of a 55-metre drop, "a combination in which the rhythm of the natural form of water and rock echoes in the rhythm of the built forms.... The steel and reinforced steel plates suspended over the waterfall giving the impression of being on the riverbed just when gravity breaks it."[45] An early pilot project for the present programme, its design success contributed to government legislation and funding support for the establishment of four National Tourist Routes in 1997, which was subsequently expanded to 18 in 2005.[46] Projects of the expanded programme continued the emphasis on design. For example, the Stegastein viewing platform (2005), by Saunders and Wilhelmsen Architects, offers an unnerving experience of the landscape via a dramatically cantilevered steel and laminated-pine structure, elevated 650 metres above Norway's longest and deepest fjord. As one architectural historian has commented, the viewpoint "leaves the landscape untouched but gives an illusion of hovering in space...[and] to make its effect more intense, its shape curves downward like a vertical toboggan, ended only by a glass that prevents the fall of the viewer."[47] Thus, while it frames a distant view of the fjord and small town of Aurland below, it is designed to produce an effect. Its daring projection far beyond the cliff face, minimal mid-height railings and glass end wall reportedly produce in anyone standing on it the feeling of being suspended in nature, evoking for some the visceral sensation of vertigo.[48] This was apparently by design; evoking a feeling of unease was intended to provoke a respect for the danger of Norway's landscape and encourage re-engagement with its scale and hazards after their possible dulling by over-familiarity.[49]

A more intimate engagement with the landscape is offered by the Tungeneset Viewing Platform (2008), by Code Arkitektur. Here, a minimal walkway is positioned on the tip of a promontory between two fjords. Seeming to simply rest on the terrain, the walkway and its descent to the sea are designed to stimulate "an intense formal dialog with the steep mountain peaks in the background."[50] The irregular path of the layered wood structure and its angled railing evoke the course of the coast and is intended to recall for some "the geological folds that have formed the coastline."[51] In echoing the landscape, the designers have aimed to enhance the experience of the place for those who follow the infrastructure's seemingly wayward course.

Extravagant form, heightened kinesthetic experience and orchestrated engagement with the landscape are all contemporary design strategies tasked with performing a double function—to serve local practices and global tourism. They must also balance the inherent tensions of conservation and access, environmental protection and commercial viability, cultural authenticity and tourist convenience.

The concept of authenticity haunts most tourist sites, including those endorsed by UNESCO. The National Scenic Routes Program has attempted to ensure an authentic Norwegian landscape experience. Many of the norms of tourist sites are avoided: Signage is minimal, capacity limited, and natural ecosystems are privileged over tourist familiarity.

TROLLSTIGEN, VISITOR CENTRE AND ASSOCIATED FACILITIES 2004-2012. REIULF RAMSTAD ARCHITECTS

Trollstigen (Troll's ladder), is a project of several discrete elements situated on a challenging watercourse that cuts through a dramatic plateau; it can only be accessed by a 100 year-old historic road. (Figure 8:11) The programme envisioned for this difficult site was complex and varied: café and visitor centre, service building, toilets, souvenir shop, walkways, viewing platform, bridges, outdoor furniture, parking, water cascade and flood barrier. The differentiated programmatic features served to answer the demands of both visitors and nature. Reiulf Ramstad Architects responded to these demands physically and metaphorically via the form, materials and siting of the various elements.

The design intention was to control architecturally the real dangers of the environment, namely the weight of snow and water in all its forms: snow melt, running and flooding.[52] Snow loads were solved via the pitch of roofs and concrete walls, and flood control via an elegant cascade, flood barrier and sustainable water treatment.[53] This ensured not only the safety of robust structures but also contributed to the experience of the landscape and natural forces. It had been the architect's intention to "add value to the site and its experience while supporting the experience of nature."[54]

All the design interventions share the same material palette and assume geological references in their form and material finish. (Figure 8:12) While poured-in-place concrete and Corten steel offer durability, an ability to withstand large static stresses, and minimum maintenance, they also provide an opportunity for metaphorical references to the landscape. The concrete is given various finishes—polished, hammered, trowelled or variously cast—in relation to its specific use and placement. The finish of the Corten steel varies as it oxidizes over time to form a patina.[55] So, while every detail is considered with respect to its durability, consideration is also given to finishes that are able to recall the natural surfaces on which the forms rest or are embedded. These natural surfaces are also considered in terms of their material qualities, such as the use of water as an architectural material in order to capture light and shape space. For some, it is water, at Trollstigen offered as "a placid surface, controlled cascade, dramatic waterfall", that is "central to Norwegian culture."[56]

Trollstigen's panoramic cultural centre has won several awards in recognition of its architecture and also for the complex ways in which it has resolved several problems: those of both giving access to and protecting the landscape; of inserting artificial structures into the fragile ecology of rock and water; and of accommodating contemporary, global viewing practices within national heritage. The successful solving of these problems, and the recognition given to this, are indicators of potential acquisition of design capital.

Clearly the structures serve more than conveniences along a highway. Their experiential qualities significantly amplified in comparison to the sheds and stark pathways that preceded them, speak to current cultural expectations. The viewing platforms, stairs and other accoutrements of the Scenic Routes Program are designed to express contemporary values of 'being in nature' and unadulterated, 'original' landscapes, although it could be argued that the artifice and ingenuity involved in effecting such immersive environments is also part of their attraction and value. The cultural value of these installations for Norwegians is part of a long history of interacting with the waterways and topographic singularities of this landscape, including the relating of built form to topography and climate that forms part of modern Norwegian architectural history.

8:12 Reiulf Ramstad Arkitekter. Trollstigen Vistor Centre (2012), More og Romsdal, Norway. Photo: Mariusz Hermandorfer, CC0, via Wikimedia Commons.

NOTES

1. Rose Marie San Juan, "Water Overflow: Contamination, Cleanliness, and the location of the fountain piazza," *Rome: a city out of print* (Minneapolis: University of Minnesota Press, 2001), 133-35.
2. San Juan, *Rome*, 137.
3. Giacomo da Marcucci, Rome 1625, quoted in San Juan, *Rome*, 140
4. The aqueduct, Acqua Vergine and the baths and households it fed were the urban initiatives of Emperor Agrippa in 19 BCE.
5. John A. Pinto, *The Trevi Fountain* (New Haven and London: Yale University Press, 1986), 22, 28-31.
6. Pinto, *Trevi Fountain*, 10.
7. The Trevi Fountain provided drinking water until it was compromised by construction along its route and it was no longer deemed potable in 1961.
8. Joe Satram, "13 Weird Moments in the History of Water Fountains. Think they're boring? Think again," *HuffPost* April 1, 2015, updated December 16, 2017.
9. Gruppo Acea, accessed October 24, 2020, https://www.gruppo.acea.it/en/serving-people/water/nasoni.
10. For a list of fountains see, Metropolitan Drinking Fountain and Cattle Trough Association, accessed October 25, 2020 ,http://www.mdfcta.co.uk.
11. La Société des Fontaines Wallace, accessed October 17, 2020, https://www.wallacefountains.org/about-sir-wallace-and-his-fountains.
12. Wallace Foundation, "Sir Richard Wallace and His Fountains." accessed October 24, 2020, https://wallacefountains.org/about-sir-wallace-and-his-fountains/.
13. Barbara Lambesis, founder and President of the Society of Wallace Fountains, "150 Years of Thirst: The Wallace Fountains of Paris," Lecture, Paris Institute of Critical Thinking Visiting Lectures III, December 5, 2019, accessed October 20, 2020, https://parisinstitute.org/pict-visiting-lectures-iii-150-years-of-thirst-the-wallace-fountains-of-paris/.
14. Urzula Nowacka-Rejzner, "Water Elements in the Creation of Public Space." IOP Conference Series. Materials Science and Engineering 603:2 (2019) 022087, https://iopscience.iop.org/article/10.1088/1757-899x/603/2/02287.
15. Gruppo Acea, "Water Houses, social and high-tech drinking fountains,"accessed October 5, 2020, https://www.gruppo.acea.it/en/serving-people/water/water-houses.
16. Augusta Pownall, "London water fountains design chosen by focus group," *Dezeen*, July 25, 2019,accessed October 26, 2020, https://www.dezeen.com/2019/07/25/london-water-fountains-design.
17. Amy Frearson, "Zaha Hadid and Hopkins among architects to design London water fountains," *Dezeen*, February 19, 2014, accessed October 25, 2020, https://www.dezeen.com/2014/02/19/zaha-hadid-hopkins-studio-weave-london-water-fountains/.
18. Sponsors for the London Drinking Fountain Co.'s Fleet Fountain were: Blue Marine Foundation, South Kensington Estates, #OneLess, Refill Organization, and London Design Festival 2018, accessed October 28, 2020, http://thelondonfountaincompany.london/partners---supporters.html.
19. Ali Morris, "Michael Anastassiades' public drinking fountains address plastic pollution during London Design Week," *Wallpaper*, September 16, 2018, accessed October 25, 2020, https://www.wallpaper.com/design/michael-anastassiades-public-drinking-fountains-london-design-festival-2018.
20. Anastassiades quoted in Morris, "Michael Anastassiades'."
21. Tim Spears, "Michael Anatassiades installs 'touchless' drinking fountain in London," *Designboom*, accessed October 28, 2020, https://www.designboom.com/design/michael-anastassiades-fleet-fountain-london.

22. Edwin Heathcote, "Drinking Fountains Quench Thirst for Sustainability, *Financial Times*, June 14, 2018, accessed October 28, 2020, https://www.ft.com/content/085f675e-6a42-11e8-aee1-39f3459514fd.
23. City of North Vancouver, "The Shipyards" Burrard Dry Dock Pier History," https://www.cnv.org/parks-recreation-and-culture/city-waterfront/the-shipyards; "Pinnacle International" *Buzz Buzz Home*, accessed October 29, 2020, http://www.buzzbuzzhome.com/ca/db/pinnacle_international.
24. Bill Pechet, Design Capital Interview with Bill Pechet, August 5, 2020, http://blogs.ubc.ca/meyboom/.
25. Pechet, Interview.
26. Pechet, Interview.
27. Pechet, Interview.
28. Future of London, accessed December 26, 2020, https://www.futureoflondon.org.uk/2019/07/08/waterways-paddington/.
29. Scheduled times are Wednesday and Friday at noon and Saturday at 2:00 pm., although this schedule is not reliable.
30. Rob Gregory, "Thomas Heatherwick, Rolling Bridge," *Architectural Review* 218 (December 2005): 56.
31. Paul Goldberger, "The Heatherwick Effect," *The New Yorker,* accessed November 18, 2020, https://www.newyorker.com/magazine/2008/05/12/the-heatherwick-effect.
32. Marcus Fairs, "Boiler Suit by Thomas Heatherwick," *Dezeen*, August 20, 2007, accessed December 27, 2020, https://www.dezeen.com/2007/08/20/boiler-suit-by-thomas-heatherwick.
33. Marcus Fairs, "Boiler Suit."
34. Goldberger, "The Heatherwick Effect."
35. Goldberger, "The Heatherwick Effect."
36. Nasjonale turisveger (Norwegian Scenic Routes), accessed December 24, 2020, https://www.nasjonaleturistveger.no/en/about-us/organization/the-scenic-route-section.
37. Nasjonale turisveger (Norwegian Scenic Routes) , accessed December 24, 2020, https://www.nasjonaleturistveger.no/en/about-us/organization/the-scenic-route-section, Also involved were the Norwegian Public Roads Administration, the Ministry of Transport and Communication, Architecture and Arts Councils and the Scenic Routes Forum.
38. Although the fact that roads with their encouragement of automobiles are the basis of the programme raises question of sustainability, the design of the roads and legislation limit the weight and length of permissible vehicles (tour buses for example are disallowed, electric vehicles are available for hire and the government has set a target for a nationwide adoption of electric vehicles.
39. https://www.nasjonaleturistveger.no/en/about-us/prizes-and-awards, accessed December 24, 2020. These include: Norway Cultural Heritage, the Norwegian Grosch Medal for architecture (Carl-Viggo Holmebakk, 2010 and Jon Olav Jensen and Borre Skodvin, 2003). While many of the awards are Norwegian, some are international, including Arch Daily Building of the year for Trollstigen in 2010, which also won the Innovation Award of Universal Design in 2011 and the European Prize for Contemporary Architecture in 2013.
40. Nasjonale turistveger, accessed December 24, 2020, https://www.nasjonaleturistveger.no/en/about-us/prizes-and-awards.
41. Janike Kampevold Larsen, "Global Tourism Practices as Living Heritage: Viewing the Norwegian Tourist Routes Project," *Future Anterior: Journal of Historic Preservation, History, Theory and Criticism* 19, no. 1 (Summer 2012): 68, https://www.jstor.org/stable/10.5749/futuante.9.1.0067. Larsen is Associate Professor at the Institute of Urbanism and Landscape, Oslo School of Architecture and Design.
42. Larsen, "Global Tourism Practices," 67-87.
43. Larsen, "Global Tourism Practices," 67.
44. "Norwegian National Tourist Routes Revisited," Norwegian Arts, accessed November 18, 2020, https://norwegianarts.org.uk/norwegian-national-tourist-routes-revisited/.
45. Iván Ricón Borrego, "Landscape Architectures in Norway: The Influence of AHO Masters on the National Tourist Routes of Norway," *Cuaderno de Notas* 20 (2019): 92.
46. See, Nasjonale turistveger, accessed December 27, 2020, https://www.nasjonaleturistveger.no/en/routes/gamle-strynefjellsvegen.

47. Ricón Borrego, "Landscape Architectures," 94.
48. Beck Roan, "The Complexity of Architecture: An Analysis of Design Intention and Theories in the Norwegian National Tourist Routes," Master of Philosophy, University of Oslo, Blindern, Norway, May 2013, 75.
49. The architect, Wilhelmsen, quoted in Roan, "The Complexity of Architecture," 75.
50. Ricón Borrego, "Landscape Architectures," 91.
51. Ricón Borrego, "Landscape Architectures," 91.
52. Reiulf Ramstad Arkitekter, accessed December 27, 2020, https://www.reiulframstadarkitekter.com.
53. Reiulf Ramstad, "National Tourist route Trollstigen," *Archello,* accessed December 27, 2020, https://archello.com/project/national-tourist-route-trollstigen.
54. Reiulf Ramstad Arkitekter, accessed December 27, 2020, https://www.reiulframstadarkitekter.com.
55. Amy Frearson "Trollstigen Tourist Route Project by Reiulf Ramstad Architects," *Dezeen,* July 7, 2012, accessed December 27, 2020, https://www.dezeen.com/2012/07/07/trollstigen-by-reiulf-ramstad-architects/.
56. Thomas Aastad, "Trollstigen Visitor's Center by Reiulf Ramstad Architects, Norway," *Wallpaper* 21 June 2012, accessed December 26, 2020, https://www.wallpaper.com/architecture/trollstigen-visitor-centre-by-reiulf-ramstad-architects-norway.

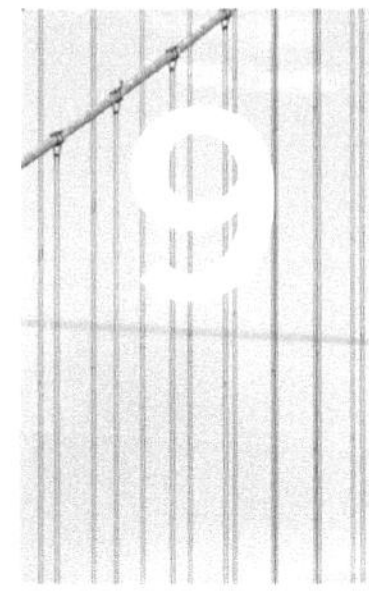
9

CASE STUDIES: MEDIUM SCALE

INTRODUCTION

As discussed in the previous chapter, it is important to understand several aspects in the design process: how the design was originally intended by those who decided to build it, how the design team interpreted what was wanted and translated this into built form, and how the design is now seen and what value it has accrued over time. In order to do so, this chapter examines case studies of how design thinking by politicians, designers and the public at large has contributed to infrastructure that has accrued design capital and looks at what form that design capital has taken.

For these medium-scale examples of design capital, we have chosen to analyze bridges. Bridges are infrastructure, but they are more discretely identifiable and less 'anonymous' than other examples of infrastructure that blend into the city fabric or landscape. A bridge often has distinct design features which can be clearly read, unlike other examples such as roadways, retaining walls or a subway entry area. Most people have some familiarity or even fondness for a bridge in their life, and therefore it is easier to imagine the value and social contribution that a bridge might bring.

Although independent structures, bridges are usually publicly funded, unlike buildings or elements in private developments. This is an important distinction for our purposes, because our claims in support of design capital are based on our argument that it serves the public good. While private developers may understand the value of design predominantly from a marketing, real estate or brand image perspective, by contrast, public spending has to answer to a broad constituency and distinct and clear arguments have to be made for these funds. As such, only a clear argument for the value of design will enable public money to be spent on design quality.

Being a complex and large-scale effort, the planning for a bridge takes a significant period of time, with a corresponding length of time needed to measure the impact of built infrastructure. It takes a minimum of three years to plan a major infrastructure project like a bridge and more likely five, owing to the need to secure environmental approvals, lengthy political decision-making processes and allowing time for the design development. Once the conceptual design and planning is complete, the project, depending on how it is tendered,[1] is handed to a design/build team who bid on it—a process of 8-12 months or longer. The actual construction takes approximately two years and only then can the bridge be opened. Once it is opened, the impact on residents, urban form, business and tourism will develop over the following years with the full impact only truly seen 5-10 years after completion. To measure impact over time, a time frame of 25 years is desirable and this will provide more data of better quality.

Bridges have a growing body of literature devoted to them, but this is varied in its focus and intention. Some authors celebrate technical and structural achievements, others embed histories of bridges within biographies of their builders, and still others categorize and evaluate bridges according to their structural rationale and material ingenuity. The case has been made for bridges as a structural art, initially in 1812 by Thomas Telford and again by David P. Billington in 1985. Telford identified a "structural aesthetic" as "three distinct yet interdependent conditions: context, design and connections" while Billington described bridge design as a combination of "efficiency, economy and elegance."[2] Linda Figg, CEO and President of FIGG Bridge Group, updated Telford's three conditions with the addition of a fourth: "people who use it."[3] Judith Dupré has plotted the history of bridges against the rise of the civil engineer and their ascending public recognition as well as more recent interdisciplinary efforts involving architects and engineers.[4] While Billington and Dupré seek to celebrate the material accomplishments of bridge construction, and to do so by reference to historical and contemporary structures, our objective is slightly different: we wish to call attention to the ability of bridges to capture design capital: the incorporation of equity in their material form in such a way that restoration, adaptation, repurposing and collective memory are all supported. However, while we are becoming more aware of the many exceptional bridges that have been endowed with substantial design budgets to produce spectacular results, the attentive design of the smaller structures of daily life and in the interests of public good should not be undervalued or overlooked. As such, we include examples of more quotidian bridges whose contribution to the everyday life of the citizen is equally important.

HOW TO DEFINE A DESIGN-SIGNIFICANT BRIDGE

Bridges have captured the popular and professional imagination. They embody within them the ability to serve as monuments or venues for entertainment and sports events, to provide platforms for gardens or viewing stations, or to act as revenue generators and national icons. This versatility of additional programmes requires design consideration so that the bridge's basic function can be augmented beyond only spanning a topographical divide.

The design and the cultural value of bridges are currently recognized in the various lists that populate the internet of the most unique, strange, amazing, largest or significant structures.[5] Here, historical and contemporary bridges are noted not only for their technical and construction ingenuity but also for their function as emblem, symbol, icon, and even entertainment. Many bridges also appear on registers of culturally significant built form. Bridges are noted as individual and ensemble features of 'universal' cultural value on the UNESCO World Heritage Register; furthermore, design is often listed among the features cited in the UNESCO statement of significance for bridges.

Bridges are attributed cultural and social significance via institutional and official agents, such as professional organizations (engineering or architectural institutes, UNESCO, etc.), special interest groups, or by tourist ratings and visitor figures. They may be assigned strategic value when assisting the expansion of nation states militarily or economically such as the extension of Roman road building accompanying the building of empire in the later decades of the BCE or the building of transport networks in the US in the 1940s and 50s. They can acquire propaganda value for kings, emperors and sultans (such as Henri IV of France , whose Pont Neuf represented his national ambitions or Sultan Süleyman whose Büyükcekmece bridge by Mimar Sinan was in part intended to showcase the Ottoman Empire's cultural equality with the West.[6] However, as history

9:1 Ponte Vecchio, (1345), Florence, Italy.
Photo: Yair Haklai.

demonstrates and Bourdieu has argued, cultural and social significance can be attributed differently by different social groups and, while not always unanimous, this significance is a powerful force in our understanding of the built environment.

The bridges considered here as socially and culturally significant have been derived from those found across several lists of notable bridges.[7] These lists perhaps originate in the references to bridges found in travel accounts as geographical signposts, and even occasionally as marvels. Leon Battista Alberti, the Renaissance theoretician, describes two bridges in De re aedificatoria (1452). One is Hadrian's Ponte Sant'Angelo in Rome (134 CE), which Alberti values for its aesthetic properties of form, geometry and ornament as well as its association with urban grandeur.[8] The second is the more contemporary Ponte Vecchio, Florence, as rebuilt in 1345 with a plaza: Alberti deemed this the chief ornament of the city, creating a place of gathering, socializing and viewing the river. (Figure 9:1) Although conventionally attributed to Taddeo Gaddi, the influence of others is also suggested, such as the Dominican Friars because of their knowledge of proportion, harmony and mathematics (gained perhaps via Vitruvian and other Roman manuscripts kept in their libraries). In the following century, Palladio included bridges in the chapter dedicated to the design of the city in his internationally influential Four Books of Architecture (1570), which distilled the classical preoccupations of Vitruvius, Alberti and other Renaissance humanists into architectural schema. His proposed design for the Rialto Bridge in Venice, although never built, is longingly recreated in the imaginative vedute of Canaletto and emulated in garden structures of 18th century Britain. Design value is implicated in such culturally assessed infrastructure.

The bestowal of UNESCO World Heritage status on so many bridges highlights both their immutable as well as mutable utilitarian and temporal functions. Cultural status is bestowed according to both durable aesthetic and location-determined economic criteria: the claim to universal importance is underpinned by local financial considerations, including the cost of site maintenance for example. Any designation of a bridge must meet historical and contemporary needs. So, while the transporter Vizcaya Bridge (Spain, 1893) and the Forth Rail Bridge (Scotland, 1890) were built to serve practical purposes and initially celebrated for their engineering advancement and as symbols of progress, by the time they were awarded

UNESCO World Heritage status (2005 and 2011 respectively) they were recognized for their symbolic value. While not the intention of its 19th century architects, the current First Minister of Scotland has deemed the Forth Bridge "an outstanding example of Scotland's built heritage,"[9] —that is, a symbol of Scotland itself.[10] Recent adaptations to augment and diversify function are justified and called forth by the design capital associated with the bridges; the original offering a kind of equity against which financing for later amendments can be justified.

HISTORIC BRIDGES

As the earliest theoretical and philosophical work known to include bridges specifically is Leon Battista Alberti's De re aedificatoria (c. 1452), we begin our historical account of bridges with the period of the Italian Renaissance and the simultaneous Ottoman hegemony.[11] While Alberti included bridges in his description of urban form, he attributed to them design and cultural significance via an attention to geometry as well as appropriately chosen ornament (to mark the proportional relationships deemed significant by classical philosophy and referential to ancient Roman achievements). Structures in the Renaissance were conceived when builders worked across the disciplines of engineering and architecture; the distinction between the two was only formalized in later centuries. Inheritors of Vitruvius' notions of design, Renaissance bridge builders attributed value to proportion, legibility and delight (beauty), with the latter often expressed in narrative or symbolic attributes. Bridge building also emulated the idea of civic grandeur and public good resulting from good design, or good "idea building" as Alberti would say. Bridges built in the Ottoman Empire of the 16th century similarly incorporated the design devices by which the values of the time might be expressed, and among those values were those of public engagement.

THE PASA SOKOLOVIC BRIDGE, BOSNIA-HERZOGOVINA, 1577. MIMAR SINAN

Mimar Sinan, working throughout the Ottoman Empire (active 1537-1588), reportedly augmented his engineering beginnings with formal appreciation for the monuments of the past, thus imbuing his bridges with aesthetic and cultural, as well as structural considerations. Sinan's conception of design is evidenced in the Mehmed Pasa Sokolovic Bridge (Figure 9:2), commissioned by the Grand Vizier Mehmed Pasa Sokolovic and built in 1577 over the Drina River in present-day Bosnia and Herzegovina. In this bridge, Sinan synthesized a design philosophy schooled in classical learning with his military experience. The Pasa Sokolovic Bridge offered an arched structure served by a convenient ramp system and a prayer niche mid-span. In addition to its practical purposes in the 16th century, it was also intended to serve as an expression of imperial prestige, to pay tribute to the region, and to be a symbol of trade and prosperity. UNESCO listed the bridge in 2007 for slightly different reasons: its strategic position amidst diverse cultures, the renown of its architect and its "unique elegance of proportions."[12]

STARI MOST (OLD BRIDGE), MOSTAR, BOSNIA-HERZEGOVINA, C. 1566. MIMAR SINAN

Likewise, the Stari Most (Old Bridge) was built by Sinan to serve the trade routes of the Ottoman Empire. It was recognized by UNESCO in 2005 for the "universal" integration of bridge and site, the Old City of Mostar, Herzegovina. (Figure 9:3) Rebuilt in 2001-04[13] after its destruction in 1993 during the conflict in the former Yugoslavia, its initial strategic value and economic role in seaward-bound trade was augmented by an appreciation of its ability to symbolize reconciliation, international cooperation and the coexistence of diverse cultural, religious and ethnic communities in the past and, hopefully, in the present and future.[14]

In these two examples, bridges that were initially designed to perform both practical and symbolic functions have continued to perform them over time even though the specific uses may have changed. These historical bridges, in their ability to sustain cultural and social value, continue to perform in the complex manner the design philosophies of the time envisioned.

9:2 Mimar Sinan. Pasa Sokolovic Bridge (1577), Visregard, Bosnia-Herzegovina. Photo: Branevgd.

9:3 Mimar Sinan /Mimar Hayruddin. Stari Most (c. 1566),Mostar, Bosnia-Herzegovina. Photo: Ramirez.

9:4 Jean Baptiste Androuet du Certeau and Guillaume Marchand. Pont Neuf (1578-1607), Paris, France. Jean-Baptiste Raguenet, A View of Paris from the Pont Neuf, 1763.

PONT NEUF, PARIS, 1578-1607, JEAN BAPTISTE ANDROUET DU CERCEAU / HENRI IV

The Pont Neuf in Paris (1578-1607) became an important place and symbol of the city in large part because of the design demands of its patron, Henri IV, and the amenities it offered, in addition to providing a convenient connection between the left and right banks of the river Seine.[15] (Figure 9:4) Henri IV had intervened in earlier proposed designs for the bridge, prompting the elimination of the initially proposed housing in order to allow viewing platforms and panoramas of the city and the provision of pedestrian ways flanking the thoroughfare (the first sidewalks in Europe since Roman times) which encouraged lingering and provided venues for the posting of notices. In addition the bridge was an achievement of unprecedented scale not only in length but also width, so that multiple events could occur simultaneously; it also included a public square, which would hold the first public statue in Paris, a commemorative bronze sculpture of Henri IV commissioned after his death, which also served to mark the identity of the Place du Pont Neuf.[16] The bridge also served as support for other urban enhancements: a water pump and house were appended to a pier near the right bank, which provided water for the fountains of the Louvre and Tuileries, and small shop owners appropriated the projecting platforms. With the completion of the Pont Neuf, "for the first time the monument that defined a city was an innovative urban work rather than a cathedral or a palace."[17]

There is no documentary evidence that Henri IV was "knowledgeable in architectural theory" or "experienced in design."[18] This suggests that his vision was filtered through the work of the supervisor of the royal works, Jean Baptiste Androuet du Cerceau, architect of many elite townhomes and civic buildings following Renaissance teachings, and the entrepreneur/master mason Guillaume Marchand.[19]

It was Henri IV's intention that the Pont Neuf should not only win the affections of his new, rebellious subjects and advance his mercantilist policies, but it should also become a symbol of a capital city of a more centralized state.[20] In establishing a location in the minds and memories of residents and visitors, the Pont Neuf performed several roles. It afforded views of and prominence to the Louvre, the monarchical seat of power; encouraged the development of the Right Bank; and attracted printers of news bulletins due to the availability of posting boards on the bridge deck. Entertainers capitalized on the abundance of passers-by while the bridge became an attraction and inspired a fledgling tourist industry. The Pont Neuf, according to historian Joan DeJean, initiated the invention of Paris as we know it and of the "Modern City" generally.[21] The Pont Neuf was also the initiator of, and integral to, larger urban redevelopment that included the adjacent Place Dauphine and the Rue Dauphine, as well as enlarged streets along the more eastern Ile St. Louis.[22] While the king paid for the bridge and its equestrian statue, private investors built the other urban interventions. Together they facilitated a real estate market and development of the Left Bank. Upon its completion the bridge was immediately celebrated in Jacque du Breul's history of the city (1608) and in later guidebooks, such as Germain Brice's guide to Paris (1684).[23] As historian Hilary Ballon asserts, the bridge was a force-shaping urban experience, and Paris itself both produced by and producing "architectural form, social forces and political vision."[24]

POL-E KHAJU BRIDGE, 1650. SHAH ABBAS II

Shah Abbas II's Pol-e Khaju (1650), Isfahan, exemplified not only engineering skill but also aesthetic achievement and the accommodation of complex social and political requirements. (Figure 9:5) The bridge shared in the aesthetic and cultural aspirations of the expansion of Isfahan with new mosques, palaces and public buildings encircling a new public square, the Mayden, and was an integral part of the vicinity's comprehensive design. As both bridge and weir, the Pol-e Khaju permitted an orderly conveyance of goods and people while its control of water flow allowed irrigation to riverine gardens. As both building and platform it provided a place for the ceremonial presentation of the shah and the public amenity of vantage points from which to observe water sports. Notions of proportion and measure shaped the structural components of the bridge and organized them in rhythmic bays punctuated by a centralized pavilion and symmetrical end projections. The multidimensional consideration of the bridge was the consequence both of recognition of the value of design for aesthetic, functional and socially integrative reasons, and of the authority of the state at the time.

9:5 Shah Abbas II. Khaju Bridge (1650), Isfahan, Tehran.
Photo : Ninara.

The two hundred years from the mid-15th to the mid-17th century witnessed a rebirth of classical knowledge and with it a desire to fuse technical ability with attention to visual appeal and cultural expression. Bridges of this period, as much as they solved fundamental structural issues (danger from flooding and the force of water surges as well as the weight and scale of new vehicular movement), also addressed aesthetic and social considerations in their design. They did so partly because their builders possessed this knowledge as part of their expertise and partly because rulers must win the hearts and minds of their subjects. Bridges engaged functional, aesthetic, social and culturally critical aspects of their construction in one concept, inviting public use in multiple ways, and contributed to the urban design of the areas in which they were built. Often, they also participated in new forms of civic publicity which arose through developments in print culture and its distribution possibilities, which saw bridges featured in prints and guide books.

BEAUTY IN FUNCTIONALITY - MODERNIST APPROACHES

SALGINATOBEL BRIDGE, SALINA GORGE, SWITZERLAND, 1930. ROBERT MAILLART

From their inception in the early 20th century, the bridges of Robert Maillart bring to the fore the role of design capital. Maillart's numerous structures have been devoted to questions of design both in engineering and artistic terms. While his work within engineering circles, such as his alma mater Eidgenössische Technische Hochschule (ETH) Zurich, was controversial during the 1920s and 30s, it was celebrated by modernist polemicists like Sigfried Giedion in his Space, Time and Architecture: The Growth of a New Tradition (1941). Giedion, an engineer and historian, had attended one of Maillart's popular lectures at ETH in 1935 on the inherent potentials of reinforced concrete; Giedion identified in this a design philosophy in keeping with modernist architectural principles which freed form from historical precedent, and for which he advocated.[25] Maillart himself published "Construction and Aesthetics of Bridges" in The Concrete Way (May/June) in 1935. In 1937, Maillart was one of the first engineers to be admitted as an

9:6 Robert Maillart. Salgiatobel Bridge (1930), Salina Gorge, Switzerland. Photo: Rama.

honorary member of the Royal Institute of British Architects. In the United States, the Museum of Modern Art in New York City held an exhibition of his bridges in 1947, as did Seattle and Portland the following year. Interest persisted with exhibitions at Princeton University Art Museum in 1972 and again in 1976.

However, by the 1970s there was also an attempt to temper this overly artistic categorization of Maillart's bridge design by emphasizing the technical and analytical basis of his design process.[26] Seeking to redress what he considered an overemphasis on the spectacular settings and "art cultist" commentary on Maillart's bridges, David P. Billington, member of Princeton University's Engineering Faculty, argues that they were in fact "technical structures par excellence and not mysterious art forms immune to calculational analysis."[27] He also attributed to Maillart the idea that engineering structure was an independent art form.[28] His larger point was, however, that Maillart combined both art and calculation, concluding that: "structures that have aesthetic and technical significance can be a part of art history."[29] The Maillart project that Billington referred to in making this claim was the Salginatobel Bridge. (Figure 9:6)

The Salginatobel Bridge of 1929-30 is a concrete hollow box, three-hinged arch with a low ratio of span to rise that allows passage across a deep gorge in the Swiss mountains. As with all his bridges, Maillart was attentive to costs, paring away material to affect the most technically advanced, but also least expensive, design of the thirteen submissions to the bridge competition. However, engineers and architectural historians, scholars and the general public find in the Salginatobel Bridge something more than mere economy and expediency; it is appreciated and evaluated in fields other than exclusively engineering ones. As indicated in Billington's 1974 article, "An Example of Structural Art: The Salginatobel Bridge of Robert Maillart," Maillart's bridges straddle the disciplines of art and engineering. Billington also wrote Robert Maillart's Bridges: The Art of Engineering (1979), which was reviewed in various engineering and science journals (ISIS, Science) as well as architectural historical journals (JSAH). After reading the latter, one reviewer concluded: "More than engineering work, bridges are often the result of great social enterprise and hence reflect societal values, and as an art form, epitomize concern for aesthetic expression."[30]

In 1991 the Salginatobel Bridge was the first concrete bridge to be designated an International Historic Civil Engineering Landmark by the American Society of Civil Engineers; in 2001, the British journal Bridge Design and Engineering voted it "the most beautiful bridge of the century."[31] It is also listed on the Swiss Inventory of Cultural Property of National and Regional Significance.

The Salginatobel Bridge accrued design capital via this conjunction of technical and aesthetic recognition. So highly valued was the bridge in both technical and aesthetic discourses by the mid-1970s that even extensive repairs carried out during 1975-76 did not tarnish its significance.[32] It was again repaired in 1991, when waterproofing and drainage were refurbished for a second time, the concrete surface completely replaced and the parapets entirely rebuilt, at a cost of 1.3 million US dollars. This second refurbishment coincided with the recognition of the Salginatobel Bridge as an International Historic Civil Engineering Landmark.

While the Salginatobel Bridge enjoys a spectacular site, many of Maillart's bridges are in typical urban settings and integral to everyday practices of coming and going. They are not only functional; they also serve to "humanize the landscape."[33]

THE GOLDEN GATE BRIDGE, SAN FRANCISCO, 1934-1937. ENGINEER JOSEPH STRAUSS AND ARCHITECTS JOHN EBERSON AND IRVING MORROW

The Golden Gate Bridge, although considered an engineering achievement upon its completion in 1937, was also deemed an aesthetic triumph. (Figure 9:7) Design was critical to its form and also in winning public support for the construction of a bridge in a site charged with historical significance and landscape preservation sentiment. The production of a bridge of structural daring and exceptional beauty had been the aspiration from its earliest conception by its chief engineer, Joseph Strauss, in 1917.[34] Many engineers and advances in metallurgy would assist Strauss in ultimately spanning the Golden Gate between San Francisco and Marin County but, as important as this engineering feat is, it is the contribution of two architects who would significantly redefine the bridge's appearance and ensure its construction. Design was at the forefront of debates in newspaper articles and the positions taken by ad hoc committees formed in response to the bridge

9:7 The Golden Gate Bridge (1933-37), San Francisco, USA.
Photo: Frank Schulenburg.

project. From the very visualizing of a bridge spanning one-and-a-half miles across the bay in 1921, fierce public opposition to its rather ungainly and utilitarian appearance made it clear that appropriate design would be necessary to win the support of the public who would, directly or indirectly, be needed to fund the audacious project.

There were sound economic arguments justifying the construction of a bridge at this location. San Francisco needed to expand, especially with increased ocean trade following the opening of the Panama Canal in 1912. Inaccessibility to the north hampered this, as did the existing ferry system across the bay which was increasingly inefficient with the increase in automobile use. There were also several factors influencing the perception of the bridge as an aesthetic object. One was a public predisposed to view the bridge aesthetically due to two influential ideas, the City Beautiful Movement and Art Deco style. Both the City Beautiful Movement and Art Deco style are recognizable references in the conceptual sketches and paintings of the envisioned bridge by consulting architects John Eberson and Irving Morrow and local artist Maynard Dixon; these were exhibited in 1930 as part of the campaign to win the approval of city voters for the bridge construction.[35]

The concern for the approaches to the bridge, its scale in relation to the landscape, and its feature as a monument against the sky were all a legacy of the City Beautiful Movement. The movement had been prominent in the previous three decades and promoted in San Francisco, particularly by Daniel H. Burnham's 1905 plan for the city.[36] The City Beautiful Movement had fostered an appreciation of spaciousness achieved via broad vistas, boulevards and parks as part of an aesthetic rather than utilitarian understanding of the city. The Art Deco style developed in the mid-1920s as an alternative to the austere modernism of the European avant-garde. It promoted forms and patterns associated with populist enthusiasms and mass entertainment (like theatre, the discovery of Mayan temples, and the automobile). Art Deco sensibilities are evident in the form of the towers, repetitive geometric detailing, emphasis on verticality, graduated colour and dramatic lighting.

The site offered unprecedented structural challenges—a more than 4000-foot span across a shipping channel, with ocean swells and the corrosive powers of salt-laden air, wind, storms, seismic instability, and the detrimental effects of fog on visibility. This was resolved via a suspension bridge and advances in metallurgy that produced durable paint, better-performing cables and steel cell structural components. The site and climatic conditions also presented design issues concerning form, colour and illumination. The challenges were to produce a bridge that had substance when viewed against the expanses of water and sky, but still appeared light-filled and spacious; that provided vistas while being substantial in form; and was beautiful as opposed to merely functional. To achieve both, the chief engineer insisted the architect's design skills were necessary.

The first consulting architect Strauss hired was a nationally prominent theatre designer and proponent of the then fashionable Art Deco style, John Eberson. Through 1929 until early 1930, he determined the basic form of the stepped-back towers with detail diminishing in scale as it ascends, creating an illusion of greater height and spaciousness. The atmospheric effects and proposed lighting added drama to the re-conceived engineered form. His 1930 view of the bridge and its south entrance approach also displays many of the strategies used by City Beautiful proponents. Eberson's sketch displayed enormous scale of conception and a composition of varied civic form: a monumental colonnade framing a plaza and the entry to the bridge deck which stretched to the Marin County headlands beyond.[37] His replacement in early 1930, local architect Irving F. Morrow, continued Eberson's general conception of the bridge. Morrow refined its Art Deco details, enhanced the illusion of verticality by accentuating the actual and illusory recession of form as the towers rose, and dramatized the form of the bridge via lighting and colour. Although most of the extensive proposals for the entry plaza of the south approach (as exhibited in 1930) were eliminated for budgetary purposes, those affecting the bridge were retained despite their added cost.

Morrow collaborated with an engineer to eliminate the crossbars of the towers and to produce a lighter appearance; heavy bracing was visually lightened by fascia plates and chevron detailing, and corbels were added to enliven the form with texture, and the geometry of components and their spacing altered to accentuate verticality.[38] The lighting and colour design were given lengthy and exacting study and widely debated among the design team, the popular press and in public forums.[39] They were clearly important aspects of the bridge's design and their discussion went beyond the functional and safety requirements of their use. Discussion included consideration of the atmospheric aspects of sea and sky on form and colour, the need to highlight detail so as to relieve the potential monotony of such an extensive form, and the aesthetic benefit of harmony with the landscape. The final colour decision, International Orange, was chosen to bring luminosity to the bridge in addition to offering a fog-cutting hue and a resilient paint formula.[40] As one citizen wrote to Morrow, "The Golden Gate Bridge is not, either in its future use or in its architectural treatment, a purely economic structure. It is perhaps the only one of the great bridges in the world in which the aesthetic element is of paramount importance."[41]

The architects directed attention to the development of an effective architectural treatment of the bridge and the added costs of these aesthetic manipulations were deemed fundamental to the dignity, character and success of the bridge. The architects designed the iconic aspects of the bridge, from street lamps and the vertical fluting of the supports to the colour palette by which the bridge gains its distinctive reference— the sunset skies of its location between the Bay of San Francisco and the Gulf of Farallones.[42] More recent maintenance and renovation of the bridge have been inspired by these early 20th century design ambitions.[43] The value of design in ensuring the cultural and historical significance of the Golden Gate Bridge is evident in the adoption of the Design Criteria Report by Donald MacDonald Architects that guides future engineering interventions.[44]

CONTEMPORARY BRIDGES

THE GATESHEAD MILLENNIUM BRIDGE, GATE HEAD-NEWCASTLE, UK, 1998. WILKINSON EYRE

Built in 1998, Gateshead Millennium Bridge, Newcastle, UK, is a modern counterpart of the Pont Neuf; it, too, was built as part of a larger civic development, provides multiple amenities and is an event in its urban context, attracting public occasions and tourists. (Figure 9:8) The architect intended that the bridge excite the spirit, create a sense of place, and evoke motion. This is achieved by geometric patterning, which makes the structure legible and also cues movement. Repeated curving patterns also intentionally harmonize the innovative arc of Gateshead with the older arched structures of nearby bridges, thus relating it to its location, while the angles of the arcing structure emphasize the actual dynamic quality of the bridge and its moving parts.[45] It has been adopted by the locals as an icon of the city, and nationally has been featured on a postage stamp and the one-pound coin.[46]

THE MILLAU VIADUCT, FRANCE, 2004. NORMAN FOSTER + PARTNERS

The Millau Viaduct (2004) was conceived as part of a highway network linking Paris to Béziers, Montpellier, the French Mediterranean, and beyond to Spain.[47] (Figure 9:9) It was intended to have as little impact on the environment as possible, improve local access to motorways as well as service the north/south summer traffic and to efficiently respond to the geological and topological features of deep ravines, high plateaus and water tables. From its first inception, it was considered a technical, architectural and financial project. The project was initiated in 1993 by a consultation with structural engineers and architects, and a group of international technical, architectural and landscape experts.[48] The designs produced via this collaboration formed the basis for a second-round competition between five teams of architects and engineers in 1995.[49] The winner, by the consortium Sogelerg Europe Etudes Ceci and Serf, engineer Michel Virlogeux and architect Norman Foster + Partners, was chosen by a jury of elected artists and experts in 1996.[50]

The cable-stayed, mast-structure of the bridge has won several technical accolades from professional organizations, such as the 2006 Outstanding Structure Award by the International Association for Bridge and Structural Engineering, and was also featured prominently in popular media such as National Geographic Channel's Richard Hammond's Engineering Connections.[51] But it has also garnered much commentary related to its aesthetic achievements. The Washington Post declared it "pure environmental sculpture," Wallpaper deemed it "spectacular when seen against the clouds" while Icon dismissed its sculptural value and declared it "a magnificent piece of infrastructure."[52] Millau Viaduct has also affected behaviour; so common was the practice of drivers to slow their vehicles to facilitate photography from the bridge deck that the speed limit on the bridge was reduced to accommodate this.

9:8 Norman Foster + Partners. The Millau Viaduct (2004), France.
Photo : Mike Locke.

9:9 WilkinsonEyre. The Gateshead Millennium Bridge, Gateshead-Newcastle (2001).
Photo Chas Thomson.

On the architects' website is a testimonial from the former President of France, Jacques Chirac, who places the bridge in the "long and great French tradition of audacious works of art."[53] Foster + Partners accompany the dramatic images of the structure with a text stating, "The architecture of infrastructure has a powerful impact on the environment."[54] This "impact on the environment" is attributed to a reading of the topography where it was seen that the elegant and economical spanning from plateau to plateau would have more expressive power than celebrating the act of crossing a river which narrowed at the site. The evaluations of all of these experts and figures of power contribute to the design capital of the Millau Viaduct.

EVERYDAY BRIDGES

While the previous examples are large spectacular projects, there are also innumerable small bridges responding to local economies and needs made viable by local support, and often local labour, that are also significant structures. They too make a location and function, as Heidegger so significantly recognized in his example of the bridge, the enabling of a place. While it could be argued that their design as not as 'important' from a tourist or media attention perspective, arguably they mean even more to people because they participate in the fabric of daily lives and the identity of place to which people have a close tie and often a personal history.

POOLEY BRIDGE, CUMBRIA, UK, 2020.
KNIGHT ARCHITECTS

A contemporary example of a small-scale bridge in the service of daily living and local economies is Pooley Bridge. (Figure 9:10) This bridge serves the approximately 100-person Pooley Bridge village (which takes its name from the original bridge) and the only slightly more populous parish of Barton, a largely rural sheep-farming community.[55] It was rebuilt after the previous three-arched stone bridge, which had stood on the same site since 1764, was destroyed by Storm Desmond in 2015. However, the bridge served more than this small community and was essential to more than an agricultural economy. The new Pooley Bridge reconnected the counties of

9:10 Knight Architects. Pooley Bridge (2020), Cumbria, UK.
Photo: Tom McNally.

Cumberland and Westmorland, re-established a needed northern access to the Lake District (recently declared a UNESCO World Heritage site) and facilitated a long-standing tourist economy. The perfunctory Bailey bridge, quickly erected as a temporary measure following Storm Desmond was inadequate for the more comprehensive functioning envisioned for the bridge by the community, client and stakeholders.

The new Pooley Bridge is a single, graceful curve of duplex stainless steel and concrete spanning 40 metres between tawny-hued stone abutments. It provides a single lane for vehicles and flanking pedestrian walkways. It is honed for resilience and practicality: elimination of mid-span supports avoids flood damage and the use of stainless steel eliminates costly maintenance. Tie-back arches compensate for the absence of suitable bedrock and a single lane calms traffic and maintains a rural pace. Although the first composite stainless steel bridge in the UK, it is quietly innovative, without fuss and fit for purpose.[56]

For all its seeming straightforwardness, Pooley Bridge is not without attention to the finessing of form for visual, social or cultural effect. While The Guardian's architectural critic, Oliver Wainwright, describes the bridge as "robust" and "pragmatic"; he also speaks of its atmospheric and experiential effects, its "gossamer elegance," and its mist-like "shimmering". Wainwright comments on the "optical trickery' in the thinness of railings that seem to dissolve, and the shaping of spandrels and angling of main beams to produce the effect of transparency and openness.[57] All of these design touches are intended to maintain views of the surrounding landscape. They are also in response to the aspirations of the community, client and stakeholders, garnered from numerous consultations.

The community wanted a bridge that served symbolic as well as practical functions:[58] a bridge of comparable quality to that destroyed by the storm, that would function as a symbol of the place and also as a tourist attraction. According to the project architect, the community wanted something "modern but not that modern."[59] For the client, Cumbria County Council, the bridge was a flagship project of a much larger initiative, a £124 million Infrastructure Recovery Programme in response to the 2015 storm.[60] The council wanted the bridge to be suited to its picturesque tourist destination and situation as entrance to the Lake District National Park, and able to represent the village and wider Cumbrian community as "beautiful and resilient."[61] Other stakeholders, The Prince's Foundation and The Lake District National Park Authority, wanted a bridge sensitive to its "uniquely beautiful landscape and in keeping with its UNESCO World Heritage site."[62]

These varied ambitions and opinions were distilled by Knight Architects into the dominant themes of their design intent: lightness and transparency, consonance with the area, elegance, flood resilience, balanced notions of modern and traditional, and open views.[63] This translated into the thinness of the steel members and their slight lateral splay, the low rise of the arch, and the inconspicuous, gentle rise of a granite curb (rather than a solid wall). It also produced a discretely articulated horizontal plane: tawny stone signals the movement from the tarmac of the highway to the bridge deck, the walkways widen at the centre as do the wood handrails, forming a space for viewing the scenery. These subtle but effective design decisions have been interpreted by the design community as signifying "resilience, beauty and respect for the surroundings, and a symbol of the resilience and aspiration of the community."[64] It was also the architects' hope that the bridge "would boost the local economy and become a tourist attraction in its own right."[65]

Knight Architects came to the project with experience in designing within national parks, and in "creating high quality bridge design in sensitive locations and in the cultural and political spotlight."[66] Statements on Knight Architects' website demonstrate an enhanced awareness of the role of infrastructure, seeing it as needing to be inclusive of cultural and environmental sensitivities as well as budgetary needs. They also recognize both the tangible and intangible values of infrastructure for clients and communities that can be achieved via intelligent design, allowing them to "create memorable and distinctive landmarks as well as understated structures, which embody 'the beautiful ordinary.'"[67] Great infrastructure design, they argue, serves communities daily, adding value year after year: "It improves quality of life and brings people together, forging connections, driving economies and helping to define an enduring sense of place."[68]

This expanded, comprehensive view of the role of design taken by Knight Architects (and the success it has brought them not only in critical acclaim but also clients) hints at a growing awareness of the role of design in infrastructure projects. Not only was the 2020 Pooley Bridge design able to convince a community and a public body of the economic benefits of a £5 million investment, it also gained their support for the future benefits of good infrastructure design.

The numerous bridges completed by Knight Architects demonstrate that there is growing recognition of the intangible value of design. It is evident in their explicit reference to the expressive opportunity for structural design to consider not only immediate functional needs but also potentials for brand identity and placemaking, landmark and gateway. Many of the sites of Knight Architects bridges are in sensitive landscape and/or post-industrial site developments in need of a strong sense of connectivity and identity. Several of their bridges have won multiple professional and popular awards (RIBA, IABSE, RICS, Civic Trust), attesting to public and professional interest in design. Such awards also serve as publicity for the bridge and the larger area in which it resides, often attracting tourists, investors and business. Knight Architects' clients—private developers, public bodies and public-private partnerships—have recognized the economic sense of the investment in design quality.

CONCLUSION

These bridges were intentionally designed to contribute to multiple social aims, necessitating significant design input. As well as connecting two sides of a topographical divide, they respond and contribute to the social and cultural fabric of the places in which they are located. This contribution was in every case the result of the ambitions of the design team throughout the bridge's development. Clearly it is possible to design in a manner that encourages the attribution of social and cultural significance to a bridge via design; that is, to accrue design capital. It is also clear that it is possible to justify good design as an integral part of bridge construction and that this could be applied to the humbler bridges of everyday life.

The case for design is clarified from the naming of the qualities that good design brings to the place in which it resides. Identifying the quality "design capital" enables the people responsible to answer to the public and the public to make the case for design consideration in bridge construction. It is through this kind of information that designers can elevate the discussion of design while addressing the issues which all parties care about—economics, cultural value and the making of place.

NOTES

1. Tendering processes vary but design-build or design-build-operate-transfer including financing are increasingly common—as opposed to the more common design-bid-build process which was used more commonly in the second half of the 20th century.
2. David P. Billington, *The Tower and the Bridge: The New Art of Structural Engineering* (Princeton NJ: Princeton University Press, 1983), 4-5.
3. Judith Dupré, Bridges: *A History of the World's Most Spectacular Spans*, rev. ed. (New York: Black Dog & Leventhan Publishers, 2017), 1. In her interview with Dupré, Figg argues that creating bridges is an art and dismisses arguments that art increases the cost, Dupré, 9.
4. Judith Dupré, Forward, *Bridges: A History.* Dupré also references the National Academy of Engineering's 2008 report "Changing the Conversation: Messages for Improving Public Understanding of Engineering," Dupré, xix.
5. For example see, Jason, "25 of the World's Most Unique Bridges," *List25*, November 21, 2018, https://www:list.com/25-of-the-worlds-most-unique-bridges.
6. Gülru Necipoglu, "Challenging the Past: Sinan and the Comparative Discourse of Early Modern Islamic Architecture," *Muqarnas*, 10, Essays in Honour of Oleg Grabar (1993), 171-72, http://www.jstor.org/stable/1523183.
7. These include lists compiled by Engineering and Architecture professional bodies, Heritage and Historical Associations, and the tourist and travel industry.
8. Leon Battista Alberti, De re aedificatoria VIII, 6, 262, quoted in Robert Tavenor, *On Alberti and the Art of Building* (New Haven: Yale University Press, 1998), 19.
9. "Forth Bridge given World Heritage Site status," *BBC News*, July 5, 2015, https://www.bbc.com/news/uk-scotland-edinburgh-east-fife-33397980.
10. This singularity of function is substantiated by the UNESCO criteria by which they were designated.
11. Note, the discussion of an Ottoman renaissance is fraught with historiographic problems. See Necipoglu, "Challenging the Past," 141-183.
12. "Sokolovic Bridge," UNESCO Heritage List, https://www.whc.unesco.org/en/list/12601.
13. It was funded by the World Bank, UNESCO, Aga Khan Trust for Culture, World Monuments Fund and several countries. See also Dupré, "Bridges: A History," 23.
14. See, UNESCO World heritage at https://www.whc.unesco.org/en/list/1260 and https://www.whc.unesco.org/en/list/946.
15. A bridge at this site had been started by Henri III, Henri IV's predecessor. Foundations had been partially built before the death of Henri III in 1579. Religious unrest delayed the resumption of work on the bridge for a decade.
16. For a full account of the Pont Neuf see, Hilary Ballon, *The Paris of Henri IV: Architecture and Urbanism* (Cambridge MA and London: The MIT Press, 1991), 114-165.
17. Joan DeJean, "The Birth of the Pont Neuf: how a simple bridge made Paris the world's first modern tourist destination," May 7, 2014, https://www.slate.com/human-interest/2014/paris-history-of-the-construction-of-the-pont-neuf.
18. Ballon, *Paris of Henri* IV, 8.
19. "Les pontes de la Cité," Le *Paris Pittoresque*, https://www.paris-pittoresque.com/monuments.
20. Ballon, *The Paris of Henri IV*, 4-5,15.
21. See Joan DeJean, *How Paris Became Paris: the invention of the modern city* (New York and London: Bloomsbury, 2014).
22. Ballon, "Place Dauphine, Pont Neuf and Rue Dauphine," *The Paris of Henri IV*, 114-165.
23. Ballon, *The Paris of Henri IV*, 122.
24. Ballon, *The Paris of Henri IV*, 13.
25. Sigfried Giedion, "Construction and Aesthetics (Notes on the Reinforced-Concrete Bridges Designed by Swiss Engineer, Robert Maillart),"

in *Circle: International Survey of Constructivist Art,* eds. J.L. Martin, Ben Nicholson, N. Gabo (London: Faber and Faber, 1937. See also, "Robert Maillart," Engineer Biography, https://www.engineering-timelines.com/who/Maillart_R/maillartRobert13.asp.

26. Most prolific in this is David P. Billington, *Robert Maillart: builder, designer and artist* (Cambridge: Cambridge University Press, 1997); *Robert Maillart's Bridges: The Art of Engineering* (Princeton: Princeton University Press, 1979); "An Example of Structural Art: The Salginatobel Bridge of Robert Maillart," *Journal of the Society of Architectural Historians* 33, no.1 (March 1974): 61-72; "Meaning in Maillart,"in *Structures Implicit and Explicit,* Via II, eds. James. Bryan and Rolf Sauer (Philadelphia, University of Pennsylvania, 1973), 29-39.
27. Billington, "Salginatobel Bridge," 61.
28. David P. Billington, *The Tower and the Bridge: The New Art of Structural Engineering* (Princeton NJ: Princeton University Press, 1983), 156.
29. Billington, "An Example of Structural Art," 63.
30. Emory L. Kemp, "Exemplars of Engineering," rev. of *Robert Maillart's Bridges: The Art of Engineering,* by David P. Billington, *Science* 208, no 4445 (May 16, 1980): 727-28. https://www.jstor.org/stable/1683862.
31. "Engineer Biography: Robert Maillart," https://www.engineeringtimelines.com/who/Maillart_R/maillartRobert9.asp.
32. Figi Heinrich, "Rehabilitation of the Salginatobel Bridge," *Structural Engineering International* 10, no.1 (2000): 21-23 (online 23 March 2018).
33. Billington, "An Example of Structural Art," 63.
34. Donald MacDonald and Ira Nadel, *Golden Gate Bridge: History and Design of an Icon* (San Francisco: Chronicle Books, 2008), 18.
35. John King, "Early Golden Gate sketches/flight of fancy," the *SFGate,* accessed May 15, 2021, https://www.sfgate.com/bayarea/place/article/Early-Golden-Gate-Bridge-sketches-flight-of-fancy-3386352.php#photo-2587323.
36. MacDonald and Nadel, 9.
37. King, "Early Golden Gate Sketches."
38. MacDonald and Nadel, *Golden Gate Bridge,* 59-71.
39. Ilrving F Morrow, of Morrow and Morrow, "Special Study in Color and Illumination," April 6, 1935. This was a year-long study, initiated in April 1934.
40. For a detailed discussion of the design development of the bridge, see MacDonald and Nadel, *Golden Gate Bridge.*
41. Letter to Irving Morrow from E.P. Meinecke February 23, 1935, reproduced in Morrow, "Special Report on Colour."
42. See Golden Gate Bridge, Highway and Transportation District, *The Golden Gate Bridge At San Francisco, California: Report of the Chief Engineer, With Architectural Studies, to the Board of Directors, Golden Gate Bridge and Highway District, August 27, 1930* (San Francisco, 1930), 50. See also, Irving Morrow, https//www.pbs.org/americanexperience/feature/biography/goldengate-morrow.
43. The artistic illumination of the towers was finally installed on the 50th anniversary of the Bridge, largely funded by the Pacific Gas & Electricity Company. The light standards retrofitted in 1972 took their cues from the original 1937 version, following the shape of the fixture but also recreating the yellow glow of the original pressure sodium lamp via the fitting of a yellow plastic lens over the new high-pressure sodium lamps (MacDonald and Nadel, *Golden Gate Bridge,* 92).
44. The Design Criteria Report was created by Donald MacDonald Architects who have offered design and aesthetic services for the Golden Gate Bridge since 1980. See, Donald Macdonald Architects, accessed May 16, 2021, http://www.donaldmacdonaldarchitects.com/projects/bridges/ggb.php.
45. See, Jim Eyre, "Movement and Geometry," in Chris Wilkinson, James Eyre and Jim Eyre, *Bridging Art and Science* (London: Booth-Clibborn, 2001, https://www.wilkinsoneyre.com/thoughts/essays/movement-and-geometry.
46. Chris Wilkinson, "Infrastructure as a Cultural Icon," *English Heritage Conservation Bulletin* 65, accessed October 19, 2020, https://www.wilkinsoneyre.com.

47. Millau Viaduct," *Structurae* https://structurae.net/en/structures/millau-viaduct; "France completes tallest bridge," *BBC News* (May 29, 2004) https://www.bbc.co.uk/2/hi/Europe/3759307.stm.
48. Ministère Georges Gillet, "le viaduc de Millau : un ouvrage exceptionnel initié par le ministre de l'équipement," Octobre 17, 2015, http://www.bv.transports.gouv.qc.ca/mono/0981378/05_Viaduc_de_Millau.pdf.
49. Government of France, Décrit du 10 janvier 1995 legiFrance.gouv.fr., https://www.legifrance.gouv.fr/jorf/id/JORFTEXT000000213396.
50. Government of France, Décrit 2001-923 du 8 octobre 2001. https://www.legifrance.gouv.fr/loda/id/JORFTEXT000000224773/.
51. "Millau Viaduct, " Wikipedia.com; "Top Gear TV supercars across France, " Part 4/4 / (series 7 episode 3) TopGear.com BBCworldwide.Ltd, October, 20 2008.
52. Kieran Long, "Millau Viaduct," Icon 021, March 2005, https://www.iconeye.com/icon-021-march-2005/millau-viaduct-icon-021-march-2005
53. Foster + Partners, "Millau Viaduct, " accessed January 3, 2020, http://www.fosterandpartners.com/projects/millau/viaduct/.
54. "Foster and Partners," accessed January 3, 2020, https://www.fostersandpartners.com.
55. Oliver Wainwright, "Sheep and Land Rovers rejoice: Pooley Bridge reunites the Lake District," *The Guardian*, November 22, 2020, accessed January 3, 2021, https://www.theguardian.com/artanddesign/2020/nov/22/pooley-bridge-reunites-the-lake-district; Cambria Crack, accessed January 3, 2021, https://www.facebook.com/knightarchitects/posts/15158285451056751.
56. Wainwright, "Pooley Bridge."
57. Wainwright, "Pooley Bridge."
58. Knight Architects, "New Pooley Bridge, UK," accessed January 3, 2021, https://www.knightarchitects.co.uk/projects/new-pooley-bridge.
59. Much quoted sentiment found in Wainwright and others. See, Hector Beade Pereda, Head of Design at Knight Architects, *Archello*, accessed January 3, 2021, https://www.Archello.com/project/pooley-bridge.
60. "Pooley Bridge," *Archello*, accessed January 3, 2021, https://www.archello.com/project/pooley-bridge 2020.
61. David S. Brown, quoted in *Archello*, accessed January 3, 2020, https://www.Archello.com/project/pooley-bridge.
62. Knight Architects, "About us." *Linkedin*, accessed January 10, 2021, https://www.linkedin.com/company/knight-architects.
63. *Cumbria Crack* accessed January 24, 2021,, https://www.cumbriacrack.com/2017/11/09/new-pooly-bridge-deign-discussed-community.
64. *Archello*, accessed January 20, 2021, https://www.archello.com/project/pooley-bridge,.
65. *Archello*, accessed January 20, 2021, https://www.archello.com/project/pooley-bridge.
66. Knight Architects, *Linkedin*, accessed January 10, 2021, https://www.linkedin.com/company/knight-architects.
67. Knight Architects, accessed January 3, 2021, https://www.knightarchitects.co.uk/studio/clients.
68. Knight Architect, accessed January 23, 2021,. https://www.knightarchitects.co.uk/studio/clients.

10

CASE STUDIES: LARGE SCALE

INTRODUCTION

The final scale of examples that we are examining are those at a very large scale. We term this 'city-scale' in reference to the overall urban implications of these case studies, which are of a neighbourhood or partial city-scale of infrastructural intervention. While there is clearly value in improving the cross section of a street—greening a street with the planting of trees, changing surface treatments and providing more generous sidewalks—there are other urban design transformations which truly enrich the public realm more systemically and/or more comprehensively. Often, these types of interventions are not usually thought of as 'design' because they are so large in scale that the individual's experience of the parts does not always reveal the design quality of the whole. In addition, effects may be 'extra' to basic function or nonessential but are nevertheless intentionally designed to enhance the city socially and culturally. As sociologist Sharon Zukin points out:

> With the disappearance of local manufacturing industries and periodic crises in government and finance, culture is more and more the business of cities - the basis of their tourist attractions and their unique competitive edge. The growth of cultural consumption (of art, food, fashion, music, tourism) and the industries that cater to it, fuels the city's symbolic economy, its visible ability to produce both symbols and space.[1]

While this is both a criticism of the current market competition of cities and their responses, what is significant is that improving the urban realm is important to people who live their lives there or are considering living there. In the same vein, another more extreme but prevalent contemporary example is the tourist district. While these districts are deliberate and transactional in purpose, they nevertheless acknowledge explicitly the value of design. Other examples, such as city-centre seawalls and transit infrastructure are more explicitly public goods, and ostensibly intended for their local residents; however, they may also directly or indirectly service visitors and tourists. While all infrastructure must justify costs, those financed by the public may have a more difficult task in persuading taxpayers to pay for costs incurred by design interventions, making influencing potentially part of the design process. More recently, as described further in the discussion of Rotterdam below, there has been a movement for sustainable development; this prioritizes local concerns while acknowledging that development may also play a role in attracting visitors and, particularly, the 'creative tourist'—the type of tourist willing to explore off the beaten track and more interested in cultural experiences.

THE CHANGING ROLE OF INFRASTRUCTURE IN THE CITY

Many cities now have a financial imperative to make themselves globally competitive and attractive to many constituents (tourists, investors, businesses and residents), not only by providing tax incentives but also by creating a distinctive identity with localized social, cultural and recreational amenities. Currently (post-COVID-19), when normal travel resumes and it is possible to move across the globe quickly and easily and for companies to locate offices internationally, the increasing necessity for cities to compete for talent in an effort to attract both investors and companies will also resume. In this, the advancing Fourth Industrial Revolution, the successful city will attract technology and other companies which can capitalize on rapidly changing technological innovations. These industries are not reliant on rivers, natural resources, or locations near agricultural or industrial production as in the past; instead, they need human talent. And it is often the case that creative responses to existing or new infrastructure play a significant role in urban development schemes.

Globally, many cities are recognizing that attracting companies and the workforce that they need is increasingly important. Becoming an attractive location for companies and their employees entails aspects such as good public transit as well as the less tangible aspects of design that contribute to identification with place and the creation of a successful public realm.

The design capital of the city as a whole comes in many forms; although it can take time for design capital to be realized, there are examples of cities who have been working for decades on enhancing the public realm and can point to the value of design and design intention on a city scale.

INFRASTRUCTURE'S IMPACT ON MAKING CITIES COMPETITIVE IN A GLOBAL MARKETPLACE

The Amazon headquarters competition, held in 2017-18, offers an insight into what successful and expanding technology companies are looking for in a city. As such, it is useful to examine the competition in more detail, especially as it pertains to city-building. Amazon's HQ2 Request for Proposal (RFP) identifies a series of factors on which cities would compete, including available real estate for their buildings, a business-friendly environment, incentives (cash, taxes, etc.) from different levels of government, a highly educated workforce with nearby training and higher education institutions, and a good public transit system as well as access to transportation to large population centres such as San Francisco, Seattle, New York or Washington, D.C. However, the request also asked for information about 'Community/Quality of Life,' which was further elaborated on:

> The Project requires a significant number of employees. We want to invest in a community where our employees will enjoy living, recreational opportunities, educational opportunities, and an overall high quality of life. Tell us what is unique about your community.[2]

Joseph Parilla, of the Brookings Institution, comments that "Amazon also indicates they want a high quality of life and a cultural community fit. These are admittedly subjective concepts, but it seems like Amazon favors sites that resemble urban Seattle—complete with a diversity of housing options and residents, walkability, and transit and entertainment options."[3] Amy Liu, also of the Brookings Institution, observes that a lesson learned from the HQ2 competition was that "[c]ities ought to invest in the attributes that matter to the modern economy," and she identifies technical talent, sustainable placemaking, globally connected infrastructure and diversity as key desirable attributes.[4]

It is clear from the Amazon building competition that the modern economy will be centred in locations where highly educated professionals want to settle because companies need this human talent to excel. The people that these companies seek are themselves looking for an "overall high quality of life," as Amazon puts it in their proposal. How can cities contribute to the creation of a high quality of life for these anticipated residents? Public transit, walkability and sustainability are qualities emphasized in the proposal, and this involves examining infrastructure enhanced by experiential considerations.

Liu comments that Virginia, who won the competition (tied with New York, who subsequently dropped out) took an innovative approach to attracting Amazon:

> Virginia threw into the package more than $1 billion in additional taxpayer funds to build a pipeline of technical workers and improved transportation. This portion of the "subsidy" will not go directly into Amazon's pockets but into Virginia schools, universities, and local agencies. It is nearly twice the amount offered to Amazon, a signal that investing in the local work force is more important than offering sweeteners to Amazon.[5]

This approach invests in the infrastructure of the place and the education of the people living there, enriching the local community and benefitting the region—potentially long past the time when Amazon is superseded by the next corporate juggernaut.

There is nothing explicitly mentioned in the Amazon proposal about cultural differentiation or placemaking. Instead, Amazon describes the outcome they are looking for as a place "where our employees will enjoy living, recreational opportunities, educational opportunities, and an overall high quality of life." They then ask, "Tell us what is unique about your community."[6] Those involved in city building or the academic study of city building, however, recognize the call for 'liveability' and the need for a distinct quality of place embedded deeply in this statement. Liu comments that cities should invest in 'sustainable placemaking' which partly addresses what Amazon is asking for in these statements.

While the Amazon RFP is a clearly articulated example of what a large global technology company is looking for in a city in which they will set up a headquarters, including defining what aspects such as infrastructure and place-defining they feel are important, there are several points which should be questioned. Firstly, Amazon says they are 'investing' in the city but have asked for massive tax breaks (incentives). Secondly, they rate a city on low crime stats, good local schools, higher education institutions, and highly educated "eligible employment pools", all of which seems to undercut their claim that they are looking for a diverse population. Thirdly, there could be consequential gentrification effects from a significantly financed, very large corporation and their employees moving into a town, depending on the scale of the city and the corporation. Overall, it is as yet unclear that the outcome for the city (or cities) chosen will be positive but we are looking at this example for what is considered 'desirable' by a corporation of the Fourth Industrial Revolution.

COPENHAGEN: BICYCLE PATHS AND PUBLIC LIFE

Copenhagen has the enviable reputation of being one of the 'happiest cities' in the world[7, 8] and one of the most liveable cities in the world.[9,10] It is also known as being one of the most bike-friendly cities in the world. Liveability, happiness and activity levels are all related to the use of public space. Here we focus on the infrastructure that enables cycling as an example of what Copenhagen has done right, and then broaden the discussion to the much larger (and less measurable) discussion of improvement in public space of the city. (Figure 10:1)

Copenhagen is known as the 'City of Cyclists'—1.4 million km are cycled per day and there are 412 km of bike paths in Copenhagen. Forty-one per cent of people bike to work in Copenhagen in 2016 and the goal is to increase this by 509% by 2024.[11] Liveability and health outcomes have been related to cycling, and cycling is highly dependent on infrastructure, making the measures of cycling mode share, liveability and health interrelated.

A comparison of Copenhagen with Stockholm—both European cities with similar population, sizes, climates and social environments—shows the bicycle mode share in Stockholm to be 7%[12] as compared to Copenhagen at 41%.[13] In the 1920s and 1930s, the bicycle modal split in these cities was comparable.[14] Copenhagen is denser than Stockholm (6200

10:1 Stroget, Copenhagen, Denmark (ca. 2021).

inhabitants/km2 compared to 4309 inhabitants/km2); however, the impact of density is usually rather small and urban design has shown to have more impact than density.[15] It can be argued that the difference in the modal split between the two cities is more to do with the quality of the infrastructure provided for cycling. Copenhagen has discrete lanes for bicycles—separated from both cars and pedestrians—with specialized crossing signals and protections at interchanges. This type of system provides a higher level of service, improved safety and greater accessibility for cyclists. The city has produced many specialized plans with specific goals for cycling, including the Copenhagen Bicycle Strategy (2011-25), which is a continuation of the Copenhagen Cycle Policy (2002-2012) and the Cycle Priority Plan 2006-16 (City of Copenhagen 2011, 2002 and 2009). Cycling infrastructure has significant design attention, not only in the planning of the routes, the design of traffic signals and the design of the separated lanes themselves, but also in such specialized features as dedicated foot rests at intersections for cyclists and particularized LED lighting, popularly known as the 'Green Wave'. The Green Wave refers to lights placed in the road that signal to cyclists to maintain a constant speed (20 km/h) so that they do not have to stop at intersections along their route.

There are several reasons that the design of bike infrastructure is better in Copenhagen than elsewhere: social priorities, governance organization, design influence and guidance (which we will discuss further). One obvious example of social priorities is that Denmark's economy is not constrained by the automotive industry in the same way as Sweden. Sweden's automotive industry indirectly contributes to more investment being made in car-related infrastructure; the political economy connected to this industry is also powerful.[16] Governance organization refers to the organization of the municipality and its internal governance. In Copenhagen, the Urban Planning and Transportation Engineering group is under one umbrella, whereas in Stockholm the Urban Planning and Transportation Engineering groups are different entities. Organizational goals are therefore not so tightly integrated in Stockholm and knowledge exchange between the departments is not as free-flowing due to fewer interactions on a daily and weekly basis.[17]

Design influence and guidance is perhaps the most interesting aspect for our discussion. There has been a significant collaboration extending back decades between Danish architect and urban designer Jan Gehl and the City of Copenhagen. Gehl has become internationally renowned for the design of excellent public space via his teaching (at the School of Architecture at the Royal Danish Academy of Fine Arts and elsewhere) and through his publication and practice (as Gehl Architects from 2000). Referencing Gehl's public life research and teaching, Bente Frost, the mayor of Copenhagen from 1994-1997, states: "Without the public life studies from the School of Architecture, we politicians wouldn't have had the courage to implement the many projects to increase the attractiveness of the city."[18]

Klaus Bondam, former mayor of Copenhagen (2006-2009), attributes Gehl with significant contributions to life in Copenhagen:

> Jan Gehl's deep involvement in new urban policies in Copenhagen have taken our city to a new level, serving as an example of how a future sustainable and people-centered development isn't a contradiction to economic growth; an example that many cities worldwide are inspired by today. Thanks to Jan Gehl-and Gehl Architects—the question and challenges of creating good urban life is integrated completely in all relevant Copenhagen policies today.[19]

Gehl's focus on the design of the public space in the city has changed over time and can be classified into three different time frames: Phase One (1960-1980) focussed on pedestrian streets and walking, while Phase Two (1980-2000) focussed on creating attractive locations to visit in the city, emphasizing places to enjoy café culture, social and cultural events, and the city in general. Phase Three (2000 onward) focuses on sports, recreation and leisure with emphasis on movement and activity of all types including, of course, biking. Through all phases, Gehl has worked in close collaboration with the City of Copenhagen and has carried out countless studies on the city's public spaces; these studies have been used as the basis for providing urban design recommendations to the city.

A large influence on Copenhagen, and by now many more cities, is Gehl's insistence that data is collected on public life, pedestrian numbers and bicycle numbers in much the same way that traffic engineers count traffic. His use of data to measure the success or failure of interventions in public space gives statistical power to the design changes enacted. As such, design can be measured—not in the way we are suggesting with 'design capital', but in tangible ways that can point to success or failure or the need for further action.[20] The power that traffic engineers wield is largely the result of having data to support their infrastructure decisions. Gehl, and then the City of Copenhagen, likewise supported the design of bicycle routes by their efforts to count both bicycle and vehicular traffic in order to determine the effectiveness of bicycle infrastructure and the need for lanes and intersection improvements.

The approach to bicycle infrastructure design can be seen from Gehl Architects blog posts:

> [T]here is more to a cyclist's experience than pedaling - there are social interactions as well. If bicycle facilities are designed with the acknowledgement that cyclists experience the world like pedestrians then they will foster social interaction. While we commonly think of the proven benefits cycling confers to personal health, environmental quality, and even the economy, this research suggests that when properly designed for, cycling can provide the additional benefits of contributing to the vitality and livability of a city.[21]

Consideration of the design of bicycle infrastructure in public space is only one small aspect of Gehl's and the city's design considerations—others include places for people to sit and watch others, interact and spend time in an enjoyable way. The intention is to have people linger in the city, enjoying spending their time in public space and socially interacting.[22]

The design of the public space of Copenhagen demonstrates design capital at a city scale. The design consideration and approach brought to the city through Gehl's research and the City's adoption of his design intent has resulted in policy and infrastructure that has been invaluable to Copenhagen—not just to its reputation and tourist attraction, but to every citizen of the country. The public space is designed for everyone and benefits everyone and all are invited to sit, walk and bike in the city. It provides an exemplar for the world in terms of public space and infrastructure design for the city.

Bjarke Ingels Group's (BIG) design of CopenHill (also known as the Amager Resource Centre) in 2017, extends the ideas of the liveable city via the design of public spaces introduced by Gehl.[23] (Figure 10:2) The resource centre is a power plant providing a waste to clean energy facility

10:2 Bjarke Ingels Group (BIG). CopenHill (2019), Copenhagen, Denmark.

on an industrial waterfront in Copenhagen; however, the utilitarian facility is augmented with social amenity and public space. Tree-lined bikeways, hiking trails, a ski slope, climbing wall and garden supplement the roof and facades. (Figure 10:3) While it is a single building, it functions within the larger city, not only by providing the district with heating for 150,000 homes a year,[24] but also by bringing the urban features of Copenhagen, such as bicycle paths and parkland, to an area otherwise deficient in them. Its design contributes to sustainability via both its technical accomplishments and its social amenities.[25] The architects designed it to be "economically, environmentally and socially profitable" and instead of considering it "an isolated architectural object [they] consider the assignment to design a façade as an opportunity for the local context."[26]

VANCOUVER: THE SEAWALL AND REPURPOSING EXISTING INFRASTRUCTURE

What began as a necessary engineering work to protect a specific stretch of urban park shoreline from further erosion, especially after storm damage on the eve of WWI, became a cross-programmed unifying feature of a downtown core: iconic landmark, urban symbol, much replicated urban design feature—and tourist attraction.[27] (Figure 10.3) The Vancouver seawall was first conceived as a practical defence against erosion along the heavily used sea channel off the coast of the substantial 405-hectare Stanley Park, a coastal peninsula on the western extremity of Vancouver city centre. Although initiated as an urgent remedial action against the natural force of tides, ordinary weather and frequent storms, it was also realized according to the prevailing cultural notions defining a park. Many among the earliest Park Board Commissioners were knowledgeable advocates of landscape design and brought this awareness to their deliberations on the seawall.[28] The role of the seawall as a larger urban amenity was realized slowly; a somewhat piecemeal approach to strategic shoreline protection became a more comprehensive park feature responsive to the changing conceptions of an urban national park as romantic wilderness retreat or recreational amenity. From its inception, the park was conceived with "aesthetic, cultural and social motivations as well."[29] As a part of the park, the seawall shared in these motivations, and design contributed to their expression. While the wall protected the integrity of the park lands, its appended walkway extended the sinuous path system of the initially envisioned romantic wilderness park and then accommodated more active recreation as the park's use was expanded.

The official encircling of the peninsular park began between 1916 and 1918, although the Stanley Park seawall, largely completed by 1971, did not include the beaches along the south-east until 1980. Its construction was sporadic, dependent on short-term funding by civic and federal governments, philanthropists and labour opportunities.[30,31] Over time the seawall was adjusted to accommodate changing expectations of a park. It was widened from its original 6 feet to 20 feet in the late 1970s due to its popularity and greatly diversified user-groups: pedestrians, cyclists, in-line skaters and skateboarders.

In this development two aspects are noteworthy. First, from its inception the design of the seawall was deliberately considered. The wall was given a generous, carefully fitted stone coursing atop its granite or concrete base and its trajectory was curved to the topography. Its ample depth offered impromptu seating as well as a protective barrier. This attention to material, detail and form remains consistent through the decades. The wall's rough-hewn granite and sinuous shape also conformed to the idea of rusticity and its paved walkway curved to afford picturesque views of mountains, ocean or harbour in keeping with the romantic notion of a wilderness park, although increasingly accommodating more active use. Second, its design (as well as its success as a public space) resulted in its expansion beyond a park feature to inform city-wide public space design.

When the industrial lands along a waterway to the south-east of Stanley Park were identified as a potential site for urban regeneration in response to both increasing population and post-industrial restructuring, one of the earliest features identified in its plan was a seawall. False Creek's seawall was proposed three years before the False Creek South Development Plan was announced in 1974.[32] It coincided with the introduction of a new planning regime at city hall that emphasized design review as well as greater public input.[33] It supported design-led (rather than developer- or business-led) design and thus the presence of a seawall, with its public amenities, was favoured by city planners.[34] The repurposing of the seawall as urban-wide public amenity coincided with the Vancouver urban planning department's new emphasis on design development in the early

10:3 Vancouver Seawall (ca. 1917-ongoing), Vancouver, Canada. Seawall near English Bay. Photo: Julian Prior.

1970s. The seawall would become factored into private development costs and an integral part of site design along the waterfront of the downtown core by the 1980s.

The seawall and variously scaled waterfront parks became part of the city's design philosophy.[35] It was highlighted in the City of Vancouver Shoreline Treatment study in the early 1990s[36] to develop both generic and site-specific approaches to Vancouver's large tide variations (up to 5 m). Among the proposed and preferred solutions was a version of the Stanley Park seawall, with the added value of viewpoints, piers and benches, all dimensioned to the megaprojects developed along the shoreline: False Creek North, Coal Harbour and False Creek Southwest.[37] False Creek North and Coal Harbour included 4.5 km of seawall and cycle paths as well as public art, seating and viewing facilities and 25 hectares of public parkland. As urban historian John Punter argues, this shoreline seawall figured in Vancouver's planning success:

> It has reclaimed its derelict industrial waterfront for public recreational use, completing the links in more that 20 kilometers of seawall and walk/cycleway encircling downtown, and linking urban and suburban beaches, parks and leisure and recreational facilities. These amenities are transforming the city into a resort in its own right, quite apart from enriching the quality of life for citizens.[38]

The seawall was also extended by the city beyond the park and new waterfront developments to traverse existing neighbourhoods as it connected waterfront public parks and beaches. These extensions were designed to augment the physical and social characteristics of the site. The seawall has morphed over time, with variants including asphalt paths edging sandy beachfront, greenways along decommissioned rail lines and boardwalks along naturalized wetlands, although invariably recalling its antecedent, the park seawall.[39] In one section the seawall becomes a narrow earth path following the shoreline at mid-height along the cliff wall paralleled by a multi-lane, multi-modal greenway above at street level, both affording picturesque views of mountains, ocean or harbour.

While the seawall is a major tourist attraction, it is also an amenity enjoyed by local residents and currently plays a role in the sustainability goals of the city. Beyond Stanley Park, the seawall extends past properties with water views; owing to their location and views, these properties demand premium prices by the local and global real-estate and property development industries. The extension of the Seaside Greenway from False Creek to westside beaches through an elite neighbourhood sparked resident opposition to the cost (approximately $6 million), imposed vehicle restrictions, loss of mature trees and the intrusion of large numbers of users.[40] Nevertheless, the extension of the Seaside Greenway—a transformed seawall—afforded citywide public access to beach and park leisure spaces. Its seating, planting and incorporation of views from enroute pocket parks recalls the initial Stanley Park seawall, both its nature-viewing practices and the debates regarding access, for whom, for what purposes and at what financial cost was this infrastructure in the public good.

The seawall has provoked controversy over its best use: passive contemplative space, sociable promenade or active bikeway. It fuelled discussion about the multiplicity of roles infrastructure might play simultaneously. And in debates about its width, material, accoutrements and context, the significance of design in infrastructure was highlighted. These debates continue and the social and cultural value recognized in its several incarnations acknowledge the design capital of its precedent, the seawall. This seawall amenity became the basis for thinking about infrastructure differently—not just as erosion prevention in a park, but as a more general urban resource. The secondary or unintended leisure outcome of the seawall in Vancouver has, over time, become its primary reason for being. The public space amenity and urban connectivity that the seawall has provided have also been recognized as advantageous for today's urban development: it is understood to further sustainability objectives and economic development by encouraging cycling, tourism, and amenities for residents. While the seawalls and greenways serve local transit and recreation, they are also serviced by bike rental outlets encouraging a tourist economy.

The seawall is infrastructure that successfully provides spatial amenity, and acquired symbolic and social value, and in its current varied forms serves both local residents and visitors, sustainability ambitions and a tourist economy. It demonstrates the ability of infrastructure to acquire value as a major element in the design vocabulary of the city. Vancouver has been voted the sixth most liveable city in the world by the Economist Intelligence Unit in 2019. This liveability was illustrated with an image of the False North Creek seawall. The Stanley Park seawall and Arbutus Greenway feature as among the top things to do in the city in the Lonely Planet guide to Vancouver.

ROTTERDAM: A CITY WITH A VISION OF THE FUTURE

Some cities have recognized the need to create an environment to attract talented young professionals; Rotterdam has made it an explicit goal since 2009. The city deliberately set out to be attractive to young, well-educated professionals, with the intention of revitalizing the city by this means. Even before making it an explicit goal, Rotterdam aimed to attract young workers by creating a vibrant area via cross-scale design. Prior to the 1980s, Rotterdam was considered a 'dull' city with limited cultural offerings. It is through design that the city is now considered 'the Capital of Cool' by CNN Travel and was named one of the ten top cities in Lonely Planet's 2016 'best in travel.'[41]

Rotterdam's Kop van Zuid district (Southern Headland) is a large redevelopment project situated on the south side of the Nieuwe Mass River and across from Rotterdam city centre. Previously the site of a port, it had become outdated and largely vacant owing to the use of larger ships and the consequent relocation of the port to accommodate these vessels; the land became derelict of any industrial activity by the mid-1980s. The Kop van Zuid project (1993-2000) included mixed-use, mixed-tenure housing, and new road, tram and metro connections to the rest of the city; these connections include the Erasmus Bridge, which is now a representative feature of Rotterdam. (Figure 10.4) The area also includes offices, restaurants, cultural attractions and residential activity.[42] Prior to the mid-1980s, the desire was to build only social housing in the area but this policy was changed by Riek Bakker, head of urban development for the City of Rotterdam at the time. She explains:

> I noticed that they only wanted to build social housing, and when I spoke to the people there, they did not gain any improvement from it [the social housing]. So, the stores and schools got worse. Everything got worse. There are few spin-offs [with social housing] ... it doesn't provide enough amenities. People don't have enough

money to spend. So you have to ensure that you provide other things.[43]

Rotterdam South had historically accommodated the port and working-class neighbourhoods, differentiating them from the socially and economically more diversified city centre across the river to the north. This created a divide—both physical and psychological—between the north and south sides of Rotterdam. As such, the make-up of the new development as well as the infrastructural connection between the two sides had to be considered very carefully and this consideration had to be carried through to the final product.

Brian Doucet argues that much of the success of the Kop van Zuid project in Rotterdam "lies in the strong vision and goal setting of key municipal leaders. This is combined with the fact that the leaders have been able to see the project through over a number of decades and have taken a more long-term view of the redevelopment."[44] He also states:

> The Kop van Zuid and its related infrastructure have helped to unify the city and Rotterdam now has a middle-class neighborhood which has proved to be a popular place to live. Office and leisure functions, though slower to develop, have, in the years leading up to the current economic crisis, been built by the private sector. Although the project has taken longer than its proponents would have liked, when measured against the goals formulated by the municipality and especially when compared to other international waterfront projects, the Kop van Zuid can be seen as a success.[45]

The vision for the project had four goals: unify north and south sides of the city, balance the exclusively working-class housing with the creation of new middle-class housing, create a new business centre and competitive business environment, and enhance the social benefits for economically disadvantaged neighbourhoods of Rotterdam South via better educational opportunities, amenities and transportation.[46] Infrastructure was clearly central to the success of the vision of Kop van Zuid, as was design.

The design vision did not happen without significant effort from many designers. An international architectural competition was held in 1981-82 in conjunction with the Architecture International Rotterdam festival, although none of the entries secured much support. In 1986, the appointment of Riek Bakker resulted in a renewed vision for the city being developed, including the Kop van Zuid. Bakker is largely credited for the area's turnaround and her process was thorough, beginning with identifying of places where interventions could be quickly realized. Dutch planner Tuen Koolhaas was commissioned to devise a comprehensive plan for the area which resulted in the notion of a "collage city" with the aim of quality, accessibility, cross-subsidization and integration. Advocacy for the scheme required economic as well as social and design goals, and this included elected local officials, a dedicated project team, and the staff and resources of the City Development Corporation and the Department of Urban Planning and Housing. Control remained within the various departments and jurisdiction of the city government.[47] To guarantee the quality of design in Kop van Zuid, an external quality team of architectural and urban experts was established.[48]

To achieve the aims of equity, accessibility and cross-subsidization, the city retained control of the project and maintained landownership in an effort to avoid hyper-speculation. Partnership with private companies included national and international property developers as well as local housing associations. Mutually beneficial outcomes were sought which would strengthen trust and a shared goal.[49] To attract private investors who were reluctant to develop office space, the municipality built government office space as an enticement to private investment.

The initial aim of the infrastructure design of Kop van Zuid was accessibility—physical and social. It focussed on transportation and public space as supports for mixed use and socially diverse development. Physical accessibility was established via road construction and public transport; the iconic and much acclaimed Erasmus Bridge linked the area to the city centre via a new major artery, while other new roads connected neighbourhoods; a distinctive tram system and a new metro station assisted public transit. Views to the water were facilitated by a dockside restructured with public promenades and public art. Visibility was enhanced by minimizing poles and signs.[50] Pedestrians, cyclists and vehicles shared a continuous road surface, without barriers between them. Streetscapes were newly serviced with level street crossings, some dedicated tram lanes were grassed, streets were lined with trees, and new lighting was installed.[51] New metro and tram services were given distinctive design and defunct buildings were transformed from supports for heavy industry to infrastructure for the tourist and leisure industries. These various scales of design decision, from street furniture to bridges and iconic buildings, to neighbourhood and city, were essential to the aspirations of Kop van Zuid to attract investment while maintaining a social mix.

More recently, Rotterdam has embarked on a project of "Inner City as a Lounge" (Gemeente Rotterdam 2008) in recognition of the advantages of high-quality spaces for socializing and short stays in a city, either for fun or for business. The strategy is to enhance public spaces and involves six conceptual areas: "residential milieus; culture and leisure; street fronts and the waterfront; green and parks; 'power to the pedestrian'; and use of architecture, cultural heritage and 'Rotterdam themes in public spaces.'"[52] Resembling what has been described by some scholars as a 'creative city' approach, it is an attempt to attract innovative workers to participate in the burgeoning creative economy.[53] Romein and Trip make the case that due to societal, economic and technological changes:

> [A] consumer market has emerged in advanced economies that is driven by an increasingly diverse and volatile demand for goods and services. Particularly the consumption of symbolic values and experiences, and the diversity and authenticity of goods and services have become important. In a broad perspective, urban atmospheres and spaces are also considered such 'goods'.[54]

Romein and Trip use Rotterdam's initiatives as an example of this and conclude,

> Current research on creative city development pays little attention to the role of intangibles and amenities, and more particularly how these are appreciated by different groups of creative talent. Surely these issues are hard to grasp, but they for a large part define the qualities (plural) of place of cities, including the growing importance of symbolic values.[55]

This recognition of the significance of symbolic values and the atmospheric aspects of urban experience for economic and social success highlights the importance of design capital.

Scholars identify Rotterdam's development, including Kop van Zuid, as a successful example of 'sustainable tourism' —namely tourism that is co-created with local stakeholders and entrepreneurs while creating facilities which both local residents and visitors enjoy.[56] This often results in tourism which is considered more authentic for the visitor as well. Rotterdam is often referenced as an example of creative placemaking and creative tourism. UNESCO (2006) defines creative tourism as "travel directed towards an engaged and authentic experience, with participative learning in the arts, heritage, or special character of a place, and it provides a connection with those who reside in this place and create this living culture."[57] Creative placemaking is considered a process in which "partners from public, private, non-profit and community sectors strategically shape the physical and social character of a neighbourhood, town, city or region around arts and cultural activities."[58]

This change of urban image from that of the 1980s, when Rotterdam was considered 'dull', to that of now is a primary example of creative placemaking and sustainable tourism. It is an example of a very well-articulated and carried out city-scale venture which resulted in a better city for residents and visitors alike, but without excessive gentrification.

CONCLUSION

City-scale infrastructures introduce a complex array of stakeholders and ambitions. While the scope for design is commensurately large, it is also complicated by its multiple roles within the city. Infrastructure has played a major role in the reimagining of a post-industrial or post-Fordist city and is of critical importance to the various design propositions as 'creative' cities seek to attract high-tech industries and 'sustainable tourist' destinations support cultural and tourist industries. These large-scale endeavours usually involve complex public-private partnerships and hence considerations of both constituents and shareholders. Consequently, the demands on infrastructure have changed: it must now perform multiple tasks simultaneously in the interest of accommodating an intended workforce, supporting an existing one and attracting tourists. It must offer value for money but also express symbolic values, offer experiential or atmospheric qualities, and is often called upon to contribute to placemaking. Success in achieving these aims is one indicator that design capital is being produced or is in circulation.

FINAL WORDS

We hope that through these examples, from small to large scale, that the significance of what is at stake can be seen. To consider cultural and social aspects in the design of infrastructure is something that every part of our cities deserves. Every neighbourhood should have design consideration for their infrastructure, as should every element in a city; in fact, everything we build in our larger environment merits this attention. All too often, however, infrastructure design only engages with social and cultural matters when it is forced to by angry citizens. These citizens sense the loss to themselves and future generations of the collective expression of their values. Financial prudence and pragmatism may express the values of economy and efficiency, but those are not the values that people desire in their living environments, nor are they the values that one would choose to leave as our legacy to future generations. We hope this book gives everyone a tool with which to identify and name these values and, if necessary, to give design an explicit economic value. In essence, we are giving design a voice by giving it a name: design capital.

NOTES

1. Sharon Zukin, *The Cultures of Cities* (Cambridge MA: Blackwell, 1995).
2. Amazon.com Archived, "Amazon's HQ2," Amazon HQ2, September 20, 2017, 2, https://web.archive.org/web/20170928031837/https://www.amazon.com/b?ie=UT-F8&node=17044620011.
3. Joseph Parilla, "Which Cities Are Well Positioned to Land Amazon's HQ2?," *Brookings* (blog), September 8, 2017, https://www.brookings.edu/blog/the-avenue/2017/09/08/which-cities-are-well-positioned-to-land-amazons-hq2/.
4. Amy Liu, "Big Tech in the City: Amazon in Arlington and the Future of Regional Economic Development" (SACRPH, Arlington, Virginia, November 2, 2019).
5. Amy Liu, "Opinion | A Better Way to Attract Amazon's Jobs," *The New York Times*, February 16, 2019, sec. Opinion, https://www.nytimes.com/2019/02/16/opinion/amazon-new-york.html.
6. Amazon.com Archived, "Amazon's HQ2."
7. National Geographic UK, "Copenhagen: The Happiest City in the World?," *National Geographic*, April 29, 2018, https://www.nationalgeographic.co.uk/travel/2018/04/copenhagen-happi-est-city-world.
8. "Cities and Happiness: A Global Ranking and Analysis," accessed January 7, 2021, http://worldhappiness.report/.
9. Copenhagen Capacity, "10 Good Rea-sons to Invest in Greater Copenhagen," accessed January 7, 2021, https://www.copcap.com/invest-in-greater-copenha-gen/10-good-reasons.
10. "Global Livability Ranking," accessed January 7, 2021, https://www.eiu.com/topic/liveability.
11. "Copenhagen City of Cyclists - Facts and Figures 2017," *Cycling Embassy of Denmark* (blog), July 4, 2017, http://www.cycling-embassy.dk/2017/07/04/copen-hagen-city-cyclists-facts-figures-2017/. "Copenhagen City of Cyclists. Facts and Figures 2017," https://international.kk.dk/sites/international.kk.dk/files/velo-city_handout.pdf.
12. "Insights City Mobility Index," Deloitte Insights, accessed January 7, 2021, https://www2.deloitte.com/us/en/insights/focus/transportation.html.
13. "Insights City Mobility Index."
14. Till Koglin, "Organisation Does Matter–Planning for Cycling in Stockholm and Copenhagen," Transport Policy 39 (2015): 56.
15. Koglin, "Organization Does Matter," 56.
16. Koglin, "Organization Does Matter, "61.
17. Koglin, "Organization Does Matter," 60.
18. Annie Matan and Peter Newman, *People Cities: The Life and Legacy of Jan Gehl* (Island Press, 2016), 48.
19. Matan and Newman, *People Cities*, 69.
20. Matan and Newman, *People Cities*, 60.
21. "Designing for the Social Experience of Bicycling - Gehl," accessed January 8, 2021. https://gehlpeople.com/blog/designing-for-the-social-experi-ence-of-bicycling.
22. Jan Gehl and Lord Richard Rogers, *Cities for People* (Washington DC, UNITED STATES: Island Press, 2010), 231, http://ebookcentral.proquest.com/lib/ubc/detail.action?docID=3317503.
23. The idea that the work of Ingels and Gehl shares similar principles is expressed by both Gehl and Thomas Ermacora in "Cities for the People of Tomorrow/ Bjarke Ingles + Jan Gehl + Thomas Ermacora December 9, 2020, accessed May 4, 2021, https://www.youtube.com/watch?v=ESNJu7aulK8
24. Lizzie Crook, "BIG opens Copenhill power plant and ski slope in Copenha-gen," *Dezeen*, October 8, 2019, accessed May 4, 2021, https://www.dezeen.com/2019/10/08/big-copenhill-power-plant-ski-slope-in-copenhagen/.
25. Crook, "BIG opens Copenhill."
26. Bjarke Ingels Group (BIG) website, accessed May 4, 2021, https://big.dk/#projects-arc.
27. Sean Kheraj. *Inventing Stanley Park: An Environmental History* (Vancouver: UBC Press, 2013), 13.
28. W.S. Rawlings, student of Allen Shake-spear Wooton, landscape architect and Park Board Secretary and then Com-missioner 1912-1936, was a supporter of the marine walkway. R. Steele, *First 100 years, 22.* English Landscape architect, Thomas Mawson visited Vancouver

and provided plans for segments of the park in 1912 and was influential in the construction of the seawall. See, Patricia Roy, *Vancouver: An Illustrated History,* 106. See, Alyssa Mulat, Our Park: An Historical Geography of Stanley Park from its Closest Neighbours, UBC Geography 429 UBC, 2018. Clavert Vaux and Frederick Law Olmsted and their design of Central Park were influential among the Park's first committee. See, Kheraj, *Inventing Stanley Park,* 96.

29. Kheraj, *Inventing Stanley Park*, 11.
30. The Federal government could be asked for funds because the harbour and waterways were part of Federal jurisdiction. Stanley Park was situated on land leased to the city by the Federal government, hence the shared financing. Elsewhere there was overlapping municipal, provincial and federal designation, for example Granville Island. A Calgary-based charity offered funding for widening the seawall as a solution to conflict between pedestrians and cyclists if matched by municipal funding in the 1970s. In the 1920s and 30s the seawall was part of a government sponsored make-work programme.
31. "Five Things You Didn't Know about the Vancouver Seawall," *Vancouver is Awesome,"* November 16, 2016, www.vancouverisawesome.com/2016/11/16/vancojver-seawall.
32. City of Vancouver, "False Creek South: Topic Workshop 1: History + Context, accessed November 11, 2019, https://vancouver.ca/files/cov/false-creek-south-history-and-context-workshop-presentation.pdf.
33. John Punter, *The Vancouver Achievement: Urban Planning and Design* (Vancouver: The University of British Columbia Press, 2003), 18.
34. Punter, *The Vancouver Achievement*, 28.
35. Punter, *The Vancouver Achievement*, 35.
36. Vancouver City Planning Department Vancouver 1991m.
37. Punter, *The Vancouver Achievement,* 202, 233.
38. Punter, *The Vancouver Achievement,* 346.
39. Ken Ohrn, "Seaside Greenway Completion and Upgrade," *Pricetags*, accessed April 23, 2021, https://pricetags.ca/2016/04/28/seaside-greenway-completion-and-upgrade/. Ohrn, for example, identifies the Greenway as part of the seawall development.
40. Ohrn, "Seaside Greenway"; CBC News "$6 M Kitsilano bike route project gets the green light," posted July 30, 2013, accessed April 23, 2021, https://www.cbc.ca/news/canada/british-columbia/6m-kitsilano-bike-route-project-gets-green-light-1.1399365; City of Vancouver "Seaside Greenway Completion and York Street Bikeway: Phase 1 of Point Grey-Cornwall Active Transportation Corridor," accessed April 23, 2021, https://vancouver.ca/files/cov/seaside-greenway-completion-york-bikeway-2013-jul.pdf.
41. Shirley Nieuwland and Mariangela Lavanga, "The Consequences of Being 'the Capital of Cool'. Creative Entrepreneurs and the Sustainable Development of Creative Tourism in the Urban Context of Rotterdam," *Journal of Sustainable Tourism*, 2020, 2.a.
42. Brian Doucet, "Variations of the Entrepreneurial City: Goals, Roles and Visions in Rotterdam's Kop van Zuid and the Glasgow Harbour Megaprojects," *International Journal of Urban and Regional Research* 37, no. 6 (2013): 2039, https://doi.org/10.1111/j.1468-2427.2012.01182.x.
43. Riek Bakker, quoted in interview with Brian Doucet, "Variations", 2040.
44. Doucet, "Variations," 2036.
45. Doucet, «Variations,» 2036.
46. Doucet, "Variations," 2040.
47. Nicholas Falk, "Case Study for Kop Van Zuid, Rotterdam," Regeneration in European Cities: Making Connections (Joseph Rowntree Foundation, 2008), 20, http://urbed.coop/sites/default/files/Case%20Study%20for%20Kop%20Van%20Zuid,%20Rotterdam.pdf.
48. Falk, "Case Study for Kop Van Zuid," 20, http://urbed.coop/sites/default/files/Case%20Study%20for%20Kop%20Van%20Zuid,%20Rotterdam.pdf.
49. Doucet, "Variations," 2042.
50. Marco van Hoek (Urban and Economic-Development Ltd.), Regeneration in European Cities: Case Study of Kop van Zuid, Rotterdam (April 2007, updated March 2008), 25.
51. Van Hoek, Regeneration in European Cities, 24.
52. Arie Romein and Jan Jacob Trip, "Key Elements of Creative City Development: An

Assessment of Local Policies in Amsterdam and Rotterdam," *City Futures' 09*, 4-6 June 2009, Madrid, 2009, 12.

53. It was a popular concept particularly promoted by Richard Florida (2002), while academics have been fairly critical of the idea and particularly the non-critical promotion of the idea without sufficient consideration of aspects such as gentrification.
54. Romein and Trip, "Key Elements," 3.
55. Romein and Trip, "Key Elements," 15.
56. Nieuwland and Lavanga, " 'the Capital of Cool'," 2.
57. UNESCO Creative Cities Network, "Towards Sustainable Strategies for Creative Tourism. Discussion Report of the Planning Meeting for 2008 International Conference on Creative Tourism," New Mexico, USA, 2006.
58. Ann Markusen and Anne Gadwa, *Creative Placemaking* (National Endowment for the Arts Washington, DC, 2010).

BIBLIOGRAPHY

Abu-Lughod, Janet, ed. *From Urban Village to East Village: The Battle for New York's Lower East Side*. Oxford: Blackwell, 1994.

Adam, Robert. "Globalization and Architecture." *Architectural Review* 222, no. 1332 (February 2002).

Aga Khan Award for Architecture. "Aga Khan Award for Architecture (1987-89 Cycle)." Accessed September 9, 2020. https://www.akdn.org/architecture/project/institut-du-monde-arabe.

Allen, Stan. *Points and Lines: Diagrams and Projects for the City*. New York: Princeton Architectural Press, 1999.

Allen, Stan, Meredith Baber, and MIT Center for Advanced Urbanism, eds. *Infrastructural Monument*. First edition. New York: Princeton Architectural Press, 2016.

Amazon.com Archived. "Amazon's HQ2." Amazon HQ2, September 20, 2017. https://web.archive.org/web/20170928031837/https://www.amazon.com/b?ie=UTF8&node=17044620011.

"An Example of Structural Art: The Salginatobel Bridge of Robert Maillart." *Journal of the Society of Architectural Historians* 33, no. 1 (March 1974): 61–72.

Appadurai, Arjun. *Globalization*. Durham and London: Duke University Press, 2001.

"Are These the World's Best Public Toilets?" Accessed November 18, 2020. https://www.visitnorway.com/plan-your-trip/travel-tips-a-z/norwegian-scenic-routes/worlds-best-toilets/.

Arrow, Kenneth, Robert Solow, Paul R Portney, Edward E Leamer, Roy Radner, Howard Schuman, and others. "Report of the NOAA Panel on Contingent Valuation." *Federal Register* 58, no. 10 (1993): 4601–14.

Atkinson, Rowland, and Gary Bridge, eds. Gentrification in a *Global Context: The New Urban Colonialism*. New York and London: Routledge, 2005.

Ballon, Hilary. *The Paris of Henri IV: Architecture and Urbanism*. Cambridge MA and London: The MIT Press, 1991.

Banham, Reyner. *Megastructures: Urban Futures of the Recent Past*. New York: Harper and Row, 1976.

———. *Theory and Design in the First Machine Age*. 2d ed. New York: Praeger, 1967.

Batt, H. William. "Infrastructure: Etymology and Import." *Journal of Professional Issues in Engineering* 110, no. 1 (January 1984). https://doi.org/htpps://doi.org/10.1061/(ASCE)1052-3928(1984)110:1(1).

Bélanger, Pierre. "Landscape as Infrastructure." *Landscape Journal* 28, no. 1 (2009): 79–95.

———. *Landscape as Infrastructure*. Routledge, 2017.

———. *Landscape Infrastructure:*

Urbanism beyond Engineering. Wageningen University, 2013.
Bell, Daniel. *The Coming of Post-Industrial Society: A Venture in Social Forecasting*. New York: Basic Books, 1976.
Bergström, Anders. "Architecture and the Rise of Practice in Education." *Architectural Theory Review* 19, no. 1 (2014). https://www.tandfonline.com/doi/abs/10.1080/13264826.2014.894604.
"Bilbao City Report." Accessed May 18, 2021. http://eprints.lse.ac.uk/3624/1/Bilbao_city_report_(final).pdf.
Billington, David P. *The Tower and the Bridge: The New Art of Structural Engineering*. Princeton NJ: Princeton University Press, 1983.
Bishop, Richard C, and Thomas A Heberlein. "Measuring Values of Extramarket Goods: Are Indirect Measures Biased?" *American Journal of Agricultural Economics* 61, no. 5 (1979): 926–30.
Black, John, Nigar Hashimzade, and Gareth Myles. *A Dictionary of Economics*. Oxford University Press, 2012.
Blundell-Jones, Peter. "Implicit and Explicit." In *Architectural History and the Studio*. London: ?uestion Press, 1966.
Borden, Iain. "Architecture, Not." In *Architectural History and the Studio*. London: ?uestion Press, n.d.
Bourdieu, Pierre. *Outline of a Theory of Practice*. Translated by Richard Nice. Cambridge, UK: Cambridge University Press, 1977.
———. "The Forms of Capital." In *Handbook of Theory and Research for the Sociology of Education*, edited by J. Richard. Westport CT.: Greenwood, 1986.
Brookshire, David S, Mark A Thayer, William D Schulze, and Ralph C d'Arge. "Valuing Public Goods: A Comparison of Survey and Hedonic Approaches." *The American Economic Review* 72, no. 1 (1982): 165–77.
Brown, Hillary. *Next Generation Infrastructure*. Washington, DC: Island Press, 2014.
Brown, Jeffrey. *Transportation Decision Making: Principles of Project Evaluation and Programming: Kumares C. Sinha and Samuel Labi. John Wiley & Sons, Hoboken, NJ, 2007. 576 Pages. $135*. Taylor & Francis, 2008.
Brown, Thomas C, Patricia A Champ, Richard C Bishop, and Daniel W McCollum. "Which Response Format Reveals the Truth about Donations to a Public Good?" *Land Economics*, 1996, 152–66.
Bryne, J.P. "Two Cheers for Gentrification." *Harvard Law Journal* 46, no. 3 (2003): 405–32.
Bunnell, Tim. "Views From Above and Below: The Petronas Twin Towers AND/IN Contesting Visions of

Development in Contemporary Malaysia." *Singapore Journal of Tropical Geography* 20, no. 1 (1999).
Burchard, John E. "Some Keys to Pandora's Jar." *Journal of Architectural Education (1947-1974)* 14, no. 2 (1959): 13–21. https://doi.org/10.2307/1424014.
———. "Some Keys to Pandora's Jug." *Journal of Architectural Education (1947-74* 14, no. 2 (Autumn) 2015 1959). https://www.jstor.org/stable/1424014.
Burkay, Pasin. "Rethinking the Design Studio-Centered Architectural Education: A Case Study at Schools of Architecture in Turkey." *The Design Journal: An International Journal for All Aspects of Design* 20, no. sup.1 (2017). https://doi.org/10.1080/14606925.2017.1352656.
Butler, Tim, and Garry Robson. "Social Capital, Gentrification and Neighbourhood Change in London: A Comparison of Three South London Neighbourhoods." *Urban Studies* 38, no. 12 (2001).
Capacity, Copenhagen. "10 Good Reasons to Invest in Greater Copenhagen." Accessed January 7, 2021. https://www.copcap.com/invest-in-greater-copenhagen/10-good-reasons.
Carlhian, Jean Paul. "The Ecole Des Beaux-Arts: Modes and Manners." *Journal of Architectural Education* 33, no. 2 (November 1, 1979): 7–17. https://doi.org/10.1080/10464883.1979.10758215.
Carpa, Mario. *The Digital Turn in Architecture 1992-2012*. Chichester: John Wiley and Sons Lts., 2013.
Carson, Richard T., W. Michael Hanemann, Raymond J. Kopp, Jon A. Krosnick, Robert C. Mitchell, Stanley Presser, Paul A. Ruud, and V. Kerry Smith. "Was the Noaa Panel Correct About Contingent Valuation?" SSRN Scholarly Paper. Rochester, NY: Social Science Research Network, 1996. https://doi.org/10.2139/ssrn.31992.
"Cities and Happiness: A Global Ranking and Analysis." Accessed January 7, 2021. http://worldhappiness.report/.
Cohen, Erik. "Authenticity and Commoditization in Tourism." *Annals of Tourism Research* 15, no. 3 (1988): 371–86.
Cohn, Scott. "Amazon Reveals the Truth on Why It Nixed New York and Chose Virginia for Its HQ2." CNBC, July 10, 2019. https://www.cnbc.com/2019/07/10/amazon-reveals-the-truth-on-why-it-nixed-ny-and-chose-virginia-for-hq2.html.
Constantinides, Panos. "Introduction: Historical Review of Infrastructure Development." In *Perspectives and Implications for the Development and Information Infrastructures,* 1–18. Hershey, PA: IGI Global, 2012.

Cycling Embassy of Denmark. "Copenhagen City of Cyclists - Facts and Figures 2017," July 4, 2017. http://www.cycling-embassy.dk/2017/07/04/copenhagen-city-cyclists-facts-figures-2017/.

Bjarke Ingels Group. "Copenhill." Accessed May 4, 2021. https://big.dk/#projects-arc.

Couch, Chris, Olivier Sykes, and Wolfgang Börstinghaus. "Thirty Years of Urban Regeneration in Britain, Germany and France: The Importance of Context and Path Dependency." *Progress in Planning* 75 (January 2011). https://doi.org/10.1016/j.progress.2010.12.001.

Crane, Diana, Nobuko Kawashima, and Ken'ichi Kawasaki, eds. *Global Culture: Media, Arts, Policy and Globalization*. London and New York: Routledge, 2002.

Crompton, John L. "The Impact of Parks on Property Values: A Review of the Empirical Evidence." *Journal of Leisure Research* 33, no. 1 (2001): 1–31.

Crompton, John L. "The Impact of Parks on Property Values: Empirical Evidence from the Past Two Decades in the United States." *Managing Leisure* 10, no. 4 (October 1, 2005): 203–18. https://doi.org/10.1080/13606710500348060.

Crook, Lizzie. "BIG Opens Copenhill Power Plant and Ski Slope in Copenhagen." *Dezeen*, October 8, 2019. https://www.dezeen.com/2019/10/08/big-copenhill-power-plant-ski-slope-in-copenhagen.

Crosbie, Michael, and Pelli Clarke Pelli Associates. *Pelli Clarke Pelli Architects*. Berlin: Birkhauser, 2013.

Crysler, C. Greig, Stephen Cairns, and Hilde Heynen, eds. *The SAGE Handbook of Architectural Theory*. Los Angeles; London; New Delhi; Singapore; Washington DC: SAGE Publications, 2012.

Cuff, Dana. *Architecture: The Story of Practice*. Cambridge, Mass: MIT Press, 1991.

Cuff, Dana, and Roger Sherman. *Fast-Forward Urbanism: Rethinking Architecture's Engagement with the City*. Princeton Architectural Press, 2011.

Czarnitzki, Dirk, Bronwyn H Hall, and Raffaele Oriani. *The Market Valuation of Knowledge Assets in US and European Firms. The Management of Intellectual Property*. Edward Elgar, 2006.

Davis, Mike. *The City of Quartz: Excavating the Future of Los Angeles*. London: Verso, 1990.

France gouvernement. "Décrit 2001-923 Du 8 Octobre 2001," October 8, 2001. https://www.legifrance.gouv.fr/loda/id/JORFTEXT000000224773/.

France gouvernement. "Décrit Du 10 Janvier 1995," January 10, 1995.

https://www.legifrance.gouv.fr/jorf/id/JORFTEXT000000213396/.

DeJean, Joan. *How Paris Became Paris: The Invention of the Modern*. New York and London: Bloomsbury, 2014.

———. "The Birth of the Pont Neuf: How a Simple Bridge Made Paris the World's First Modern Tourist Destination." Slate, May 7, 2014. https://www.slate.com/human-interest/2014/paris-history-of-the-construction-of-the-pont-neuf.

"Designing for the Social Experience of Bicycling - Gehl." Accessed January 8, 2021. https://gehlpeople.com/blog/designing-for-the-social-experience-of-bicycling/.

D'Hooghe, Alexander. "The Objectification of Infrastructure: Elements of a Different Space and Aesthetic for Suburban America." *PROJECTIONS* 10, 2011, 85.

Diamond, Peter A, and Jerry A Hausman. "Contingent Valuation: Is Some Number Better than No Number?" *Journal of Economic Perspectives* 8, no. 4 (1994): 45–64.

Doucet, Brian. "Variations of the Entrepreneurial City: Goals, Roles and Visions in Rotterdam's Kop van Zuid and the Glasgow Harbour Megaprojects." *International Journal of Urban and Regional Research* 37, no. 6 (2013): 2035–51. https://doi.org/10.1111/j.1468-2427.2012.01182.x.

Metropolitan Drinking Fountain and Cattle Trough Association. "Drinking Fountains." Accessed October 25, 2020. http://www.mdfcta.co.uk.

Dupré, Judith. *Bridges: A History of the World's Most Spectacular Spans.* Revised. New York: Black Dog & Leventhan Publishers, 2017.

Easterling, Keller. *Extrastatecraft: The Power of Infrastructure Space.* Verso Books, 2014.

Journal of the American Institute of Architects. "Erasmus Bridge, UN Studio," December 20, 2013.

Fabre, Thierry. "L'institut Du Monde Arabe: Entre Deux Rives." *Vingtième Siècle : Revue d'histoire,* no. 32 (11 1991). http://www.jstor.com/stable/3770000.

Falk, Nicholas. "Case Study for Kop Van Zuid, Rotterdam." Regeneration in European Cities: Making Connections. Joseph Rowntree Foundation, 2008. http://urbed.coop/sites/default/files/Case%20Study%20for%20Kop%20Van%20Zuid,%20Rotterdam.pdf.

City of Vancouver. "False Creek South: Topic Workshop 1: History + Context," November 11, 2019. https://vancouver.ca/files/cov/false-creek-south-history-and-context-workshop-presentation.pdf.

Figi, Heinrich. "Rehabilitation of the Salginatobel Bridge." *Structural Engineering International* 10, no. 1 (2000).

Vancouver is Awesome. "Five Things You Didn't Know about the Vancouver Seawall," November 16, 2016. www.vancouverisawesome.com/2016/11/16/vancojver-seawall.

Fontana-Giusti, Gordana. *Foucault for Architects.* London and New York: Routledge, 2004.

"Foreign Missions Get Creative | The Star." Accessed July 14, 2020. https://www.thestar.com.my/news/nation/2020/07/11/foreign-missions-get-creative.

MoMA. "Foreign Office Architects (FOA), London, Farshid Moussavi, Alejandro Zaero-Polo, Yokohama International Port Terminal," 2000. https://www.moma.org/collection/works/95092.

BBC News. "Forth Bridge given World Heritage Site Status," July 5, 2015. https://www.bbc.com/news/uk-scotland-edinburgh-east-fife-33397980.

Frampton, Kenneth. "Patricia and John Patkau. Tecto-Totemic." *Perspecta* 28 (1997): 180–89.

———. "Towards a Critical Regionalism." In *The Anti-Aesthetic: Essays on Postmodern Culture,* edited by Hal Foster, 1st ed. Port Townsend, Wash: Bay Press, 1983.

BBC News. "France Completes Tallest Bridge," May 29, 2004. https://www.bbc.co.uk/2/hi/Europe/3759307.stm.

François, Des Rosiers, Thériault Marius, Kestens Yan, and Villeneuve Paul. "Landscaping and House Values: An Empirical Investigation." *Journal of Real Estate Research* 23, no. 1–2 (January 1, 2002): 139–62. https://doi.org/10.1080/10835547.2002.12091072.

Frearson, Amy. "Zaha Hadid and Hopkins among Architects to Design London Water Fountains." *Dezeen,* February 19, 2014. https://www.dezeen.com/2014/02/19/zaha-hadid-hopkins-studio-weave-london-water-fountains.

Freeman, A Myrick. "Hedonic Prices, Property Values and Measuring Environmental Benefits: A Survey of the Issues." In *Measurement in Public Choice,* 13–32. Springer, 1981.

Freeman, Cristina Garduño. *Participatory Culture and the Social Value of an Architectural Icon: Sydney Opera House.* Routledge, 2018.

Gardner, Ethel Bernie. "Seabird Island Community School: Unique Features of an Indian Band School." Master of Education, University of British Columbia, 1986.

Gehl, Jan, and Lord Richard Rogers. *Cities for People.* Washington DC, USA: Island Press, 2010. http://

ebookcentral.proquest.com/lib/ubc/detail.action?docID=3317503.

"Gentrification, Housing Differentiation and Urban Regeneration: 'Going for Broke' in Newcastle upon Tyne." *Urban Studies* 40, no. 12 (2003): 2367–82.

Giedion, S. *Space, Time and Architecture: The Growth of a New Tradition.* 5th ed., rev.Enl. The Charles Eliot Norton Lectures 1938–1939. Cambridge: Harvard University Press, 1967.

Giedion, Sigfried. "Construction and Aesthetics (Notes on the Reinforced-Concrete Bridges Designed by Swiss Engineer, Robert Maillart." In *Circle: International Survey of Constructivist Art,* edited by J.L. Martin, Ben Nicholson, and N. Gabo. London: Faber and Faber, 1937.

———. "History and the Architect." *Journal of Architectural Education,* no. 12:2 (1957): 14–16.

Gillet, Georges. "Le Viaduc de Millau." transports Quebec, October 17, 2015. http://www.bv.transports.gouv.qc.ca/mono/0981378/05_Viaduc_de_Millau.pdf.

Glass, Ruth. "Introduction: Aspects of Change." In *London: Aspects of Change,* edited by Centre for Urban Studies. London: MacKibbon and Kee, 1964.

Glendinning, Miles. *Architecture's Evil Empire? The Triumph and Tragedy of Global Modernism.* London: Reaktion Books, 2010.

"Global Liveability Ranking." Accessed January 7, 2021. https://www.eiu.com/topic/liveability.

Goldberger, Paul. "The Heatherwick Effect." *The New Yorker,* November 18, 2008.

Donald MacDonald Architects. "Golden Gate Bridge." Accessed May 15, 2021. http://www.donaldmacdonaldarchitects.com/projects/bridges/ggb.php.

Graham, Steve and Marvin, Simon. *Splintering Urbanism: Networked Infrastructures, Technological Mobilities and the Urban Condition.* New York: Routledge, 2001.

Gregory, Rob. "Thomas Heatherwick, Rolling Bridge." *Architectural Review* 218 (December 2005): 56.

Gruppo acea. "Serving People." Gruppo Acea. Accessed October 24, 2020. https://www.gruppo.acea.it/en/serving-people/water/nasoni.

Habermas, Jürgen. *The Divided West.* Cambridge UK: Polity Press, 2006.

Habibu, Sira. "Foreign Missives Get Creative." *The Star.* July 11, 2020. https://www.thestar.com.my/news/nation/2020/07/11/foreign-missions-get-creative.

Hanemann, W Michael. "Valuing the Environment through Contingent Valuation." *Journal of Economic Perspectives* 8, no. 4 (1994): 19–43.

Harrington, Kevin. *Changing Ideas*

on Architecture in the "Encyclopédie," 1750-1776. Ann Arbor: UMI Research Press, 1985.
Harvey, David. *The Limits to Capital.* Oxford: Blackwell, 1982.
———. *The Condition of Post Modernity.* Oxford: Blackwell, 1989.
Hayllar, Bruce, Tony Griffin, and Deborah Edwards. *City Spaces-Tourist Places*. Routledge, 2010.
Heidegger, M. *Martin Heidegger, Poetry, Language, Thought. Trans. Albert Hofstadter.* New York: Harper & Row, 1971.
Hejinskik, Roy. "The Iconic Value of Infrastructure Projects: A Case Study to the Iconic Value of the Erasmus Bridge." Master's, TUDelft, 2015. http://resolver.tudelft.nl/uuid:d9ee66a8-6c45-472a-b586-31b01d56836f.
Heylighen, Ann, and Genviève Martin. "That Elusive Concept of Concept in Architecture. A First Snapshot During Design." In *Computing and Cogmitiomn'04,* edited by J.S. Gero. Dordrecht: Kluwer Publishers, 2004.
Deloitte Australia. "How Do You Value an Icon? | Deloitte Australia | Economic Value of Sydney Opera House, Cultural and Digital Value, Deloitte Access Economics." Accessed May 7, 2021. https://www2.deloitte.com/au/en/pages/sydney-opera-house/articles/value-an-icon-sydney-opera-house.html.
Deloitte Insights. "Insights City Mobility Index." Accessed January 7, 2021. https://www2.deloitte.com/us/en/insights/focus/transportation.html.
"Irving Morrow." Accessed May 15, 2021. https//www.pbs.org/americanexperience/feature/biography/goldengate-morrow.
Jacobs, Jane. "Jane Jacobs." *The Death and Life of Great American Cities,* 1961.
James-Chakrabarty, Kathleen. "From Isolationism to Internationalism: American Acceptance of the Bauhaus." In *Bauhaus Culture: From Weimar to the Cold War,* edited by Kathleen James-Chakrabarty. Minneapolis and London: University of Minnesota Press, 2006.
Jason. "25 of the World's Most Unique Bridges." List25, November 21, 2018. https://www:list.com/25-of-the-worlds-most-unique-bridges.
Jayne, Mark. *Cities of Consumption*. New York and London: Routledge, 2006.
Jencks, Charles. "Toward an Iconography of the Present." *Log*, Fall 2004.
———. "The Iconic Building Is Here to Stay." *City* 10, no. 1 (April 2006).
Johnson, Randal. "Editor's Introduction." In *The Field of Cultural Production,* by Pierre Bourdieu. New York: Columbia University Press, 1993.
Kaplan, Rachel, and Stephen Kaplan.

The Experience of Nature: A Psychological Perspective. Cambridge University Press, 1989.

Kealy, Mary Jo, John F Dovidio, and Mark L Rockel. "Accuracy in Valuation Is a Matter of Degree." *Land Economics* 64, no. 2 (1988): 158–71.

Kemp, Emory L. "Exemplars of Engineering Review. of *Robert Maillart's Bridges: The Art of Engineering*, by David P. Billington,." *Science* 208, no. 4445 (May 16, 1980): 727–28.

Kherai, Sean. *Inventing Stanley Park: An Environmental History.* Vancouver: UBC Press, 2013.

King, Anthony D., ed. *Culture, Globalization and the World System: Contemporary Conditions for the Representation of Identity.* Minneapolis: University of Minnesota Press, 1997.

———. *Spaces of Global Cultures: Architecture, Urbanism, Identity.* London and New York: Routledge, 2004.

King, John. "Early Golden Gate Sketches/Flight of Fancy." The SFGate. Accessed May 15, 2021. https://www.sfgate.com/bayarea/place/article/Early-Golden-Gate-Bridge-sketches-flight-of-fancy-3386352.php#photo-2587323.

Klingmann, Anna. *Brandscapes: Architecture in the Experience Economy.* Cambridge, MA: The MIT Press, 2007.

Knight Architects. "About Us." Linkedin. Accessed January 10, 2021. https://www.linkedin.com/company/knight-architects.

Knight Architects. "Knight Architects." Accessed January 3, 2021. https://www.knightarchitects.co.uk/studio/clients.

Koglin, Till. "Organisation Does Matter–Planning for Cycling in Stockholm and Copenhagen." *Transport Policy* 39 (2015): 55–62.

Kruft, Hanno-Walter. *History of Architectural Theory.* Princeton Architectural Press, 1994.

Krutilla, John V. "Conservation Reconsidered." *The American Economic Review* 57, no. 4 (1967): 777–86.

Kuhn, Sarah. "Learning from the Architecture Studio: Implications for Project-Based Pedagogy." *International Journal of Engineering Education* 17, no. 4/5 (2001): 349–52.

La Société des Fontaines Wallace. "Sir Wallace and His Fountains." La Société des Fontaines Wallace, October 2020. www.wallacefountains.org/about-sir-wallace-and-his-fountains.

Lambesis, Barbara. "150 Years of Thirst: The Wallace Fountains of Paris." Paris Institute, December 5, 2019. https://parisinstitute.org/pict-visiting-lectures-iii-150-years-of-thirst-the-wallace-fountains-of-paris/.

Langdon, David. "AD Classics: Yokohama International Passenger Terminal/ Foreign Office Architects (FOA)." *ArchDaily*, 2014. https://www.archdaily.com/554132'ad-classics-yokohama-international-passenger-terminal-foreign-office-architects.

Lanvin, Sylvia. "Re: Reading the Encyclopedia: Architectural Theory and the Formation of the Public in Late-Eighteenth-Century France." *Journal of the Society of Architectural Historians* 53, no. 2 (June 1994): 184–92.

Larsen, Janike Kampevold. "Global Tourism Practices as Living Heritage: Viewing the Norwegian Tourist Route Project." *Future Anterior: Journal of Historic Preservation, History, Theory, and Criticism* 9, no. 1 (2012): 67–87. https://doi.org/10.5749/futuante.9.1.0067.

Laska, Shirley Bradway, and Daphne Spain, eds. *Back to the City: Issues in Neighborhood Renovation*. New York: Pergamon Press, 1980.

Lawson, Bryan. *How Designers Think*. Routledge, 2006.

Leary, Michael E, and John McCarthy. *The Routledge Companion to Urban Regeneration*. Routledge, 2013.

Leary, Michael, and John McCarthy. "Part 3: Public Infrastructure and Public Space." In *The Routledge Companion to Urban Regeneration*, edited by Michael Leary and John McCarthy. London and New York: Routledge, 2013.

Lees, Loretta, Tom Slater, and Elvin Wyly. *Gentrification*. New York and London: Routledge, 2008.

Le Paris Pittoresque. "Les Pontes de La Cité." Accessed October 12, 2020. https://www.paris-pittoresque.com/monuments.

Lever, W.F. "Chapter 17: The Post-Fordist City." In *Handbook of Urban Studies*, edited by Ronan Paddison. Thousand Oaks: Sage Books, 2000.

Liu, Amy. "Big Tech in the City: Amazon in Arlington and the Future of Regional Economic Development." Presented at the SACRPH, Arlington, Virginia, November 2, 2019.

———. "Opinion | A Better Way to Attract Amazon's Jobs." *The New York Times*, February 16, 2019, sec. Opinion. https://www.nytimes.com/2019/02/16/opinion/amazon-new-york.html.

Long, Kieran. "Millau Viaduct." *Icon* 021, May 2005. https://www.iconeye.com/icon-021-march-2005/millau-viaduct-icon-021-march-2005.

Loomis, John, Thomas Brown, Beatrice Lucero, and George Peterson. "Evaluating the Validity of the Dichotomous Choice Question Format in Contingent Valuation." *Environmental and Resource Economics* 10, no. 2 (September 1, 1997): 109–23. https://doi.org/10.1023/A:1026403916622.

Lynch, Kevin, Kevin R Lynch, and

others. *The Image of the City*. Vol. 11. MIT press, 1960.
Lynn, Greg, and Farshid Moussavi. *Yokohama International Port Terminal*. Montreal: Canadian Centre for Architecture, 2018.
Markusen, Ann, and Anne Gadwa. *Creative Placemaking*. National Endowment for the Arts Washington, DC, 2010.
Masdin, Marta, and Josep Fuses. "Reconceptualizing the Design Studio in Architectural Education: Distance Learning and Blended Learning as Transformation Factors." *International Journal of Architectural Research* 11, no. 2 (July 2017).
Massey, Doreen. *For Space*. London, England: Sage Publications Ltd, 2005.
Matan, Annie, and Peter Newman. *People Cities: The Life and Legacy of Jan Gehl*. Island Press, 2016.
Meijer, M. "Capturing the Young and the Restless," August 13, 2010. https://thesis.eur.nl/pub/7769.
Meyboom, AnnaLisa. *Driverless Urban Futures: A Speculative Atlas for Autonomous Vehicles*. Routledge, 2018.
Structurae. "Millau Viaduct." Accessed May 29, 2020. https://structurae.net/en/structures/millau-viaduct.
Foster + Partners. "Millau Viaduct." Accessed January 3, 2021. http://www.fosterandpartners.com/projects/millau-viaduct/.
Mills, Karen, and Jan W. Rivkin. "Amazon's HQ2 (A)," February 4, 2018. https://www.hbs.edu/faculty/Pages/item.aspx?num=53989.
Millward, Robert. "European Governments and the Infrastructure Industries, c.1840-1914." *European Review of Economic History* 8, no. 1 (April 2004).
Milojovic, Michael. "An Architecture of Difference: Some New Places of Learning for British Columbia's First Nations." *Australian-Canadian Studies* 15, no. 1 (1997): 85–89.
Mitchell, Robert Cameron, Richard T Carson, and Richard T Carson. *Using Surveys to Value Public Goods: The Contingent Valuation Method*. Resources for the Future, 1989.
Morris, Ali. "Michael Anastassiades' Public Drinking Fountains Address Plastic Pollution during London Design Week." *Wallpaper*, 9016 2018. https://www.wallpaper.com/design/michael-anastassiades-public-drinking-fountains-london-design-festival-2018.
Mostafavi, Mohsen, and Gareth Doherty. *Ecological Urbanism*. Lars Müller Publishers, Baden, 2010.
Moussavi, Farshid. "Yokohama International Port Terminal." Farshid Moussavi Architecture. Accessed September 23, 2020. https://www.farshimoussavi.com/node/15#yokohama_international_port_terminal_yokohama_japan.

Mulat, Alyssa. "Our Park: An Historical Geography of Stanley Park Form Its Closest Neighbours." University of British Columbia, 2018.

Nam, Seungmin, Sae-eun Park, and Hong-Chul Shin. "Accessing the Economic Value of Night View of Bridge Using Contingent Valuation Method: The Case of South Korea's Han-River Bridge." *International Journal of Culture, Tourism and Hospitality Research*, 2015.

National Geographic UK. "Copenhagen: The Happiest City in the World?" *National Geographic*, April 29, 2018. https://www.nationalgeographic.co.uk/travel/2018/04/copenhagen-happiest-city-world.

Necipoglu, Gülru. "Challenging the Past: Sinan and the Comparative Discourse of Early Modern Islamic Architecture." *Muqarnas* 10 (1993): 169–82.

Network, UNESCO Creative Cities. "Towards Sustainable Strategies for Creative Tourism. Discussion Report of the Planning Meeting for 2008 International Conference on Creative Tourism." *New Mexico, USA*, 2006.

Knight Architects. "New Pooley Bridge, UK." Accessed January 3, 2021. https://www.knightarchitects.co.uk/projects/new-pooley-bridge.

Nieuwland, Shirley, and Mariangela Lavanga. "The Consequences of Being 'the Capital of Cool'. Creative Entrepreneurs and the Sustainable Development of Creative Tourism in the Urban Context of Rotterdam." *Journal of Sustainable Tourism*, 2020, 1–18.

Norberg-Schulz, Christian. "Genius Loci: Towards a Phenomenology of Architecture (1979)." *Historic Cities: Issues in Urban Conservation* 8 (2019): 31.

Nouvel, Jean. "Institut Du Monde Arab." Ateliers Jean Nouvel. Accessed October 23, 2020. https://www.jeannouvel.com/projects/institut-du-monde-arab-ima,.

Nouvel, Jean, and Jack Lang. "Jean Nouvel et Jack Lang at the JDD : L'institut Du Monde Arabe Est Agressé." *Le Blog de l'IMA* (blog). Accessed March 10, 2020. https//:www.imarabe.org/fr/blog/2020/01/jean-nouvel-et-jack-land-au-jdd-l-instut-du-monde-arabe-est-agressé.

Nowacka-Rejzner, Urzula. "Water Elements in the Creation of Public Space." *Materials Science and Engineering*, 2019. https://iopscience.iop.org/article/10.1088/1757-899x/603/2/02287.

Ockman, Joan, and Rebecca Williamson, eds. *Architecture School: Three Centuries of Educating Architects in North America*. Cambridge, Mass. : Washington, D.C: MIT Press ; Association of Collegiate Schools of Architecture, 2012.

Ohrn, Ken. "Seaside Greenway: $6 M Kitsilano Bike Route Project Gets the Green Light." CBC News, July 30, 2013. https://www.cbc.ca/news/canada/british-columbia/6m-kitsilano-bike-route-project-gets-green-light-1.1399365.

———. "Seaside Greenway Completion and Upgrade." *Pricetags*, April 28, 2016. https://pricetags.ca/2016/04/28/seaside-greenway-completion-and-upgrade/.

Palen, J. John, and Bruce London. *Gentrification, Displacement and Neighborhood Revitalization*. Albany: State University of New York, 1974.

Parilla, Joseph. "Which Cities Are Well Positioned to Land Amazon's HQ2?" *Brookings* (blog), September 8, 2017. https://www.brookings.edu/blog/the-avenue/2017/09/08/which-cities-are-well-positioned-to-land-amazons-hq2/.

Patkau, John. "Patkau Architects Investigations into the Particular." *The Journal of the International Institute* 3, no. 2 (Winter 1996). https://quod.lib.umich.edu/j/jii/4750978.0003.2*?/-patkau-architects-investigation-into-the-particular .

Pearson, Clifford A. "Other than Their Status as the World's Tallest Buildings, What Else Do Cesar Pelli's Petronas Towers Have..." *Architectural Record,* January 1999. https://www.archrecord.com.

Pechet, Bill. Design Capital Interview with Bill Pechet, August 5, 2020. http://blogs.ubc.ca/meyboom/.

Pelli, Cesar, Charles Thornton, and Leonard Joseph. "The World's Tallest Building: Malaysian Petronas Twin Towers Serve as Both a Cultural and Economic Symbol." *Scientific America* 277, no. 6 (December 1997).

Pereda, Hector Beade. "Pooley Bridge." *Archello*. Accessed January 3, 2021. https://www.archello.com/project/pooley-bridge 2020.

Perry, Andre M. "Cities Bidding for Amazon HQ2 Should Have Played Their Own Game." *Brookings* (blog), October 24, 2017. https://www.brookings.edu/blog/the-avenue/2017/10/24/cities-bidding-for-amazon-hq2-should-have-played-their-own-game/.

Tripadvisor. "Petronas Twin Towers (Kuala Lumpur) - All You Need to Know BEFORE You Go - Updated 2020." Accessed October 4, 2020. https://www.tripadvisor.ca/Attraction_Review-g298570-d2373838-Reviews-Kuala_Lumpur_City_Gallery-Kuala_Lumpur_Wilayah_Persekutuan.html.

Pigou, Arthur Cecil. *The Economics of Welfare*. Second Edition. London: Palgrave Macmillan, 1924.

Pinto, John A. *The Trevi Fountain.* New Haven and London: Yale

University Press, 1986.
Ploger, Jorg. “Bilbao City Report.” Monograph. London, UK: Centre for Analysis of Social Exclusion, London School of Economics and Political Science, 2008. http://sticerd.lse.ac.uk/case/.
Archello. “Pooley Bridge.” Accessed January 20, 2021. https://www.archello.com/project/pooley-bridge.
Powers, Alan. “Teaching History in Schools of Architecture in the Age of Eclecticism.” In *Architectural History and the Studio,* edited by Adam Hardy and Necdet Teymur. London: ?uestion Press, 1966.
Pownall, Augusta. “London Water Fountains Design Chosen by Focus Group.” *Dezeen*, July 25, 2019. https://www.dezeen.com/2019/07/25/london-water-fountains-design.
Punter, John. *The Vancouver Achievement: Urban Planning and Design.* Vancouver: The University of British Columbia Press, 2003.
Rajagopalan, Mrinalini. “Preservation and Modernity: Competing Perspectives, Contested Histories and the Question of Authenticity.” In *The Sage Handbook of Architectural Theory.* Los Angeles ; London ; New Delhi ; Singapore ; Washington DC: SAGE Publications, 2012.
Rapson, Ralph. “Objectives of Architectural Education.” *Journal of Architectural Education* 14, no. 2 (1959). https://doi.org/DOI: 10.1080/10464883.1959.11102411 http:dx.org/10.1080/104 6883.1959.11102411.
Ricón Borrego, Iván I. “Landscape Architectures in Norway: The Influence of AHO Masters on the National Tourist Routes of Norway.” *Cuaderno de Notas* 20 (2019).
Roan, Beck. “The Complexity of Architecture: An Analysis of Design Intention and Theories in the Norwegian National Tourist Routes.” Master of Philosophy, University of Oslo, 2013.
Engineer Biography. “Robert Maillart.” Accessed October 10, 2020. http://www.engineering-timelines.com/who/Maillart_R/maillartRobert.asp.
Romein, Arie, and Jan Jacob Trip. “Key Elements of Creative City Development: An Assessment of Local Policies in Amsterdam and Rotterdam.” City Futures’ 09, 4-6 June 2009, Madrid, 2009.
Rosen, Sherwin. “Hedonic Prices and Implicit Markets: Product Differentiation in Pure Competition.” *Journal of Political Economy* 82, no. 1 (1974): 34–55.
Rowe, Colin. *Character and Compositions: Or Some Vicissitudes of Architectural Vocabulary in the Nineteenth Century,* 1974.
Royal Architectural Institute of Canada.

"Royal Architectural Institute of Canada College of Fellows," 2011. https://raic.org/sites/raic.org/files/raic/documents/2011fellows.pdf.

Ruby, Andreas, and Ilka Ruby. *Infrastructure Space.* Ruby Press, 2017.

San Juan, Rose Marie. "Rome: A City out of Print." In *Rome: A City out of Print.* Minneapolis: University of Minnesota Press, 2001.

Sassen, Saskia. *The Global City: New York, London, Tokyo.* 2nd ed. Princeton and Oxford: Princeton University Press, 2001.

Satram, Joe. "13 Weird Moments in the History of Water Fountains. Think They're Boring? Think Again." *HuffPost,* April 1, 2015.

———. "13 Weird Moments in the History of Water Fountains. Think They're Boring? Think Again." *HuffPost,* December 16, 2017. https://www.huffpost.com/entry/history-of-water-fountains_n_6357064.

Savich, H.V. *Post Industrial Cities: Politics and Planning in New York, London and Paris.* Princeton NJ: Princeton University Press, 2014.

Scerri, Moira, Deborah Edwards, and Carmel Foley. "The Value of Architecture to Tourism." In *Proceedings of 26th Annual CAUTHE Conference,* 1–21, 2016.

Scorse, Jason. *What Environmentalists Need to Know about Economics.* Springer, 2010.

Patkau Architects. "Seabird Island School." Accessed October 3, 2020. https://patkau.ca.

"Seaside Greenway: $6 M Kitsilano Bike Route Project Gets the Green Light," n.d.

City of Vancouver. "Seaside Greenway Completion and York Street Bikeway: Phase 1 of Point Grey-Cornwall Active Transportation Corridor."," July 2013. https://vancouver.ca/files/cov/seaside-greenway-completion-york-bikeway-2013-jul.pdf.

Shangquan, Gao. "Economic Globalization: Trends, Risks and Risk Prevention." United Nations Background Paper NO.1 ST/ESA/2000/CPP/1, 2000. https://www.un.org/en/development/desa/policy/cdp/cdp_background_papers/bp2000_1.pdf.

Shaw, Douglas v. "Chapter 18: The Post-Industrial City." In *Handbook of Urban Studies,* edited by Ronan Paddison. Thousand Oaks: Sage Books, 2000.

Sheppard, Benedict, Garen Kouyoumjian, Hugo Sarrazin, and Fabricio Dore. "The Business Value of Design." McKinsey & Company, October 2018.

Sherman, Roger. "Battery Power: Recharging Architecture's Causes and Effects." In *Infrastructural Monument.* New York: Princeton Architectural Press, 2016.

Wallace Foundation. "Sir Richard Wallace and His Fountains." Accessed October 24, 2020. https://wallacefountains.org/about-sir-wallace-and-his-fountains/.

Sklair, Leslie. "Iconic Architecture and Capitalist Globalization." *City* 10, no. 1 (2006): 21–47.

"Slashed." Accessed July 15, 2020. https://www.e-flux.com/architecture/history-theory/159236/slashed/.

Smit, Annet Jantien. "The Influence of District Visual Quality on Location Decisions of Creative Entrepreneurs." *Journal of the American Planning Association* 77, no. 2 (April 15, 2011): 167–84. https://doi.org/10.1080/01944363.2011.567924.

Smith, Neil. "New Globalism, New Urbanism: Gentrification as Global Urban Strategy." *Antipode* 34, no. 4 (2002).

Smith, Neil, and Peter Williams. *Gentrification of the City.* Boston: Allen and Unwin, 1986.

Smithson, Alison, ed. *Team Ten Primer.* Cambridge, AM: The MIT Press, 1968.

Sokol, David. "Over Site: How Caracas's New Cable-Car System Is Making the City's Favelas More Visible." *Architonic*, July 29, 2010. https://www.architonic.com/en/story/david-sokol-over-site-how-caracas-s-new-cable-car-system-is-making-the-city-s-favelas-more-visible/7000511.

UNESCO Heritage List. "Sokolovic Bridge." Accessed October 10, 2020. https://www.whc.unesco.org/en/list/12601.

Spears, Tim. "Michael Anatassiades Installs 'Touchless' Drinking Fountain in London." *Designboom.* Accessed October 28, 2020. https://www.designboom.com/design/michael-anastassiades-fleet-fountain-london.

Stathaki, Emily. "Norwegian National Tourist Routes Revisited." *Norwegian Arts.* Accessed November 18, 2020. https://norwegianarts.org.uk/norwegian-national-tourist-routes-revisited/.

"Stockholm | CIVITAS." Accessed January 7, 2021. https://civitas.eu/eccentric/stockholm.

"Stockholm_GlobalCityMobility_WEB.Pdf." Accessed January 7, 2021. https://www2.deloitte.com/content/dam/insights/us/articles/4331_Deloitte-City-Mobility-Index/Stockholm_GlobalCityMobility_WEB.pdf.

Stoll, Katrina, and Scott Lloyd, eds. *Infrastructure as Architecture: Designing Composite Networks.* Berlin: Jovis, 2010.

Stó:lō nation. "Stó:Lō Nation." Accessed March 20, 2021. https://www.stolonation.bc.ca.

Strauss, Joseph. "The Golden Gate Bridge At San Francisco, California: Report of the Chief Engineer, With Architectural Studies, to the Board of Directors, Golden Gate Bridge and Highway District, August 27, 1930." San Francisco, 1930.

Szenab, Imre, and Timothy Kaposy, eds. *Cultural Theory: An Anthology.* Chichester: Wiley-Blackwell, 2011.

Tallon, A. *Urban Regeneration in the UK.* London: Routledge, 2010.

Tavenor, Robert. *On Alberti and the Art of Building.* New Haven: Yale University Press, 1998.

The London Fountain Company. "The London Fountain Company." Accessed October 28, 2020. http://thelondonfountaincompany.london/partners---supporters.html.

The World Health Organization. "Topics: Globalization." Accessed June 1, 2020. https://www.who.int/topics/globalization/en.

Tibbetts, John, and Charles J Fausold. *Open Space Conservation.* Lincoln Institute of Land Policy, 1998.

Tokman, Lyla Y., and Rusen Yamacli. "Reality-Based Design Studio in Architectural Education." *Journal of Architecture and Planning Research* 24, no. 3 (2007).

Tomer, Adie. "Does Transportation Even Matter to Amazon and HQ2?" *Brookings* (blog), January 19, 2018. https://www.brookings.edu/blog/the-avenue/2018/01/19/does-transportation-even-matter-to-amazon-and-hq2/.

"Top Gear TV Supercars across France." *Top Gear.* BBC, October 20, 2008.

Tuan, Yi-Fu. *Space and Place: The Perspective of Experience.* U of Minnesota Press, 1977.

Uitermark, Justus, Jan Willem Duyvendak, and Reinout Kleinhans. "Gentrification as a Governmental Strategy: Social Control and Social Cohesion in Hoogvleit, Rotterdam." *Environment and Planning A:1*, 2007, 125–41.

UN Studio. "Erasmus Bridge." *Architect Magazine.* Accessed May 18, 2021. https://www.architectmagazine.com/project-gallery/erasmus-bridge.

Urban and Economic Development, and Marco van Hoek. "Regeneration in European Cities: Making Connections. Case Study of Kop van Zuid, Rotterdam (The Netherlands)." Rotterdam, April 2007.

Architectural Record. "Urban-Think Tank." Accessed May 18, 2021. https://www.architecturalrecord.com/articles/6448-urban-think-tank?v=preview.

Urry, John. "The Consumption of Tourism." *Sociology* 24, no. 1 (1990): 23–35.

Vidler, Anthony, Bernard Tschumi, and Jacques Derrida. *Tschumi Parc de*

La Villette. London: Artifice, 2004.
Wainwright, Oliver. "Sheep and Land Rovers Rejoice: Pooley Bridge Reunites the Lake District." *The Guardian*, November 22, 2020. https://www.theguardian.com/artanddesign/2020/nov/22/pooley-bridge-reunites-the-lake-district.
Waldheim, Charles. "Landscape Urbanism: A Genealogy." *Praxis: Journal of Writing + Building* 4 (2002): 10–17.
———. *The Landscape Urbanism Reader.* Princeton Architectural Press, 2006.
La Société des Fontaines Wallace. "Wallace Fountains." Accessed October 17, 2020. https://www.wallacefountains.org/about-sir-wallace-and-his-fountains.
Wallis Miller. "Architecture, Building and the Bauhaus," In *Bauhaus Culture: From Weimar to the Cold War,* edited by Kathleen James-Chakrabarty. Minneapolis and London: University of Minnesota Press, 2006.
Webster, Helena. *Bourdieu for Architects*. London and New York: Routledge, 2011.
Weder, Adele. "Architecture of Hope Revisited." the Tyee, February 27, 2009. https://thetyee.ca/Photo/2009/02/27/ArchHope/print.html.
Weigher, John C., and Robert H. Zerbst. "The Externalities of Neighborhood Parks: An Empirical Investigation." *Land Economics* 49, no. 1 (1973): 99–105. https://doi.org/10.2307/3145337.
Whyte, William Hollingsworth and others. "The Social Life of Small Urban Spaces," 1980.
Wilkinson, Chris. "Bridging Art and Science." Wilkonsoneyre, 2001. www.wilkinsoneyre.com/thoughts/essays/movement-and-geometry.
Wilkonson, Chris. "Infrastructure as a Cultural Icon." English Heritage Conservation Bulletin 65. Accessed May 15, 2020. https://www.wilkinsoneyre.com.
CICA (Comité International des Critiques d'Architecture / International Committee of Architectural Critic). "Y.I.P.T.," 2019. https://cicarchitecture.org/2019/07/25/the-yokohama-international-port-terminal.
"Yokohama International Port Terminal/ 4 Competition Entries by AA Members." *AA Files* 29 (Summer 1995). . https://www-jstor-org-ezproxy.library.ubc.ca/.
Zukin, Sharon. *The Cultures of Cities.* Oxford: Blackwell, 1995.

LIST OF FIGURES

Cover: Robert Maillart. Salgiatobel Bridge (1930), Salina Gorge, Switzerland. Photo: Rama, CC BY-SA 2.0, via Wikimedia Commons.
1.1 Patrick Berger. Viaduc des Arts (1988-96), Paris, France. Courtesy of Patrick Berger.
1.2 Patrick Berger. Viaduc des Arts (1988-96), Paris, France. Courtesy of Patrick Berger.
1.3 Diba Tensile Architecture. Tabiat Pedestrian Bridge (2014), Tehran, Iran. Courtesy of DIBA Group.
1.4 UN Studio. Erasmus Bridge (1990-96), Rotterdam, The Netherlands. Photo: Ronald Tileman.
3.1 Bilbao, Spain with Frank Gehry's Bilbao Guggenheim in foreground. Photo: Brianna Laugher.
3.2 Renzo Piano. The Shard (2012) London, UK. Photo: Daniel Chapman, CC BY 2.0 Wikimedia Commons.
3.3 Urban Think Tank (U-TT). Caracas Metrocable (2010). Photo: Iwan Baan.
3.4 Estudio Teddy Cruz + Fonna Forman. UCSD-Casa Community Station: Living Rooms at the Border (2020), San Ysidro, California, US. Courtesy of Teddy Cruz and Fonna Forman.
4.1 Pechet and Robb art and architecture with PWL Partnership Landscape Architects. Granville Street Lighting (2010), Vancouver, Canada. Photo: Clayton Perry.
5.1 Diagram: Method of economic estimation of the value of the Sydney Opera House, reproduced by permission from Moira Scerri, Deborah Edwards and Carmel Foley, "Design, Architecture and the Value to Tourism" Tourism Economics 25, no.5 (2019): 700, as cited in Deloitte, *How Do You Value and Icon? The Sydney Opera House Sydney:* Cultural and Design Value, 2013), 3.
7.1 Jean Nouvel, Gilbert Lézénès, Pierre Soria, Architecture Studio. Institut du Monde Arabe, (1981-87), Paris, France. Photo : Auguste Fischer.
7.2 Jean Nouvel, Gilbert Lézénès,Pierre Soria, Architecture Studio, Institut du Monde Arabe, (1981-87), Paris France. Courtesy of Jean Nouvel, Pierre Soria, Architecture Studio.
7.3 Patkau Architects. Seabird Island School (1988-91), Agassiz, Canada. Courtesy of Patkau Architects.
7.4 Patkau Architects. Seabird Island School (1988-91), Agasszi, Canada. Courtesy of Patkau Architects.
7.5 César Pelli. Petronas Twin Towers (1998), Kuala Lumpur. Photo: Marcin Konsek, CC BY-SA 4.0, via Wikimedia Commons.
7.6 Foreign Office Architects (FOA). Yokohama Passenger Terminal (2002), Yokohama, Japan. Photo: Tony Wu.

8.1 Nicola Salvi. Trevi Fountain, (1762) Rome. Photo: David Liff, CC BY-SA 3.0, via Wikimedia Commons.

8.2 Site Plan of the Trevi Fountain. (A) Aqua Virgo; (B) arch of Aqua Virgo; (c) medieval portico; (D) ss. Vincenzo e Anastasio. Trevi Fountain stippled area: Alberti , 1453-1643; thick outline: Bernini, 1643-1732; thin outline: Slavi, 17320-1762. Original A. Ceen in John A. Pinto, *The Trevi Fountain* (New Haven and London: Yale University Press, 1986), 26. Courtesy of Yale University Press.

8.3. Charles-August Lebourg. Wallace Fountain in Montmartre (1872), Paris France. Photo: Martin Robson, CC BY-SA 2.0, via Wikimedia Commons.

8.4. Nasone, Via Casilina, (ca. 1870s-), Rome, Italy. Photo: Martin Koppenhöfer (dieterdreist) CC BY-SA 4.0, via Wikimedia Commons.

8.5. Michael Anastassiades for Fountain London. Fleet Fountain (2018), London, UK. Photo: Andy Stagg. Image courtesy of The London Fountain Co.

8.6. Pechet and Robb Art and Architecture. Seating at the Burrard Shipyards Pier (2010), North Vancouver, Canada.

8.7. PECHET Studio with PWL Partnership Landscape Architects Inc. Granville Street Bollards (2012), Vancouver, Canada. Photo: PECHET Studio.

8.8 Heatherwick Studio. Rolling Bridge (2004) London. Photo: Steve Speller. Courtesy of Steve Speller and Heatherwick Studio.

8.9 Heatherwick Studio. Rolling Bridge. Rolling Bridge (2004) London. Courtesy of Heatherwick Studio.

8.10 Heatherwick Studio. Boiler Suit, Guy's Hospital (2007), London, UK. Photo: Steven Speller.

8.11 Reiulf Ramstad Arkitekter. Trollstigen Visitor Cente (2012), More og Romsdal, Norway. Possible: Photo: Chell Hill, CC BY-SA 3.0, via Wikimedia Commons.

8. 12 Reiulf Ramstad Arkitekter. Trollstigen Visitor Centre (2012), More og Romsdal, Norway. Possible. Photo: Mariusz Hermandorfer, CC0, via Wikimedia Commons.

9.1 Ponte Vecchio, (1345), Florence, Italy. Photo: Yair Haklai, CC BY-SA 4.0, via Wikipedia Commons.

9.2 Mimar Sinan. Pasa Sokolovic Bridge (1577), Visregard, Bosnia-Herzegovina. Photo: Branevgd, CC BY-SA 4.0, via Wikimedia Commons.

9.3 Mimar Sinan /Mimar Hayruddin Stari Most (c. 1566), Mostar, Bosnia-Herzegovina. Photo: Ramirez CC BY-SA 4.0, via Wikimedia Commons.

9.4 Jean Baptiste Androuet du Certeau and Guillaume Marchand. Pont Neuf (1578-1607), Paris, France. Jean-Baptiste Raguenet, *A View of Paris from the Pont Neuf, 1763.*

Image courtesy of The J. Paul Getty Museum, Los Angeles, 71.PA.26

9.5 Shah Abbas II. Khaju Bridge (1650), Isfahan, Tehran. Photo: Ninara, CC BY 2.0, via Wikimedia Commons.

9.6 Robert Maillart. Salgiatobel Bridge (1930), Salina Gorge, Switzeland. Photo: Rama, CC BY-SA 2.0, via Wikimedia Commons.

9.7 The Golden Gate Bridge (1933 37), San Francisco, USA. Photo: Frank Schulenburg, CC BY-SA 4.0, via Wikimedia Commons.

9.8 Norman Foster + Partners. The Millau Viaduct (2004), France. Photo: Mike Locke.

9.9 WilkinsonEyre. The Gateshead Millennium Bridge, Gateshead-Newcastle (2001). Photo: Chas Thomson, CC BY-SA 2.0, via Wikimedia Commons.

9.10 Knight Architects. Pooley Bridge (2020), Cumbria, UK. Photo: Tom McNally.

10.1 Stroget, Copenhagen, Denmark (ca. 2021). Courtesy of City Clock Magazine.

10.2 Bjarke Ingels Group (BIG CopenHill (2019), Copenhagen, Denmark. Courtesy of Bjarke Ingels Group (BIG).

10.3 Vancouver Seawall(ca.1917-ongoing), Vancouver, Canada. Seawall near English Bay. Photo: Julian Prior.

INDEX